Practice*Planners*

Arthur E. Jongsma, Jr., Series Editor

Helping therapists help their clients...

Treatment Planners cover all the necessary elements for developing formal treatment plans, including detailed problem definitions, long-term goals, short-term objectives, therapeutic interventions, and DSM-IV™ diagnoses.

❑ The Complete Adult Psychotherapy Treatment Planner, Third Edition ....0-471-27113-6 / $49.95
❑ The Child Psychotherapy Treatment Planner, Third Edition..............................0-471-27050-4 / $49.95
❑ The Adolescent Psychotherapy Treatment Planner, Third Edition ....0-471-27049-0 / $49.95
❑ The Addiction Treatment Planner, Third Edition...0-471-72544-7 / $49.95
❑ The Couples Psychotherapy Treatment Planner ....0-471-24711-1 / $49.95
❑ The Group Therapy Treatment Planner..0-471-25469-X / $49.95
❑ The Family Therapy Treatment Planner..0-471-34768-X / $49.95
❑ The Older Adult Psychotherapy Treatment Planner ....0-471-29574-4 / $49.95
❑ The Employee Assistance (EAP) Treatment Planner ....0-471-24709-X / $49.95
❑ The Gay and Lesbian Psychotherapy Treatment Planner ....0-471-35080-X / $49.95
❑ The Crisis Counseling and Traumatic Events Treatment Planner ....0-471-39587-0 / $49.95
❑ The Social Work and Human Services Treatment Planner ....0-471-37741-4 / $49.95
❑ The Continuum of Care Treatment Planner ....0-471-19568-5 / $49.95
❑ The Behavioral Medicine Treatment Planner...0-471-31923-6 / $49.95
❑ The Mental Retardation and Developmental Disability Treatment Planner ....0-471-38253-1 / $49.95
❑ The Special Education Treatment Planner...0-471-38872-6 / $49.95
❑ The Severe and Persistent Mental Illness Treatment Planner...........................0-471-35945-9 / $49.95
❑ The Personality Disorders Treatment Planner ....0-471-39403-3 / $49.95
❑ The Rehabilitation Psychology Treatment Planner ....0-471-35178-4 / $49.95
❑ The Pastoral Counseling Treatment Planner..0-471-25416-9 / $49.95
❑ The Juvenile Justice and Residential Care Treatment Planner ....0-471-43320-9 / $49.95
❑ The School Counseling and School Social Work Treatment Planner.............0-471-08496-4 / $49.95
❑ The Psychopharmacology Treatment Planner ....0-471-43322-5 / $49.95
❑ The Probation and Parole Treatment Planner..0-471-20244-4 / $49.95
❑ The Suicide and Homicide Risk Assessment
   and Prevention Treatment Planner ....0-471-46631-X / $49.95
❑ The Speech-Language Pathology Treatment Planner...0-471-27504-2 / $49.95
❑ The College Student Counseling Treatment Planner ....0-471-46708-1 / $49.95
❑ The Parenting Skills Treatment Planner ....0-471-48183-1 / $49.95
❑ The Early Childhood Intervention Treatment Planner ....0-471-65962-2 / $49.95
❑ The Co-Occurring Disorders Treatment Planner...0-471-73081-5 / $49.95

The **Complete Treatment and Homework Planners** series of books combines our bestselling *Treatment Planners* and *Homework Planners* into one easy-to-use, all-in-one resource for mental health professionals treating clients suffering from the most commonly diagnosed disorders.

❑ The Complete Depression Treatment and Homework Planner....................0-471-64515-X / $39.95
❑ The Complete Anxiety Treatment and Homework Planner ....0-471-64548-6 / $39.95

NEW!

Over 500,000 Practice*Planners*® sold ...

Ⓦ WILEY

Practice*Planners*®

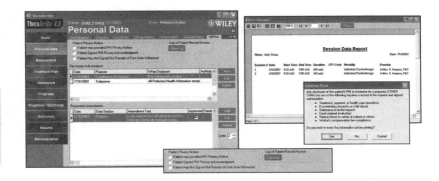

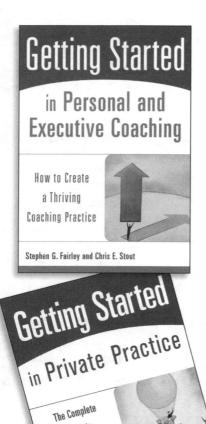

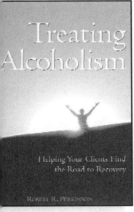
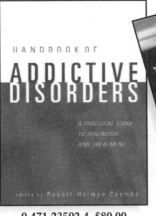

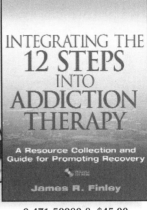
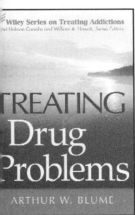

The Addiction
Treatment Planner

Practice*Planners*® Series

Treatment Planners

The Complete Adult Psychotherapy Treatment Planner, Third Edition
The Child Psychotherapy Treatment Planner, Third Edition
The Adolescent Psychotherapy Treatment Planner, Third Edition
The Addiction Treatment Planner, Third Edition
The Continuum of Care Treatment Planner
The Couples Psychotherapy Treatment Planner
The Employee Assistance Treatment Planner
The Pastoral Counseling Treatment Planner
The Older Adult Psychotherapy Treatment Planner
The Behavioral Medicine Treatment Planner
The Group Therapy Treatment Planner, Second Edition
The Gay and Lesbian Psychotherapy Treatment Planner
The Family Therapy Treatment Planner
The Severe and Persistent Mental Illness Treatment Planner
The Mental Retardation and Developmental Disability Treatment Planner
The Social Work and Human Services Treatment Planner
The Crisis Counseling and Traumatic Events Treatment Planner
The Personality Disorders Treatment Planner
The Rehabilitation Psychology Treatment Planner
The Special Education Treatment Planner
The Juvenile Justice and Residential Care Treatment Planner
The School Counseling and School Social Work Treatment Planner
The Sexual Abuse Victim and Sexual Offender Treatment Planner
The Probation and Parole Treatment Planner
The Psychopharmacology Treatment Planner
The Speech-Language Pathology Treatment Planner
The Suicide and Homicide Risk Assessment & Prevention Treatment Planner
The College Student Counseling Treatment Planner
The Parenting Skills Treatment Planner
The Early Childhood Intervention Treatment Planner
The Co-Occurring Disorders Treatment Planner

Progress Notes Planners

The Child Psychotherapy Progress Notes Planner, Second Edition
The Adolescent Psychotherapy Progress Notes Planner, Second Edition
The Adult Psychotherapy Progress Notes Planner, Second Edition
The Addiction Progress Notes Planner
The Severe and Persistent Mental Illness Progress Notes Planner
The Couples Psychotherapy Progress Notes Planner
The Family Therapy Progress Notes Planner

Homework Planners

Brief Therapy Homework Planner
Brief Couples Therapy Homework Planner
Brief Adolescent Therapy Homework Planner
Brief Child Therapy Homework Planner
Brief Employee Assistance Homework Planner
Brief Family Therapy Homework Planner
Grief Counseling Homework Planner
Group Therapy Homework Planner
Divorce Counseling Homework Planner
School Counseling and School Social Work Homework Planner
Child Therapy Activity and Homework Planner
Addiction Treatment Homework Planner, Second Edition
Adolescent Psychotherapy Homework Planner II
Adult Psychotherapy Homework Planner
Parenting Skills Homework Planner

Client Education Handout Planners

Adult Client Education Handout Planner
Child and Adolescent Client Education Handout Planner
Couples and Family Client Education Handout Planner

Complete Planners

The Complete Depression Treatment and Homework Planner
The Complete Anxiety Treatment and Homework Planner

PracticePlanners®

Arthur E. Jongsma, Jr., Series Editor

The Addiction Treatment Planner, Third Edition

Robert R. Perkinson

Arthur E. Jongsma, Jr.

WILEY

JOHN WILEY & SONS, INC.

This publication is designed to provide accurate and authoritative information in regard to the subject matter covered. It is sold with the understanding that the publisher is not engaged in rendering professional services. If legal, accounting, medical, psychological or any other expert assistance is required, the services of a competent professional person should be sought.

Designations used by companies to distinguish their products are often claimed as trademarks. In all instances where John Wiley & Sons, Inc. is aware of a claim, the product names appear in initial capital or all capital letters. Readers, however, should contact the appropriate companies for more complete information regarding trademarks and registration.

All references to diagnostic codes are reprinted with permission from the *Diagnostic and Statistical Manual of Mental Disorders, Fourth Edition, Text Revision.* Copyright 2000. American Psychiatric Association.

For general information on our other products and services please contact our Customer Care Department within the United States at (800) 762-2974, outside the United States at (317) 572-3993 or fax (317) 572-4002.

Wiley also publishes its books in a variety of electronic formats. Some content that appears in print may not be available in electronic books. For more information about Wiley products, visit our Web site at www.wiley.com.

ISBN-10 0471-72544-7
ISBN-13 978-0471-72544-2

Printed in the United States of America

10 9 8 7 6 5 4 3 2

CONTENTS

CONTENTS LISTED BY ASAM ASSESSMENT DIMENSIONS

PRACTICE*PLANNERS*® SERIES PREFACE

The practice of psychotherapy has a dimension that did not exist 30, 20, or even 15 years ago—accountability. Treatment programs, public agencies, clinics, and even group and solo practitioners must now justify the treatment of patients to outside review entities that control the payment of fees. This development has resulted in an explosion of paperwork. Clinicians must now document what has been done in treatment, what is planned for the future, and what the anticipated outcomes of the interventions are. The books and software in this Practice*Planners* series are designed to help practitioners fulfill these documentation requirements efficiently and professionally.

The Practice*Planners* series is growing rapidly. It now includes not only the original *Complete Adult Psychotherapy Treatment Planner,* Third Edition, *The Child Psychotherapy Treatment Planner,* Third Edition, and *The Adolescent Psychotherapy Treatment Planner,* Third Edition, but also Treatment Planners targeted to specialty areas of practice, including: addictions, juvenile justice/residential care, couples therapy, employee assistance, behavioral medicine, therapy with older adults, pastoral counseling, family therapy, group therapy, neuropsychology, therapy with gays and lesbians, special education, school counseling, probation and parole, therapy with sexual abuse victims and offenders, and more.

Several of the Treatment Planner books now have companion Progress Notes Planners (e.g., Adult, Adolescent, Child, Addictions, Severe and Persistent Mental Illness, Couples, Family). More of these planners that provide a menu of progress statements that elaborate on the client's symptom presentation and the provider's therapeutic intervention are in production. Each Progress Notes Planner statement is directly integrated with "Behavioral Definitions" and "Therapeutic Interventions" items from the companion Treatment Planner.

The list of therapeutic Homework Planners has grown to include Adult, Adolescent, Child, Couples, Group, Family, Addictions, Divorce, Grief, Parenting Skills, Employee Assistance, and School Counseling/School Social Work Homework Planners. Each of these books can be used alone or in conjunction with their companion Treatment Planner. Homework assignments are designed around each presenting problem (e.g., Anxiety, Depression, Chemical Dependence, Anger Management, Panic, Eating Disorders) that is the focus of a chapter in its corresponding Treatment Planner.

Client Education Handout Planners, a new branch in the series, provides brochures and handouts to help educate and inform adult, child, adolescent, couples, and family clients on a myriad of mental health issues, as well as life-skills techniques. The list of presenting problems for which information is provided mirrors the list of presenting problems in the Treatment Planner of the title similar to that of the Handout Planner. Thus, the problems for which educational material is provided in the *Child and Adolescent Client Education Handout Planner* reflect the presenting problems listed in *The Child* and *The Adolescent Psychotherapy Treatment Planner* books. Handouts are included on CD-ROMs for easy printing and are ideal for use in waiting rooms, at presentations, as newsletters, or as information for clients struggling with mental illness issues.

In addition, the series also includes Thera*Scribe*®, the latest version of the popular treatment planning, clinical record-keeping software. Thera*Scribe* allows the user to import the data from any of the Treatment Planner, Progress Notes Planner, or Homework Planner books into the software's expandable database. Then the point-and-click method can create a detailed, neatly organized, individualized, and customized treatment plan along with optional integrated progress notes and homework assignments.

Adjunctive books, such as *The Psychotherapy Documentation Primer,* and *Clinical, Forensic, Child, Couples and Family, Continuum of Care,* and *Chemical Dependence Documentation Sourcebook* contain forms and resources to aid the mental health practice management. The goal of the series is to provide practitioners with the resources they need in order to provide high-quality care in the era of accountability—or, to put it simply, we seek to help you spend more time on patients, and less time on paperwork.

ARTHUR E. JONGSMA, JR.
Grand Rapids, Michigan

The Addiction
Treatment Planner

INTRODUCTION

PLANNER FOCUS

The Addiction Treatment Planner has been written for individual, group, and family counselors and psychotherapists who are working with adults who are struggling with addictions to mood-altering chemicals, gambling, abusive eating, nicotine, or sexual promiscuity. The problem list of chapter titles reflects those addictive behaviors and the emotional, behavioral, interpersonal, social, personality, legal, medical, and vocational issues associated with those addictions. Whereas the focus of the original *Chemical Dependence Treatment Planner* was limited exclusively to substance abuse and its associated problems, the focus of later editions has been expanded to include other common addictive behaviors. The original problem chapters have been altered slightly from the first edition to be more generic in their language so as to include these other addictions.

This third edition has added chapters for Chronic Pain, Dangerousness/Lethality, Opioid Dependence, and Self-Care Deficits—Primary, Self-Care Deficits—Secondary, and Social Anxiety/Skills Deficits. We have also reordered the Objectives and Interventions in every presenting problem chapter in an attempt to strengthen the associations between each Objective and the Intervention aligned with it. We have added Objectives and Interventions in each chapter to encourage pre-and posttesting to measure outcome of treatment. An Objective/Intervention for assessing client satisfaction has also been added to each chapter. Additionally, we have included support material for client satisfaction surveys (Appendix C). Examples of satisfaction surveys are provided for easy reference.

This edition of the *Addiction Treatment Planner* has also given special attention to the Patient Placement Criteria (PPC) developed by the American Society of Addiction Medicine (ASAM). In the Contents table we have listed our presenting problem chapters under each of the six assessment dimensions:

Dimension One: Acute intoxication and/or withdrawal potential
Dimension Two: Biomedical conditions and complications

Dimension Three: Emotional, behavioral, or cognitive conditions and complications
Dimension Four: Readiness to change
Dimension Five: Relapse, continued use, or continued problem potential
Dimension Six: Recovery/Living environment

The Addiction Treatment Planner has treatment planning content applicable to problems discovered in all of the six assessment dimensions.

Also included (Appendix D) is a form that can be used to assess the client under the six ASAM dimensions. The checklist provides material for efficient evaluation of the client on each of the six dimensions. This form has been developed and is utilized by the staff at Keystone Treatment Center, Canton, South Dakota, where Dr. Perkinson is the Clinical Director. It is not copyrighted and may be used or adapted for use by our readers.

Interventions can be found in each chapter that reflect a 12-step recovery program approach, but you will also find interventions based on a broader psychological and pharmacological model. Because addiction treatment is often done in a residential setting through a team approach, interventions have been created that can be assigned to staff members of various disciplines and modalities: nursing, medical, group counseling, family therapy, or individual therapy. We hope that we have provided a broad, eclectic menu of objectives and interventions from which you can select to meet your client's unique needs. Hopefully, we have also provided a stimulus for you to create new objectives and interventions from your own clinical experience that have proven to be helpful to addictive clients.

HISTORY AND BACKGROUND

Since the early 1960s, formalized treatment planning has gradually become a vital aspect of the entire health care delivery system, whether it is treatment related to physical health, mental health, child welfare, or substance abuse. What started in the medical sector in the 1960s spread into the mental health sector in the 1970s, as clinics, psychiatric hospitals, treatment agencies, and so on began to seek accreditation from bodies such as the Joint Commission on Accreditation of Healthcare Organizations (JCAHO) to qualify for third-party reimbursements. For most treatment providers to achieve accreditation, they had to begin developing and strengthening their documentation skills in the area of treatment planning. Previously, most mental health and substance abuse treatment providers had, at best, a bare-bones plan that looked similar for most of the individuals they treated. As a result, clients were uncertain as to what they were trying to attain in treatment. Goals were vague, objectives were nonexistent, and interventions were applied equally to all clients. Outcome data were not measurable, and neither the treatment provider nor the client knew exactly when treatment was complete. The initial development of rudimentary treatment plans made inroads toward addressing some of these issues.

With the advent of managed care in the 1980s, treatment planning has taken on even more importance. Managed care systems *insist* that clinicians move rapidly from assessment of the problem to the formulation and implementation of the treatment plan. The primary goal of most managed care companies is to expedite the treatment process by prompting the client and treatment provider to focus on identifying and changing behavioral problems as quickly as possible. Treatment plans must be specific as to the problems and interventions, individualized to meet the client's needs and goals, and measurable in terms of setting milestones that can be used to chart the patient's progress. Pressure from third-party payors, accrediting agencies, and other outside parties has therefore increased the need for clinicians to produce effective, high-quality treatment plans in a short time frame. However, many mental health providers have little experience in treatment plan development. Our purpose in writing this book is to clarify, simplify, and accelerate the treatment planning process.

TREATMENT PLAN UTILITY

Detailed, written treatment plans can benefit not only the client, therapist, treatment team, insurance community, and treatment agency, but also the overall psychotherapy profession. The client is better served by a written plan because it stipulates the issues that are the focus of the treatment process. It is very easy for both provider and client to lose sight of what the issues were that brought the patient into therapy. The treatment plan is a guide that structures the focus of the therapeutic contract. Since issues can change as therapy progresses, the treatment plan must be viewed as a dynamic document that can and must be updated to reflect any major change of problem, definition, goal, objective, or intervention.

Clients and therapists benefit from the treatment plan, which forces both to think about therapy outcomes. Behaviorally stated, measurable objectives clearly focus the treatment endeavor. Clients no longer have to wonder what therapy is trying to accomplish. Clear objectives also allow the patient to channel effort into specific changes that will lead to the long-term goal of problem resolution. Therapy is no longer a vague contract to just talk honestly and openly about emotions and cognitions until the client feels better. Both client and therapist are concentrating on specifically stated objectives using specific interventions.

Providers are aided by treatment plans because they are forced to think analytically and critically about those therapeutic interventions that are best suited for objective attainment for the patient. Therapists were traditionally trained to follow the patient, but now a formalized plan is the guide to the treatment process. The therapist must give advance attention to the technique, approach, assignment, or cathartic target that will form the basis for interventions.

Clinicians also benefit from clear documentation of treatment because it provides a measure of added protection from possible patient litigation. Malpractice suits are increasing in frequency and insurance premiums are soaring. The first line of defense against malpractice allegations is a complete clinical record detailing the treatment process. A written, individualized, formal treatment plan that is the guideline for the therapeutic process, that has been reviewed and signed by the client, and that is coupled with problem-oriented progress notes is a powerful defense against exaggerated or false claims.

A well-crafted treatment plan that clearly stipulates presenting problems and intervention strategies facilitates the treatment process carried out by team members in inpatient, residential, or intensive outpatient settings. Good communication between team members about what approach is being implemented and who is responsible for specific interventions is critical. Team meetings to discuss patient treatment used to be the only source of interaction between providers; often, therapeutic conclusions or assignments were not recorded. Now, a thorough treatment plan stipulates in writing the details of objectives and the varied interventions (pharmacologic, milieu, group therapy, didactic, recreational, individual therapy, etc.) and who will implement them.

Every treatment agency or institution is constantly looking for ways to increase the quality and uniformity of the documentation in the clinical record. A standardized, written treatment plan with problem definitions, goals, objectives, and interventions in every client's file enhances that uniformity of documentation. This uniformity eases the task of record reviewers inside and outside the agency. Outside reviewers, such as JCAHO, insist on documentation that clearly outlines assessment, treatment, progress, and discharge status.

The demand for accountability from third-party payers and health maintenance organizations (HMOs) is partially satisfied by a written treatment plan and complete progress notes. More and more managed care systems are demanding a structured therapeutic contract that has measurable objectives and explicit interventions. Clinicians cannot avoid this move toward being accountable to those outside the treatment process.

The psychotherapy profession stands to benefit from the use of more precise, measurable objectives to evaluate success in mental health treatment. With the advent of detailed treatment plans, outcome data can be more easily collected for interventions that are effective in achieving specific goals.

HOW TO DEVELOP A TREATMENT PLAN

The process of developing a treatment plan involves a logical series of steps that build on each other, much like constructing a house. The foundation of any effective treatment plan is the data gathered in a thorough biopsychosocial assessment. As the client presents himself or herself for treatment, the clinician must sensitively listen to and understand what the client struggles with in terms of family of origin issues, current stressors, emotional status, social network, physical health, coping skills, interpersonal conflicts, self-esteem, and so on. Assessment data may be gathered from a social history, physical exam, clinical interview, psychological testing, or contact with a client's significant others. The integration of the data by the clinician or the multidisciplinary treatment team members is critical for understanding the client, as is an awareness of the basis of the client's struggle. We have identified six specific steps for developing an effective treatment plan based on the assessment data.

Step One: Problem Selection

Although the client may discuss a variety of issues during the assessment, the clinician must ferret out the most significant problems on which to focus the treatment process. Usually a *primary* problem will surface, and *secondary* problems may also be evident. Some other problems may have to be set aside as not urgent enough to require treatment at this time. An effective treatment plan can only deal with a few selected problems or treatment will lose its direction. *The Addiction Treatment Planner* offers 42 problems from which to select those that most accurately represent your client's presenting issues.

As the problems to be addressed become clear to the clinician or the treatment team, it is important to include opinions from the client as to his or her prioritization of issues for which help is being sought. A client's motivation to participate in and cooperate with the treatment process depends, to some extent, on the degree to which treatment addresses his or her greatest needs.

Step Two: Problem Definition

Each individual client presents with unique nuances as to how a problem behaviorally reveals itself in his or her life. Therefore, each problem that is selected for treatment focus requires a specific definition about how it is evidenced in the particular client. The symptom pattern should be associated with diagnostic criteria and codes such as those found in the *Diagnostic and Statistical Manual* or the *International Classification of Diseases*. The *Planner*, following the pattern established by *DSM-IV*, offers such behaviorally specific definition statements to choose from or to serve as a model for your own personally crafted statements. You will find several behavior symptoms or syndromes listed that may characterize one of the 42 presenting problems.

Step Three: Goal Development

The next step in treatment plan development is that of setting broad goals for the resolution of the target problem. These statements need not be crafted in measurable terms but can be global, long-term goals that indicate a desired positive outcome to the treatment procedures. The *Planner* suggests several possible goal statements for each problem, but one statement is all that is required in a treatment plan.

Step Four: Objective Construction

In contrast to long-term goals, objectives must be stated in behaviorally measurable language. It must be clear when the client has achieved the established objectives; therefore, vague, subjective objectives are not acceptable. Review agencies (e.g., JCAHO), HMOs, and managed care organizations insist that psychological treatment outcome be measurable. The objectives presented in this *Planner* are designed to meet this demand for accountability. Numerous alternatives are presented to allow construction of a variety of treatment plan possibilities for the same presenting problem. The clinician must exercise professional judgment as to which objectives are most appropriate for a given client.

Each objective should be developed as a step toward attaining the broad treatment goal. In essence, objectives can be thought of as a series of steps that, when completed, will result in the achievement of the long-term goal. There should be at least two objectives for each problem, but the clinician may construct as many as are necessary for goal achievement. Target attainment dates should be listed for each objective. New objectives should be added to the plan as the individual's treatment progresses. When all the necessary objectives have been achieved, the client should have resolved the target problem successfully.

Step Five: Intervention Creation

Interventions are the actions of the clinician designed to help the client complete the objectives. There should be at least one intervention for every objective. If the client does not accomplish the objective after the initial intervention, new interventions should be added to the plan.

Interventions should be selected on the basis of the client's needs and the treatment provider's full therapeutic repertoire. *The Addiction Treatment Planner* contains interventions from a broad range of therapeutic approaches, including cognitive, dynamic, behavioral, motivational enhancement, pharmacologic, family-oriented, and client-centered therapy. Other interventions may be written by the provider to reflect his or her own training and experience. The addition of new problems, definitions, goals, objectives, and interventions to those found in the *Planner* is encouraged, because doing so adds to the database for future reference and use.

Some suggested interventions listed in the *Planner* refer to specific books that can be assigned to the client for adjunctive bibliotherapy. Appendix A contains a full bibliographic reference list of these materials. The books are arranged under each problem for which they are appropriate as assigned reading for clients. When a book is used as part of an intervention plan, it should be reviewed with the client after it is read, enhancing the application of the content of the book to the client's specific circumstances. For further information about self-help books, mental health professionals may wish to consult *The Authoritative Guide to Self-Help Resources in Mental Health, Revised Edition* (Guilford, 2003) by Norcross, Santrock, Zuckerman, Campbell, Smith, and Sommer.

Assigning an intervention to a specific provider is most relevant if the patient is being treated by a team in an inpatient, residential, or intensive outpatient setting. Within these settings, personnel other than the primary clinician may be responsible for implementing a specific intervention. Review agencies stipulate that the responsible provider's name be supplied for every intervention.

Step Six: Diagnosis Determination

The determination of an appropriate diagnosis is based on an evaluation of the client's complete clinical presentation. The clinician must compare the behavioral, cognitive, emotional, and interpersonal symptoms that the client presents to the criteria for diagnosis of a mental illness condition as described in *DSM-IV*. The issue of differential diagnosis is admittedly a difficult one, which research has shown to have rather low interrater reliability.

Psychologists have also been trained to think more in terms of maladaptive behavior than disease labels. In spite of these factors, diagnosis is a reality that exists in the world of mental health care, and it is a necessity for third-party reimbursement. (However, recently, managed care agencies are more interested in behavioral indices that are exhibited by the client than the actual diagnosis.) It is the clinician's thorough knowledge of *DSM-IV* criteria and a complete understanding of the client's assessment data that contribute to the most reliable and valid diagnosis. An accurate assessment of behavioral indicators will also contribute to more effective treatment planning.

HOW TO USE THIS PLANNER

Our experience has taught us that learning the skills of effective treatment plan writing can be a tedious and difficult process for many clinicians. It is even more stressful to try to develop this expertise when under the pressures of increased patient load and short time frames placed on clinicians today by managed care systems. The documentation demands can be overwhelming when we must move quickly from assessment to treatment plan to progress notes. In the process, we must be very specific about how and when objectives can be achieved, and how progress is exhibited in each client. *The Addiction Treatment Planner* was developed as a tool to aid clinicians in writing a treatment plan in a rapid manner that is clear, specific, and highly individualized according to the following progression:

1. Choose one presenting problem (Step One) that you have identified through your assessment process. Locate the corresponding page number for that problem in the *Planner's* table of contents.
2. Select two or three of the listed behavioral definitions (Step Two) and record them in the appropriate section on your treatment plan form. Feel free to add your own defining statement if you determine that your client's behavioral manifestation of the identified problem is not listed. (Note that while our design for treatment planning is vertical, it will work equally well on plan forms formatted horizontally.)
3. Select a single long-term goal (Step Three) and again write the selection, exactly as it is written in the *Planner* or in some appropriately modified form, in the corresponding area of your own form.
4. Review the listed objectives for this problem and select the ones that you judge to be clinically indicated for your client (Step Four). Remember, it is recommended that you select at least two objectives for each problem. Add a target date or the number of sessions allocated for the attainment of each objective.
5. Choose relevant interventions (Step Five). The *Planner* offers suggested interventions related to each objective in the parentheses following the objective statement. But do not limit yourself to those interventions. The entire list is eclectic and may offer options that are more tailored to your theoretical approach or preferred way of working with clients. Also, just as with definitions, goals, and objectives, there is space allowed for you to enter your own interventions in the *Planner*. This allows you to refer to these entries when you create a plan around this problem in the future. You will have to assign responsibility to a specific person for implementation of each intervention if the treatment is being carried out by a multidisciplinary team.
6. Several *DSM-IV* diagnoses are listed at the end of each chapter that are commonly associated with a client who has this problem. These di-

agnoses are meant to be suggestions for clinical consideration. Select a diagnosis listed or assign a more appropriate choice from the *DSM-IV* (Step Six).

Note: To accommodate those practitioners who tend to plan treatment in terms of diagnostic labels rather than presenting problems, Appendix B lists all of the *DSM-IV* diagnoses that have been identified in the various presenting problem chapters as suggestions for consideration. Each diagnosis is followed by the presenting problem that has been associated with that diagnosis. The provider may look up the presenting problems for a selected diagnosis to review definitions, goals, objectives, and interventions that may be appropriate for clients with that diagnosis.

Congratulations! You should now have a complete, individualized treatment plan that is ready for immediate implementation and presentation to the client. It should resemble the format of the sample plan, presented on page 10.

A FINAL NOTE

One important aspect of effective treatment planning is that each plan should be tailored to the individual client's problems and needs. Treatment plans should not be mass produced, even if clients have similar problems. The individual's strengths and weaknesses, unique stressors, social network, family circumstances, and symptom patterns *must* be considered in developing a treatment strategy. Drawing upon our own years of clinical experience, we have put together a variety of treatment choices. These choices can be combined in thousands of permutations to develop detailed treatment plans. Relying on their own good judgment, clinicians can easily select the statements that are appropriate for the individuals they are treating. In addition, we encourage readers to add their own definitions, goals, objectives, and interventions to the existing samples. It is our hope that *The Addiction Treatment Planner* will promote an effective, creative treatment planning process that will ultimately benefit the client, clinician, and mental health community.

SAMPLE TREATMENT PLAN

SUBSTANCE ABUSE/DEPENDENCE

Definitions: Demonstrates a maladaptive pattern of substance use manifested by increased tolerance and withdrawal.

Fails to stop or reduce the use of mood-altering drug once started, despite the verbalized desire to do so and the negative consequences continued use brings.

Denies that chemical dependence is a problem despite feedback from significant others that the use of the substance is negatively affecting them and others.

Experiences frequent blackouts as a result of substance abuse.

Continues substance use despite knowledge of experiencing persistent physical, legal, financial, vocational, social, or relationship problems that are directly caused by the use of the substance.

Reports suspension of important social, recreational, or occupational activities because they interfere with using.

Goals: Accept one's powerlessness and unmanageability over mood-altering substances, and participate in a recovery-based program.

Establish and maintain total abstinence while increasing knowledge of the disease and of the process of recovery.

OBJECTIVES

1. Provide honest and complete information for a chemical dependence biopsychosocial history.

2. Complete psychological testing or objective questionnaires for assessing substance abuse/dependence.

INTERVENTIONS

1. Complete a thorough family and personal biopsychosocial history that focuses on addiction.

1. Administer to the client psychological instruments designed to assess substance abuse/dependence (e.g., Substance Abuse Subtle Screening Inventory-3, [SASSI-3], Addiction Severity Index [ASI], Substance Use Disorders Diagnostic Schedule-IV [SUDDS-IV]); give the client feedback regarding the results of the assessment.

3. Cooperate with a medical assessment and an evaluation of the necessity for pharmacological intervention.

1. Refer the client to a physician to perform a physical exam and write treatment orders including, if necessary, prescription of medications.

2. Ask the physician to monitor the side effects and effectiveness of medication, titrating as necessary.

4. Take prescribed medications as directed by the physician, and report as to compliance, effectiveness, and side effects.

1. Direct the staff to administer the client's prescription medications.

2. Monitor the client's prescribed psychotropic medications for compliance, effectiveness, and side effects.

5. Report acute withdrawal symptoms.

1. Assess and monitor the client's condition during withdrawal using a standardized procedure (e.g., Clinical Institute of Withdrawal Scale) as needed.

6. Attend didactic sessions and read assigned material in order to increase knowledge of addiction and of the process of recovery.

1. Assign the client to attend a chemical dependence didactic series to increase his/her knowledge of the patterns and effects of chemical dependence; ask him/her to identify and process several key points from each didactic.

2. Assign the client to read substance abuse literature (e.g., *Cannabis and Cognitive Functioning* by N. Solowij, *Cocaine Addiction* by A. Washton, or *Alcohol Abuse* by P. Sales); process five key points that were gained from the reading.

7. Attend group therapy sessions focused on addiction.

1. Assign the client to attend group therapy that is focused on addiction issues.

2. Direct group therapy that facilitates the sharing of causes for, consequences of, feelings about, and alternatives to addiction.

8. Verbally admit to powerlessness over the mood-altering substances.

    1. Assign the client to complete a 12-step recovery program's Step One paper, admitting to powerlessness over mood-altering chemicals and present it in group or individual therapy for feedback.

9. Verbalize an understanding of the problems that are caused by the use of mood-altering substances and, therefore, the need to stay in treatment.

    1. Ask the client to make a list of the ways in which chemical use has negatively impacted his/her life; process the list in individual or group session.

    2. Assist the client in listing reasons why he/she should stay in chemical dependence treatment and be abstinent from addiction.

10. List the reasons for substance abuse, and list the ways in which the same things can be attained in an adaptive manner.

    1. Assist the client in clarifying why he/she was using substances; teach him/her how to get good things out of life without mood-altering substances.

11. Practice stress management skills to attain a feeling of relaxation and comfort.

    1. Using progressive relaxation or biofeedback, teach the client how to relax; assign him/her to relax twice a day for 10–20 minutes.

12. Make a written plan to cope with each high-risk or relapse trigger situation.

    1. Explore with the client how addiction was used to escape from stress, physical and emotional pain, and boredom; confront the negative consequences of this pattern.

    2. Using a 12-step recovery progam's relapse prevention exercise, help the client uncover his/her triggers for relapse.

    3. Teach the client about high-risk situations (e.g., negative emotions, interpersonal conflict, positive emotions, test of personal control); assist him/her in making a written plan to cope with each high-risk situation.

13. Complete a readministration of objective tests of substance abuse/dependence as a means of assessing treatment outcome.

1. Assess the outcome of treatment by readministering to the client objective tests of substance abuse/dependence; evaluate the results and provide feedback to the client.

Diagnosis: 303.9   Alcohol Dependence

ADULT-CHILD-OF-AN-ALCOHOLIC (ACOA) TRAITS

BEHAVIORAL DEFINITIONS

1. Has a history of being raised in an alcoholic home, which resulted in having experienced emotional abandonment, role confusion, abuse, and a chaotic, unpredictable environment.
2. Reports an inability to trust others, share feelings, or talk openly about self.
3. Demonstrates an over-concern with the welfare of other people.
4. Passively submits to the wishes, wants, and needs of others; is too eager to please others.
5. Verbalizes chronic fear of interpersonal abandonment and desperately clings to destructive relationships.
6. Tells other people what they want to hear, rather than the truth.
7. Verbalizes persistent feelings of worthlessness and a belief that being treated with disdain is normal and to be expected.
8. Reports strong feelings of panic and helplessness when faced with being alone as a close relationship ends.
9. Chooses partners and friends who are chemically dependent or have other serious problems.
10. Demonstrates distrust of authority figures—only trusts peers.
11. Takes on the parental role in a relationship.
12. Reports feeling less worthy than those who have a more normal family life.

—. _____
   _____

—. _____
   _____

—. _____
   _____

LONG-TERM GOALS

1. Implement a plan for recovery from addiction that reduces the impact of adult-child-of-an-alcoholic traits on sobriety.
2. Decrease dependence on relationships while beginning to meet his/her own needs, build confidence, and practice assertiveness.
3. Reduce the frequency of behaviors that are exclusively designed to please others.
4. Become competent to choose partners and friends who are responsible, respectful, and reliable.
5. Overcome fears of abandonment, loss, and neglect as the source of these feelings—being raised in an alcoholic home—become clear.
6. Reduce feelings of alienation by learning similarity to others who were raised in a more normal home.

—. _____

_____

—. _____

_____

—. _____

_____

SHORT-TERM OBJECTIVES	THERAPEUTIC INTERVENTIONS
1. Acknowledge the feelings of powerlessness that result from ACOA traits and addiction. (1)	1. Probe the feelings of powerlessness that the client experienced as a child in the alcoholic home, and explore similarities to his/her feelings when abusing chemicals.
2. Verbalize the relationship between being raised in an addictive family and repeating the pattern of addiction now. (2)	2. Teach the client the relationship between his/her childhood experience in an addictive family and how this increased the likelihood of repeating the addictive behavior pattern as an adult.
3. Complete psychological testing or objective questionnaires for assessing traits associated with being an adult child of an alcoholic. (3)	3. Administer to the client psychological instruments designed to objectively assess the strength of traits associated with being an adult child of an alcoholic (e.g.,

Symptom Checklist-90-Revised [SCL-90-R], Children of Alcoholics Screening Test [CAST]); give the client feedback regarding the results of the assessment.

4. Verbalize the rules of "don't talk, don't trust, don't feel," which were learned as a child, and how these rules have made interpersonal relationships more difficult. (4, 5)

4. Explore how the dysfunctional family rules led to uncomfortable feelings and an escape into addiction.

5. Educate the client about the ACOA rules of "don't talk, don't trust, don't feel;" explain how these rules make healthy relationships impossible.

5. Verbalize an understanding of how ACOA traits contributed to addiction. (6, 7)

6. Teach the client the effects that modeling, fear, and shame have on choosing a lifestyle of addiction.

7. Assist the client in identifying his/her ACOA traits and the relationship between ACOA traits and addiction.

6. Identify the causes of the fear of abandonment that were experienced in the alcoholic home. (8, 9)

8. Probe the client's fear of violence, abandonment, unpredictability, and embarrassment when the parent was abusing chemicals.

9. Explore specific situations when the client experienced fear of abandonment or feelings of rejection during childhood.

7. Identify how the tendency to take on the parental role in interpersonal relationships is related to maintaining a feeling of security and control. (10, 11)

10. Assist the client in understanding how his/her early childhood experiences led to fears of abandonment, rejection, neglect, and to an assumption of the caretaker role, which is detrimental to intimate relationships.

11. Assist the client in identifying the many ways in which he/she takes on the parental role of caretaker.

8. Share the feeling of worthlessness that was learned in the alcoholic home, and directly relate this feeling to abuse of substances as a coping mechanism. (12, 13)

9. Verbalize a basis for increased feelings of self-worth. (14, 15)

10. Identify the pattern in the alcoholic family of being ignored or punished when honest feelings were shared. (5, 16)

11. List five qualities and behaviors that should be evident in others before interpersonal trust can be built. (17)

12. Increase the frequency of telling the truth rather than saying only what the client thinks the other person wants to hear. (18, 19)

12. Explore the client's feelings of worthlessness; assess their depth and origins.

13. Teach the client how low self-esteem results from being raised in an alcoholic home, due to experiencing emotional rejection, broken promises, abuse, neglect, poverty, and lost social status.

14. Assign the client to list his/her positive traits and accomplishments; reinforce these as a foundation for building self-esteem.

15. Emphasize to the client his/her inherent self-worth as a human being; relate this to his/her acceptance of a higher power.

5. Educate the client about the ACOA rules of "don't talk, don't trust, don't feel;" explain how these rules make healthy relationships impossible.

16. Probe how the client's family responded to expressions of feelings, wishes, and wants and why it became dangerous for the client to share feelings with others.

17. Assist the client in developing a set of character traits to be sought in others (e.g., honesty, sensitivity, kindness) that qualify them as trustworthy.

18. Teach the client that the behavior of telling other people what we think they want to hear rather than speaking the truth is based on fear of rejection, which was learned in the alcoholic home; use modeling, role-playing, and behavior rehearsal to teach the client more honest communication skills.

13. List the steps to effectively and independently solve problems. (20)

14. Acknowledge the resistance to sharing personal problems; share at least one problem in each therapy session. (5, 16, 21, 22)

15. Verbalize an understanding of how ACOA traits contribute to choosing partners and friends that have problems and need help. (10, 23)

19. Assign the client to keep a journal of incidents in which he/she told the truth rather than saying only what others want to hear.

20. Teach the client problem-solving skills (e.g., identify the problem, brainstorm alternate solutions, examine the advantages and disadvantages of each option, select an option, implement a course of action, evaluate the result); role-play solving a current problem in his/her life.

5. Educate the client about the ACOA rules of "don't talk, don't trust, don't feel;" explain how these rules make healthy relationships impossible.

16. Probe how the client's family responded to expressions of feelings, wishes, and wants and why it became dangerous for the client to share feelings with others.

21. Educate the client about healthy interpersonal relationships based on openness, respect, and honesty; explain the necessity of sharing feelings to build trust and mutual understanding.

22. Explore the client's pattern of resistance to sharing personal problems and preferring, instead, to focus on helping others with their problems.

10. Assist the client in understanding how his/her early childhood experiences led to fears of abandonment, rejection, neglect, and to an assumption of the caretaker role, which is detrimental to intimate relationships.

16. Initiate the encouragement of others in recovery, to help reestablish a feeling of self-worth. (24, 25)

17. List reasons why regular attendance at recovery group meetings is necessary to arrest ACOA traits and addiction. (26)

18. Discuss fears that are related to attending recovery group meetings, and develop specific written plans to deal with each fear. (27)

19. Verbalize how a recovery group can become the healthy family that one never had. (24, 28, 29)

23. Help the client to understand that his/her strong need to help others is based on low self-esteem and the need for acceptance, which was learned in the alcoholic family-of-origin; relate this caretaking behavior to choosing friends and partners who are chemically dependent and/or psychologically disturbed.

24. Teach the client that active involvement in a recovery group can aid in building trust in others and confidence in himself/herself.

25. Assist the client in developing an aftercare plan that is centered around regular attendance at Alcoholics Anonymous/Narcotics Anonymous (AA/NA) meetings.

26. Assist the client in listing reasons why 12-step recovery group attendance is helpful to overcome ACOA traits.

27. Probe the relationship between ACOA traits and the fear of attending recovery group meetings; assist the client in developing coping strategies to cope with the fear (e.g., give self positive messages regarding self-worth, use relaxation techniques to reduce tension, use meditation to induce calm and support from a higher power).

24. Teach the client that active involvement in a recovery group can aid in building trust in others and confidence in himself/herself.

28. Discuss how the home group of AA/NA can function as the

healthy family the client never had; help him/her realize why he/she needs such a family to recover.

29. Educate the client about the family atmosphere in a home AA/NA recovery group, and how helping others can aid in recovery and reestablish a feeling of worth.

20. List five ways in which belief in and interaction with a higher power can reduce fear and aid in recovery. (30, 31)

30. Teach the client how faith in a higher power can aid in recovery and arrest ACOA traits and addiction.

31. Assign the client to read the Alcoholics Anonymous *Big Book* on the topic of spirituality and the role of a higher power; process the material in an individual or group therapy session.

21. Verbalize the feeling of serenity that results from turning out-of-control problems over to a higher power. (32)

32. Review problematic circumstances in the client's life that could be turned over to a higher power to increase serenity.

22. Practice assertiveness skills and share how these skills were used in interpersonal conflict. (33, 34)

33. Use modeling, behavior rehearsal, and role-playing to teach the client healthy, assertive skills; apply these skills to several current problem situations, and then ask the client to journal his/her assertiveness experiences.

34. Teach the client the assertive formula of "I feel____ when you____. I would prefer it if____"; role-play several applications in his/her life and then assign him/her to use this formula three times per day.

23. Share the personal experiences of each day with one person that day. (35, 36)

35. Teach the client the *share check* method of building trust, in which the degree of shared information is related to a proven level of trustworthiness; use behavior

rehearsal of several situations in which the client shares feelings.

36. Review and reinforce instances when the client has shared honestly and openly with a trustworthy person.

24. Cooperate with a physician's evaluation for psychopharmacological intervention. (37)

37. Refer the client to a physician to evaluate whether psychopharmacological interventions are warranted.

25. Take medications as prescribed, and report on their effectiveness and side effects. (38, 39)

38. Medical staff administer medications as prescribed.

39. Monitor medications for effectiveness and side effects.

26. Complete a re-administration of objective tests of traits associated with being an adult child of an alcoholic as a means of assessing treatment outcome. (40)

40. Assess the outcome of treatment by re-administering to the client objective tests of ACOA traits; evaluate the results and provide feedback to the client.

27. Complete a survey to assess the degree of satisfaction with treatment. (41)

41. Administer a survey to assess the client's degree of satisfaction with treatment.

—. _____

—. _____

_____

_____

—. _____

—. _____

_____

_____

—. _____

—. _____

_____

_____

DIAGNOSTIC SUGGESTIONS:

Axis I:	311	Depressive Disorder NOS
	300.00	Anxiety Disorder NOS
	309.81	Posttraumatic Stress Disorder
	V61.20	Parent-Child Relational Problem
	_____	_____
	_____	_____

Axis II: 301.82   Avoidant Personality Disorder
                       301.6   Dependent Personality Disorder
                       301.9   Personality Disorder NOS

                       _____   _____

                       _____   _____

ANGER

BEHAVIORAL DEFINITIONS

1. Has a history of explosive, aggressive outbursts, particularly when intoxicated, that lead to assaultive acts or destruction of property.
2. Abuses substances to cope with angry feelings and to relinquish responsibility for aggression.
3. Passively withholds feelings, then explodes in a violent rage.
4. Angry overreaction to perceived disapproval, rejection, or criticism.
5. Demonstrates a tendency to blame others rather than accept responsibility for own problems.
6. Persistent pattern of challenging or disrespecting authority figures.
7. Body language of tense muscles (e.g., clenched fists or jaw, glaring looks, or refusal to make eye contact).
8. Views aggression as a means of achieving needed power and control.
9. Uses verbally abusive language.

—. _____
   _____
—. _____
   _____
—. _____
   _____

LONG-TERM GOALS

1. Maintain a program of recovery that is free of addiction and violent behavior.
2. Decrease the frequency of occurrence of angry thoughts, feelings, and behaviors.

3. Implement specific assertive skills that are necessary to solve problems in a less aggressive and more constructive manner.
4. Think positively in anger-producing situations.
5. Stop blaming others for problems, and accept responsibility for own feelings, thoughts, and behaviors.
6. Learn and implement stress management skills to reduce the level of stress and the irritability that accompanies it.
7. Understand the relationship between angry feelings and the feelings of hurtfulness and worthlessness that are experienced in the family of origin.
8. Learn the assertive skills that are necessary to reduce angry feelings, and solve problems in a less aggressive and more constructive manner.

—. _____
   _____
   _____
—. _____
   _____
   _____
—. _____
   _____

SHORT-TERM OBJECTIVES

1. Verbalize an increased awareness of the depth and frequency of one's anger expression. (1)

2. Complete psychological testing or objective questionnaires for assessing anger expression. (2)

THERAPEUTIC INTERVENTIONS

1. Assign the client to keep a log of situations that precipitate angry feelings, noting the thoughts, feelings, and depth of anger (rate on a scale from 1 to 100); process the anger log and assist in identifying those dysfunctional thoughts that trigger anger.

2. Administer to the client psychological instruments designed to objectively assess anger expression (e.g., Anger, Irritability, and Assault Questionnaire [AIAQ], Buss-Durkee Hostility Inventory [BDHI], State-Trait Anger Expression Inventory [STAXI]); give the client feedback regarding the results of the assessment.

3. Verbalize an understanding of the relationship between the feelings of worthlessness and hurtfulness that were experienced in the family of origin and the current feelings of anger. (3, 4)

4. Verbalize an understanding of how anger has been reinforced as a coping mechanism for stress. (5)

5. Verbalize regret and remorse for the harmful consequences of anger. (6)

6. Decrease the frequency of negative, self-defeating thinking, and increase the frequency of positive, self-enhancing self-talk. (7, 8)

7. Increase the frequency of assertive behaviors while reducing the frequency of aggressive behaviors. (9, 10)

3. Assign the client to list painful experiences of his/her life that have led to anger and resentment.

4. Probe the client's experience with his/her family of origin and help him/her to see how these experiences led to a tendency to see people and situations as dangerous and threatening.

5. Teach the client how anger blocks the awareness of pain, discharges uncomfortable feelings, erases guilt, and places the blame for problems on others.

6. Use modeling and role reversal to make the client more aware of how his/her aggressive behavior has had negative consequences on others (e.g., spouse, children) who have been the targets of or witness to violence.

7. Help the client to develop a list of positive, self-enhancing statements to use daily in building a positive and accurate self-image; use role-playing and modeling to demonstrate implementation of positive self-talk.

8. Highlight the client's positive traits and accomplishments whenever they are apparent; reinforce the client's use of positive words to describe himself/herself.

9. Teach assertiveness and its benefits through the use of role-playing and modeling, assigning appropriate reading material (e.g., *Your Perfect Right* by Alberti and Emmons) or participating in an assertiveness training group.

8. Verbalize an understanding of the need for and process of forgiving others so as to reduce anger. (11, 12)

10. Explore the opportunities the client has had for implementing assertiveness in place of aggressiveness in his/her daily life; reinforce success and redirect for failure.

11. Assist the client in identifying whom he/she needs to forgive, and educate him/her as to the long-term process that is involved in forgiveness versus a magical single event; recommend reading books on forgiveness (e.g., *Forgive and Forget* by Smedes).

12. Review the client's progress in beginning the process of forgiving perpetrators of pain; reinforce success and assess its impact on anger reduction.

9. Verbalize an understanding of how angry thoughts and feelings can lead to increased risk of addiction. (13, 14)

13. Educate the client about his/her tendency to engage in addictive behavior as a means of relieving uncomfortable feelings; develop a list of several instances of occurrence.

14. Teach the client about high-risk situations of strong negative emotions, social pressure, interpersonal conflict, strong positive emotions, and testing personal control; discuss how anger, as a strong negative emotion, places him/her at a high risk for addiction.

10. List those thoughts that trigger angry feelings, and replace each one with a more positive and accurate thought that is supportive to self and recovery. (1, 15, 16)

1. Assign the client to keep a log of situations that precipitate angry feelings, noting the thoughts, feelings, and depth of anger (rate on a scale from 1 to 100); process the anger log and assist in identifying those dysfunctional thoughts that trigger anger.

11. Practice relaxation skills twice a day for 10 to 20 minutes per session. (17, 18)

12. Verbalize an understanding of the concept of a higher power and the benefits of acceptance of such a concept. (19)

13. Implement regular physical exercise to reduce tension. (20)

14. Attend 12-step recovery group meetings regularly, and share feelings with others there. (21)

15. Implement proactive steps to meet the needs of self, without expecting other people to meet those needs and then angrily blaming them when they fail. (22, 23)

15. Educate the client about how the thoughts of abandonment and rejection trigger feelings of worthlessness, hurt, and then anger.

16. Assist the client in identifying a list of distorted thoughts that trigger feelings of anger; teach him/her to replace such thoughts with positive, realistic thoughts.

17. Teach the client progressive relaxation skills, and encourage their utilization twice a day for 10 to 20 minutes.

18. Review the client's application of relaxation skills; reinforce success and redirect for failure.

19. Teach the client about the 12-step recovery program concept of a higher power, and how to turn over perpetrators of pain to his/her higher power for judgment.

20. Teach the client the benefits of regular physical exercise; assign a program of implementation.

21. Teach the client the importance of actively attending 12-step recovery meetings, getting a sponsor, reinforcing people around him/her, and sharing feelings.

22. Assist the client in identifying a list of pleasurable leisure activities that he/she could engage in to reduce stress and increase enjoyment of life; solicit a contract to engage in one or two such activities per week.

23. Assist the client in developing a list of his/her own needs and wishes and then the personal actions necessary to attain these,

16. Implement cognitive and behavioral techniques designed to stop the impulsive angry reaction when feeling angry. (24, 25, 26)

rather than being angry with others for not meeting his/her needs and wishes.

24. Teach the client the impulse control skill of "stop, look, listen, think, and plan" before reacting with anger.

25. Using modeling, role-play, and behavior rehearsal, show the client how to stop the impulse to react with anger (e.g., relax muscles; use positive, comforting self-talk; implement a time out procedure; and speak softly in frustrating, threatening, or hurtful situations).

26. Teach the client a time out procedure to interrupt escalating angry interactions between the client and his/her significant other; role-play, applying the time out procedure in five different anger-producing situations, and ask the client to keep a log of implementation of the technique in daily life.

17. Cooperate with a physician's evaluation regarding whether psychopharmacological intervention is warranted. (27)

27. Refer the client to a physician for evaluation if psychopharmacological interventions are warranted.

18. Take medications as prescribed, and report as to the effectiveness as well as side effects. (28, 29)

28. Medical staff administer medications as prescribed.

29. Monitor medications for effectiveness and side effects.

19. Read books on coping with anger and implement newly learned techniques. (30)

30. Recommend that the client read books on coping with anger (e.g., *Of Course You're Angry* by Rosellini and Worden; *The Angry Book* by Rubin; *Anger Work-Out Book* by Weisinger); process his/her implementation of coping techniques, reinforcing success and redirecting for failure.

20. Develop an aftercare program that details healthy, constructive alternatives to impulsive, destructive anger expression. (31)

21. Complete a re-administration of objective tests of anger expression as a means of assessing treatment outcome. (32)

22. Complete a survey to assess the degree of satisfaction with treatment. (33)

—. _____

_____

—. _____

_____

—. _____

_____

31. Help the client develop a list of what adaptive actions he/she is going to take to cope with angry feelings during aftercare (e.g., calling a sponsor, being assertive but not aggressive, taking a time-out, implementing relaxation, practicing positive self-talk, praying to a higher power) to avoid relapse.

32. Assess the outcome of treatment by re-administering to the client objective tests of anger expression (e.g., Anger, Irritability, and Assault Questionnaire [AIAQ], Buss-Durkee Hostility Inventory [BDHI], State-Trait Anger Expression Inventory [STAXI]); evaluate the results and provide feedback to the client.

33. Administer a survey to assess the client's degree of satisfaction with treatment.

—. _____

_____

—. _____

_____

—. _____

_____

DIAGNOSTIC SUGGESTIONS:

Axis I:	312.8	Conduct Disorder
	313.81	Oppositional Defiant Disorder
	296.xx	Bipolar I Disorder
	296.89	Bipolar II Disorder
	312.34	Intermittent Explosive Disorder
	312.30	Impulse Control Disorder NOS
	309.4	Adjustment Disorder with Mixed Disturbance of Emotions and Conduct
	V71.01	Adult Antisocial Behavior

	V71.02	Child or Adolescent Antisocial Behavior
	_____	_____
	_____	_____

Axis II:	301.0	Paranoid Personality Disorder
	301.7	Antisocial Personality Disorder
	301.83	Borderline Personality Disorder
	301.9	Personality Disorder NOS
	301.81	Narcissistic Personality Disorder
	_____	_____
	_____	_____

ANTISOCIAL BEHAVIOR

BEHAVIORAL DEFINITIONS

1. Has a history of breaking the rules or the law (often under the influence of drugs or alcohol) to get his/her own way.
2. Exhibits a pervasive pattern of disregard for and violation of the rights of others.
3. Consistently blames other people for his/her own problems and behaviors.
4. Uses aggressive behavior to manipulate, intimidate, or control others.
5. Demonstrates a chronic pattern of dishonesty.
6. Lives a hedonistic, self-centered lifestyle, with little regard for the needs and welfare of others.
7. Verbalizes a lack of empathy for the feelings of others, even if they are friends or family.
8. Presents a pattern of criminal activity and addiction, going back to one's adolescent years.
9. Engages in dangerous, thrill-seeking behavior, without regard for the safety of self or others.
10. Makes decisions impulsively, without giving thought to the consequences for others.

—. _____

_____

—. _____

_____

—. _____

_____

LONG-TERM GOALS

1. Develop a program of recovery that is free from addiction and the negative influences of antisocial behavior.
2. Learn the importance of helping others in recovery.
3. Learn how antisocial behavior and addiction is self-defeating.
4. Understand criminal thinking and develop self-talk that respects the welfare and rights of others.
5. Understand the importance of a program of recovery that demands rigorous honesty.
6. Take responsibility for one's own behavior.

__. _____

_____

__. _____

_____

__. _____

_____

SHORT-TERM OBJECTIVES

1. Verbalize an acceptance of powerlessness and unmanageability over antisocial behavior and addiction. (1, 2)

2. Complete psychological testing or objective questionnaires for assessing antisocial behavior. (3)

THERAPEUTIC INTERVENTIONS

1. Help the client to understand the self-defeating nature of antisocial behavior and addiction.

2. Help the client to see the relationship between antisocial behavior and addiction.

3. Administer to the client psychological instruments designed to objectively assess antisocial behavior, impulsivity, and/or aggression rating instruments (e.g., Psychopathy Checklist Revised [PCL-R], Aggressive Acts Questionnaire [AAQ], Barratt Impulsiveness Scale-11 [BIS-11]); give the client feedback regarding the results of the assessment.

3. State how antisocial behavior and addiction are associated with irrational thinking (AA's "insanity"). (4)

4. Help the client to understand how doing the same things over and over but expecting different results is irrational—what AA calls "insane."

4. Consistently follow all rules. (5)

5. Assign appropriate consequences when the client fails to follow rules or expectations.

5. Identify and verbalize the negative consequences that failure to comply with the rules/limits has had on self and others. (6, 7, 8)

6. Review with the client several examples where his/her rule and/or limit breaking led to negative consequences to self and others.

7. Use role reversal techniques to sensitize the client to his/her lack of empathy for others by revisiting the consequences of his/her behavior on others.

8. Teach the client that many negative consequences are preceded by decisions that are based on criminal thinking; ask the client to list five times that antisocial behavior led to negative consequences and list the many decisions that were made along the way.

6. List the ways dishonesty is self-defeating. (9)

9. Assist the client in understanding why dishonesty results in more lies, loss of trust from others, and, ultimately, rejection.

7. List the reasons why criminal activity leads to a negative self-image. (10)

10. Help the client to understand why criminal activity leads to feelings of low self-esteem (e.g., loss of respect from others, broken relationships, legal problems, lack of achievement).

8. Verbalize how criminal thinking is used to avoid responsibility and to blame others. (11)

11. Teach the client how criminal thinking (e.g., super-optimism, little empathy for others, power orientation, sense of entitlement, self-centeredness) avoids personal

9. Decrease the frequency of statements blaming others or circumstances while increasing the frequency of statements accepting responsibility for one's own behavior, thoughts, and feelings. (12, 13, 14)

responsibility and leads to blaming others.

12. Help the client to understand how blaming others results in a failure to learn from one's mistakes, and therefore making the same mistakes over again.

13. Explore with the client the reasons for blaming others for one's own problems and behaviors, and how he/she may have learned this behavior in a punishing family environment.

14. Confront the client's projection of blame for his/her behavior, feelings, and thoughts; reinforce his/her acceptance of personal responsibility.

10. Develop a list of prosocial behaviors and practice one of these behaviors each day. (15)

15. Teach the client the difference between antisocial and prosocial behaviors, then help him/her develop a list of prosocial behaviors (e.g., helping others) to practice each day.

11. Write a list of typical criminal thoughts; then replace each thought with one that is respectful of self and others. (16, 17)

16. Confront the client's antisocial beliefs about his/her lack of respect for the rights and feelings of others, and model thoughtful attitudes and beliefs about the welfare of others.

17. Assist the client in identifying his/her typical antisocial thoughts; list an alternate, respectful, and trusting empathic thought.

12. List five ways AA/NA meetings and a higher power can assist in overcoming antisocial behavior and addiction. (18)

18. Discuss with the client the various ways recovery groups and a belief in a higher power can assist him/her in recovery (e.g., provide emotional support, provide social relationships, relieve anxiety, reinforce self-worth, provide guidance).

13. Receive feedback/redirection from staff/therapist without making negative gestures or remarks. (19)

14. Develop a written plan to address all pending legal problems in a constructive manner. (20)

15. Encourage at least one person in recovery each day. (21, 22)

16. Articulate the antisocial and addiction behaviors that have resulted in pain and disappointment to others and, therefore, a loss of their trust. (23, 24, 25)

17. Verbalize a desire to keep commitments to others, and list ways to prove oneself to be responsible, reliable, loyal, and faithful. (26)

18. Write an aftercare plan that includes a sponsor, AA meetings, and counseling. (27, 28)

19. Confront the client when he/she breaks the rules, blames others, or makes excuses.

20. Assist the client in addressing each legal problem honestly, taking responsibility for his/her behavior.

21. Teach the client why it is essential to attend recovery groups and to learn how to help others.

22. Using modeling, role-playing, and behavior rehearsal, practice with the client how he/she can encourage others in recovery.

23. Assist the client in developing a list of reasons why the trust of others is important as a basis for any relationship.

24. Encourage the client to be honest in acknowledging how he/she has hurt others.

25. Confront any denial of responsibility for irresponsible, self-centered, and impulsive behaviors.

26. Discuss with the client the importance of keeping commitments and promises to others and ways to prove himself/herself as trustworthy in relationships.

27. Introduce the client to his/her AA/NA sponsor or encourage him/her to ask a stable recovery person to be a sponsor; teach him/her the many ways a sponsor can be used in recovery.

28. Help the client develop an aftercare program that specifically outlines what AA meetings will be attended and the psychotherapist he/she will be working with.

19. Family members develop an aftercare plan that focuses on what they are expected to do to help the client recover. (29, 30, 31, 32)

29. Teach the family members about criminal thinking and show them how to help the client correct his/her inaccurate thoughts.

30. Teach the family the need to overcome their denial of making excuses for reinforcing or being intimidated by the client's anti-social behavior.

31. Use behavior rehearsal, modeling, and role-playing to teach the family members conflict resolution skills.

32. Assist each family member in identifying and listing how to encourage the client to recover from antisocial behavior and addiction.

20. Complete a re-administration of objective tests of antisocial behavior, impulsivity, and aggression as a means of assessing treatment outcome. (33)

33. Assess the outcome of treatment by re-administering to the client objective tests of antisocial behavior, impulsivity, and aggression (e.g., Psychopathy Checklist Revised [PCL-R], Aggressive Acts Questionnaire [AAQ], Barratt Impulsiveness Scale-11 [BIS-11]); evaluate the results and provide feedback to the client.

21. Complete a survey to assess the degree of satisfaction with treatment. (34)

34. Administer a survey to assess the client's degree of satisfaction with treatment.

__. _____

__. _____

__. _____

__. _____

__. _____

__. _____

DIAGNOSTIC SUGGESTIONS:

Axis I:

312.8	Conduct Disorder
313.81	Oppositional Defiant Disorder
309.3	Adjustment Disorder with Disturbance of Conduct
312.34	Intermittent Explosive Disorder
V71.01	Adult Antisocial Behavior
V71.02	Child or Adolescent Antisocial Behavior

_____   _____

_____   _____

Axis II:

301.7	Antisocial Personality Disorder
301.83	Borderline Personality Disorder
301.81	Narcissistic Personality Disorder

_____   _____

_____   _____

ANXIETY

BEHAVIORAL DEFINITIONS

1. Demonstrates excessive fear and worry regarding several life circumstances, which has no factual or logical basis.
2. Constantly worries about family, job, social interactions, and/or health.
3. Has a tendency to blame self for the slightest imperfection or mistake.
4. Expresses a fear of saying or doing something foolish in a social situation due to a lack of confidence in social skills.
5. Reports symptoms of autonomic hyperactivity (e.g., cardiac palpitations, shortness of breath, sweaty palms, dry mouth, trouble swallowing, nausea, diarrhea).
6. Demonstrates symptoms of motor tension (e.g., restlessness, tiredness, shakiness, muscle tension).
7. Abuses substances in an attempt to control anxiety symptoms.
8. Reports symptoms of hypervigilance (e.g., feeling constantly on edge, difficulty concentrating, sleep problems, irritability).

—. _____
_____
—. _____
_____
—. _____
_____

LONG-TERM GOALS

1. Maintain a program of recovery, free from addiction and excessive anxiety.
2. End addiction as a means of escaping anxiety and practice constructive coping behaviors.

3. Decrease anxious thoughts and increase positive, self-enhancing self-talk.
4. Reduce overall stress levels, reducing excessive worry and muscle tension.
5. Learn to relax and think accurately and logically about events.
6. Resolve the conflict that is at the source of anxiety.

—. _____
   _____
   _____
—. _____
   _____
   _____
—. _____
   _____

SHORT-TERM OBJECTIVES

THERAPEUTIC INTERVENTIONS

1. Acknowledge the powerlessness and unmanageability caused by excessive anxiety and addiction. (1, 2)

1. Help the client to see how anxiety and powerlessness over addiction has made his/her life unmanageable.

2. Teach the client about the relationship between anxiety and addiction (e.g., how the substance was used to treat the anxious symptoms and why more substance use became necessary).

2. Complete psychological testing or objective questionnaires for assessing client's level of anxiety. (3)

3. Administer an objective anxiety assessment instrument to the client (e.g., Beck Anxiety Inventory [BAI], Hamilton Anxiety Rating Scale [HARS], State-Trait Anxiety Inventory [STAI]); evaluate the results and give feedback to him/her.

3. Verbalize an understanding of the principle of how irrational thoughts may be the basis for anxiety and addiction. (4, 5)

4. Teach the client about the 12-step program concept of *insanity*, and help him/her to see how anxiety and addictive behavior are insane.

5. Assist the client in understanding the irrational nature of his/her

thoughts that underlie his/her fears.

4. Use logic and reasoning to replace irrational thoughts with reasonable ones. (6, 7, 8, 9)

6. Assign the client to keep a daily record of anxiety, including each situation that caused anxious feelings, the negative thoughts precipitating the anxiety, and a ranking of the severity of the anxiety from 1 to 100.

7. Process the client's anxiety journal in order to help him/her to identify the distorted thoughts that fueled his/her anxiety.

8. Facilitate the client's use of logic and reasoning to challenge the irrational thoughts associated with unreasonable worries and to replace those thoughts with reasonable ones.

9. Reinforce the client's implementation of reality-based cognitive messages that will increase his/her self-confidence in coping with fears and anxieties.

5. List 10 positive, self-enhancing statements that will be read several times per day, particularly when feeling anxious. (10, 11, 12)

10. Assist the client in developing a list of ten positive statements to read to himself/herself several times per day, particularly with feeling anxious.

11. Assign the client to read material on positive self-talk (e.g., *What to Say When You Talk to Yourself* by Helmstetter); process key ideas learned from the reading.

12. Reinforce the client's use of more realistic, positive messages to himself/herself in interpreting life events.

6. Comply with a physician's evaluation to determine if

13. Physician will determine if psychopharmacological intervention

psychopharmacological intervention is warranted; take any medications as directed. (13, 14, 15)

13. is warranted, and order and titrate medication.

14. Staff will administer prescribed medication as directed by the physician.

15. Monitor the client's use of prescribed medication for effectiveness as well as for side effects.

7. Report on instances that worries and anxieties have been turned over to a higher power. (16, 17, 18)

16. Teach the client the benefits of turning his/her will and life over to the care of a higher power of his/her own understanding.

17. Using a 12-step program's Step Three exercise, show the client how to turn over problems, worries, and anxieties to a higher power and to trust that the higher power is going to help him/her resolve the situation.

18. Review the client's implementation of turning anxieties over to a higher power; reinforce success and redirect for failure.

8. Identify the fears that were learned in the family of origin, and relate these fears to current anxiety levels. (19, 20, 21)

19. Probe the client's family-of-origin experiences for fear-producing situations; help him/her relate these past events to current anxious thoughts, feelings, and behaviors.

20. Encourage and support the client's verbal expression and clarification of his/her feelings that are associated with past rejection experiences, harsh criticism, abandonment, or trauma.

21. Assign the client to read books on resolving painful early family experiences (e.g., *Healing the Shame That Binds You* by Bradshaw or *Facing Shame* by Fossum and Mason); process key concepts learned from the reading.

9. Write a specific plan to follow when anxious and subsequently craving substance use. (8, 10, 17, 22)

8. Facilitate the client's use of logic and reasoning to challenge the irrational thoughts associated with unreasonable worries and to replace those thoughts with reasonable ones.

10. Assist the client in developing a list of 10 positive statements to read to himself/herself several times per day, particularly with feeling anxious.

17. Using a 12-step program's Step Three exercise, show the client how to turn over problems, worries, and anxieties to a higher power and to trust that the higher power is going to help him/her resolve the situation.

22. Help the client develop an alternative constructive plan of action (e.g., relaxation exercises, physical exercise, calling a sponsor, going to a meeting, calling the counselor, talking to someone) when feeling anxious and craving substance use.

10. Develop a leisure program that will increase the frequency of engaging in pleasurable activities and will affirm client's sense of self. (23)

23. Help the client develop a plan of engaging in pleasurable leisure activities (e.g., clubs, hobbies, church, sporting activities, social activities, games) that increase enjoyment of life and affirm himself/herself.

11. Practice relaxation techniques twice per day for 10 to 20 minutes. (24)

24. Using relaxation techniques (e.g., progressive relaxation, guided imagery, biofeedback) teach the client how to completely relax; assign him/her to relax twice per day for 10 to 20 minutes per session.

12. Exercise at least three times per week at a training heart rate for at least 20 minutes. (25)

25. Using the client's current physical fitness levels, increase his/her exercise by 10 percent per week,

13. Write an autobiography, detailing those behaviors in the past that are related to current anxiety or guilt, and the subsequent abuse of substances as a means of escape. (19, 26)

until he or she is exercising three times per week at a training heart rate for at least 20 minutes.

19. Probe the client's family-of-origin experiences for fear-producing situations; help him/her relate these past events to current anxious thoughts, feelings, and behaviors.

26. Using a 12-step program's Step Four exercise, have the client write an autobiography detailing the exact nature of his/her mistakes; teach the client how to begin to forgive himself/herself and others.

14. Increase specific assertive behaviors to deal more effectively and directly with stress, conflict, and responsibilities. (27, 28)

27. Teach assertiveness skills to help the client communicate thoughts, feelings, and needs more openly and directly.

28. Use role-playing, modeling, and behavior rehearsal to help the client apply assertiveness to his/her daily life situations; review progress in implementation, reinforcing success and redirecting for failure.

15. Increase the frequency of speaking up with confidence on social situations. (28, 29)

28. Use role-playing, modeling, and behavior rehearsal to help the client apply assertiveness to his/her daily life situations; review progress in implementation, reinforcing success and redirecting for failure.

29. Teach social skills to the client (see *Intimate Connections* by Burns and *Shyness* by Zimbardo).

16. Develop a program of recovery that includes regularly helping others at recovery group meetings. (30)

30. Help the client develop a structured program of recovery that includes regularly helping others at 12-step program recovery groups.

17. Family members verbalize an understanding of anxiety and addiction, and discuss the ways they and the client can facilitate the recovery process. (31, 32, 33)

31. Assist each family member in developing a list of three things that he or she can do to assist the client in recovery; hold a family session to facilitate communication of the actions on the list.

32. Provide the family members with information about anxiety disorders and the tools that are used to assist the client in recovery.

33. Discuss with the family the connection between anxiety and addiction.

18. Complete a re-administration of objective tests of anxiety as a means of assessing treatment outcome. (34)

34. Assess the outcome of treatment by re-administering to the client objective tests of anxiety (e.g., Beck Anxiety Inventory [BAI], Hamilton Anxiety Rating Scale [HARS]); evaluate the results and provide feedback to the client.

19. Complete a survey to assess the degree of satisfaction with treatment. (35)

35. Administer a survey to assess the client's degree of satisfaction with treatment.

—. _____

—. _____

—. _____

—. _____

—. _____

—. _____

—. _____

—. _____

DIAGNOSTIC SUGGESTIONS:

Axis I:	309.21	Separation Anxiety Disorder
	291.89	Alcohol-Induced Anxiety Disorder
	292.89	Other (or Unknown) Substance-Induced Anxiety Disorder
	296.90	Mood Disorder NOS
	300.01	Panic Disorder without Agoraphobia
	300.21	Panic Disorder with Agoraphobia

	300.29	Specific Phobia
	300.23	Social Phobia
	300.3	Obsessive-Compulsive Disorder
	309.81	Posttraumatic Stress Disorder
	308.3	Acute Stress Disorder
	300.02	Generalized Anxiety Disorder

_____   _____

_____   _____

Axis II:	301.0	Paranoid Personality Disorder
	301.83	Borderline Personality Disorder
	301.50	Histrionic Personality Disorder
	301.82	Avoidant Personality Disorder
	301.6	Dependent Personality Disorder
	301.9	Personality Disorder NOS

_____   _____

_____   _____

ATTENTION-DEFICIT/HYPERACTIVITY DISORDER (ADHD)

BEHAVIORAL DEFINITIONS

1. Demonstrates a pattern of restlessness and hyperactivity leading to attention deficits or learning disability.
2. Is unable to focus attention long enough to learn appropriately.
3. Often fidgets with hands or squirms in seat.
4. Often leaves seat in situations where sitting is required.
5. Moves about excessively in situations in which it is inappropriate.
6. Demonstrates inability to exclude extraneous stimulation.
7. Blurts out answers before questions have been completed.
8. Has difficulty waiting in lines or waiting his/her turn.
9. Often intrudes or talks excessively.
10. Acts too quickly on feelings without thought or deliberation.
11. ADHD traits increase vulnerability to addictive behaviors.

—. _____
   _____

—. _____
   _____

—. _____
   _____

LONG-TERM GOALS

1. Maintain a program of recovery from addiction, and reduce the negative effects of Attention-Deficit Hyperactivity Disorder on learning, social interaction, and self-esteem.
2. Develop the coping skills necessary to improve Attention-Deficit Hyperactivity Disorder and eliminate addiction.

3. Understand the relationship between Attention-Deficit Hyperactivity Disorder symptoms and addiction.

4. Develop the skills necessary to bring Attention-Deficit Hyperactivity Disorder symptoms under control, so normal learning can take place.

5. Decrease impulsivity by learning how to stop, think, and plan before acting.

—. _____

_____

—. _____

_____

—. _____

_____

SHORT-TERM OBJECTIVES

THERAPEUTIC INTERVENTIONS

1. Complete psychological testing or objective questionnaires for assessing ADHD and substance abuse. (1)

1. Administer to the client psychological instruments designed to objectively assess ADHD (e.g., Conners' Adult ADHD Rating Scales [CAARS], Substance Abuse Subtle Screening Inventory-3 [SASSI-3]); give the client feedback regarding the results of the assessment.

2. Complete psychological testing to rule out emotional factors or learning disabilities as the basis for maladaptive behavior. (2, 3)

2. Arrange for psychological testing to rule out emotional factors or learning disabilities as the basis for the client's maladaptive behavior.

3. Give feedback to the client and his/her family regarding psychological testing results.

3. Identify the symptoms of ADHD and their impact on daily living. (4, 5)

4. Teach the client how to monitor ADHD symptoms and rate the severity of symptoms on a scale of 1 to 100 each day.

5. Explore the client's pattern of ADHD symptoms and their impact on his/her daily living.

4. Verbalize the powerlessness and unmanageability that resulted from treating ADHD symptoms with addiction. (6)

5. Verbalize the relationship between ADHD and addiction. (7)

6. Implement a program of recovery structured so as to bring ADHD and addiction under control. (8)

7. List five ways a higher power can be used to assist in recovery from ADHD and addiction. (9)

8. Comply with a physician evaluation to determine if a psychotropic intervention is warranted and take any medications as directed. (10, 11)

9. Implement remedial procedures for any learning disabilities that add to client's frustration. (12)

10. Reduce environmental stimulation so as to facilitate concentration and learning. (13, 14)

6. Using a 12-step recovery program's Step One exercise, help the client to accept his/her powerlessness and unmanageability over ADHD symptoms and addiction.

7. Using a biopsychosocial approach, teach the client about the relationship between ADHD symptoms and the use of substances to control symptoms.

8. Help the client to develop a program of recovery that includes the elements necessary to bring ADHD and addiction under control (e.g., medication, behavior modification, environmental controls, aftercare meetings, further therapy).

9. Teach the client about the AA concept of a higher power and how this power can assist him/her in recovery.

10. Arrange for a physician to order psychotropic medications as warranted, to titrate medications, and to monitor for side effects.

11. Direct the staff to administer medications as ordered by the physician and monitor for side effects.

12. Refer the client to an educational specialist to design remedial procedures for any learning disabilities that may be present in addition to ADHD.

13. Help the client to create an environment that is free enough of extraneous stimulation that learning can occur.

14. Using modeling, role-playing, and behavior rehearsal, show the

11. Keep lists and make a calendar as reminders about daily appointments and obligations. (15)

12. Practice extending concentration in gradual increments, and self-reinforce each extension. (16)

13. Verbalize an understanding of the importance of learning in small increments of time, and of taking breaks. (17)

14. Reduce impulsive behavior and demonstrate the ability to stop, think, and plan before acting. (18, 19)

15. Verbalize the feelings of shame and frustration that accompany failure to learn because of ADHD. (20)

16. List the negative messages given to oneself in a learning situation and replace each with an encouraging, affirming message. (21, 22)

17. Verbalize constructive coping mechanisms to use when the negative emotions associated

client how to take time-outs and breaks when feeling restless and/or irritable.

15. Teach the client how to make lists and keep a calendar to remind him/her about appointments and daily obligations.

16. Show the client how to extend periods of concentration in small increments; then teach him/her how to reinforce himself/herself each time.

17. Assist the client in setting up learning periods in small increments of time, taking enough breaks to keep ADHD symptoms under control.

18. Using modeling, role-playing, and behavior rehearsal, show the client how to stop, think, and plan before acting.

19. Review the client's impulsive behavior pattern and the negative consequences that have resulted from it.

20. Explore the negative emotions associated with a failure to learn.

21. Assist the client in identifying the distorted, negative self-talk that he/she engages in within any learning situation.

22. Train the client to replace negative expectations and disparaging self-talk with positive self-talk in learning situations.

23. Review specific instances of failure to learn and the negative emotions associated with the ex-

with failure are a trigger for addiction. (23, 24)

perience; focus on how addictive behavior was used to escape from negative emotions.

24. Role-play and model constructive alternative coping behaviors to use in failure-to-learn situations (e.g., cognitive focusing, deep breathing, make lists, reduce distractions, shorten learning sessions, repeat instructions verbally).

18. Increase the frequency of positive interaction with peers. (25, 26)

25. Using role-playing, modeling, and behavior rehearsal, teach the client social skills that control impulsivity, reduce alienation, and build self-esteem (e.g., calm tones, respectful timing of verbal contribution, comments thoughtful of impact, appropriate humility).

26. Direct group therapy sessions that focus on social skill enhancement, getting feedback from peers for the client's socialization behavior.

19. Verbalize feeling pleased with self and others regarding "fitting in" socially. (26, 27)

26. Direct group therapy sessions that focus on social skill enhancement, getting feedback from peers for the client's socialization behavior.

27. Reinforce positive social interaction with peers and explore the positive self-esteem that results from successful interactions.

20. Report instances when relaxation techniques reduced tension and frustration while increasing focus in a learning situation. (28, 29, 30)

28. Using techniques like progressive relaxation, guided imagery, or biofeedback, teach the client how to relax completely; assign him/her to relax twice per day for 10 to 20 minutes per session.

29. Encourage the client to implement relaxation skills as a coping and focusing mechanism when feeling tense and frustrated by a learning situation.

21. Develop and implement an exercise program that includes exercising at a training heart rate for at least 20 minutes at least three times per week. (31)

22. Develop an aftercare program that includes regular attendance at recovery group meetings, getting a sponsor, and continuing the therapy necessary to bring ADHD and addiction under control. (32)

23. Family members verbalize an understanding of the connection between ADHD and addiction. (33, 34, 35)

24. Complete a re-administration of objective tests of ADHD and addiction as a means of assessing treatment outcome. (36)

25. Complete a survey to assess the degree of satisfaction with treatment. (37)

30. Review the client's implementation of relaxation techniques; reinforce success and redirect for failure.

31. Help the client develop an exercise program; increase the exercise by 10 percent each week until the client is exercising at a training heart rate for at least 20 minutes, at least three times a week.

32. Help the client to develop an aftercare program that includes regular attendance at recovery group meetings, getting a sponsor, and continuing the therapy necessary to bring ADHD and addictive behavior under control.

33. Discuss with the family members the connection between ADHD and addictive behavior.

34. In a family session, go over what each family member can do to assist the client in recovery (e.g., attend recovery group meetings, reinforce positive coping skills, be patient, keep expectations realistic, go to ADHD support group).

35. Provide family members with information about ADHD (e.g., *You Mean I'm Not Lazy, Stupid, or Crazy?* by Kelly and Ramundo).

36. Assess the outcome of treatment by re-administering to the client objective tests of ADHD; evaluate the results and provide feedback to the client.

37. Administer a survey to assess the client's degree of satisfaction with treatment.

—. _____   —. _____
   _____   _____
—. _____   —. _____
   _____   _____
—. _____   —. _____
   _____   _____

DIAGNOSTIC SUGGESTIONS:

Axis I:	314.01	Attention-Deficit/Hyperactivity Disorder, Combined Type
	314.01	Attention-Deficit/Hyperactivity Disorder, Predominantly Hyperactive-Impulsive Type
	314.9	Attention-Deficit/Hyperactivity Disorder NOS
	312.8	Conduct Disorder
	313.81	Oppositional-Defiant Disorder
	300.4	Dysthymic Disorder
	312.9	Disruptive Behavior Disorder NOS
	312.30	Impulse-Control Disorder NOS

_____   _____

_____   _____

Axis II:	301.7	Antisocial Personality Disorder
	301.83	Borderline Personality Disorder

_____   _____

_____   _____

ATTENTION-DEFICIT/INATTENTIVE DISORDER (ADD)

BEHAVIORAL DEFINITIONS

1. Demonstrates inability to sustain attention long enough to learn normally at work or school.
2. Fails to give sufficient attention to detail and tends to make careless mistakes.
3. Has difficulty sustaining attention at work, school, or play.
4. ADD symptoms and the frustration associated with them increase vulnerability to addictive behavior.
5. Often does not seem to listen when spoken to directly.
6. Often does not follow through on instructions and fails to finish tasks.
7. Reports difficulty organizing events, material, or time.
8. Avoids tasks and activities that require concentration.
9. Becomes too easily distracted by extraneous stimulation.
10. Often forgets daily obligations.

—. _____

_____

—. _____

_____

—. _____

_____

LONG-TERM GOALS

1. Maintain a program of recovery, free from addiction and the negative effects of Attention-Deficit Disorder.
2. Demonstrate sustained attention and concentration for consistently longer periods of time.

3. Understand the negative influence of Attention-Deficit Disorder on substance use.
4. Structure a recovery program sufficient to maintain abstinence and reduce the negative effects of Attention-Deficit Disorder on learning and self-esteem.
5. Develop positive self-talk when faced with problems caused by Attention-Deficit Disorder or addiction.

—. _____
   _____
   _____

—. _____
   _____
   _____

—. _____
   _____

SHORT-TERM OBJECTIVES

1. Complete psychological testing or objective questionnaires for assessing ADD. (1)

2. Complete psychological testing to rule out emotional factors or learning disabilities as the basis for maladaptive behavior. (2)

3. Verbalize several reasons why attention deficit symptoms lead to addiction. (3, 4)

THERAPEUTIC INTERVENTIONS

1. Administer to the client psychological instruments designed to objectively assess ADD and substance abuse (e.g., Conners' Adult ADHD Rating Scales [CAARS]); give the client feedback regarding the results of the assessment.

2. Arrange for psychological testing to rule out emotional factors or learning disabilities as the basis for the client's maladaptive behavior; give feedback to the client and his/her family regarding psychological testing results.

3. List the ways that using addictive behavior to cope with the symptoms of ADD and the feelings that result from it leads to powerlessness and unmanageability.

4. Probe the feelings the client had when trying to deal with the failure to learn due to symptoms of

4. List the ways that using addiction to cope with symptoms of ADD and the feelings that result from it leads to powerlessness and unmanageability. (5)

5. Verbalize the interpersonal difficulties caused or exacerbated by symptoms of ADD and substance abuse. (6, 7)

6. List the negative messages given to oneself in a learning situation and replace each with an encouraging, affirming message. (8, 9)

7. Identify specific instances when the negative emotions associated with failure to learn were a trigger for addiction, and verbalize constructive coping mechanisms to use in future learning situations. (10, 11)

ADD, and discuss how chemical abuse was used to avoid uncomfortable feelings.

5. Using a12-step Step One exercise, help the client to correlate ADD and addiction with powerlessnes and unmanageability.

6. Probe the client's relationship problems caused or exacerbated by ADD and addiction.

7. Confront statements in which the client blames others for his/her impulsive behaviors and fails to accept responsibility for the consequences of his/her actions.

8. Assist the client in identifying distorted, negative self-talk with positive self-talk in a learning situation.

9. Train the client to replace negative expectations and disparaging self-talk with positive self-talk in a learning situation.

10. Review specific instances of the client's failure to learn and the negative emotions associated with the experience; note if these emotions triggered addictive behavior as an escape.

11. Role play and model constructive alternative coping behaviors (e.g., cognitive focusing, deep breathing, make lists, reduce distractions, shorten learning sessions, repeat instructions verbally) to deal with difficult and frustrating learning situations.

8. List how working a program of recovery can assist in eliminating the negative effects of ADD and addiction. (12, 13)

12. Help the client to see how working a program of recovery can aid in reducing the negative influences of ADD and addiction (e.g., going to meetings, talking regularly with a sponsor, and enjoying recreation with a new recovery peer group).

13. Help the client to understand the AA concept of a higher power and teach the client the ways a higher power can assist him/her in recovery (e.g., turn problems over to God, practice regular prayer, and meditation).

9. Comply with a physician's evaluation to determine if psychopharmacological intervention is warranted; then take any medications as directed. (14, 15)

14. Refer the client to a physician to determine if psychopharmacological intervention is warranted, and to order medications as indicated, titrate medications, and observe for side effects.

15. Direct the staff to administer medications as ordered by the physician and to monitor for side effects and effectiveness.

10. Implement remedial procedures for learning disabilities that add to frustration. (16)

16. Refer the client to a special educator who will design remedial procedures for any learning disabilities that may be present in addition to ADD.

11. Keep lists of all scheduled activities and obligations and mark off each item as it is completed. (17)

17. Assist the client in developing calendars and lists to carry that detail activities and obligations.

12. List techniques that can be used to reduce the negative effects of ADD. (18)

18. Help the client to develop a list of the things he/she can do to reduce the negative effects of ADD (e.g., reduce extraneous stimulation, make lists and reminders, take medication, utilize relaxation techniques, talk to someone, go to AA/NA meetings, engage in physical exercise).

13. Create and utilize a learning environment that is free enough of extraneous stimulation that productive learning can take place. (19)

14. Implement coping skills when experiencing ADD symptoms or craving for addiction. (20, 21, 22, 23)

15. Family members verbalize what each person can do to assist the client in recovery. (24, 25)

19. Help the client develop a quiet place that is free of extraneous stimulation, where he/she can concentrate and learn.

20. Teach the client relapse prevention techniques of going to meetings, talking to someone, calling a sponsor, utilizing relaxation skills, engaging in physical exercise, and turning worries over to a higher power.

21. Using relaxation techniques (e.g., progressive relaxation, guided imagery, biofeedback), teach the client how to relax; assign him/her to relax twice a day for 10 to 20 minutes.

22. Encourage the client to implement relaxation skills as a coping and focusing mechanism when feeling tense and frustrated by a learning situation or when tempted to relapse into addictive behavior.

23. Help the client develop an exercise program, increasing the exercise until he/she is exercising at a training heart rate at least three times a week for at least 20 minutes; encourage exercise as a means of reducing the level of stress and frustration or when tempted to relapse into addictive behavior.

24. In a family session, teach the family members the connection between ADD and addiction, going over what each family member can do to assist the client in recovery (e.g., go to Alanon meetings, reinforce positive coping skills, keep expectations realistic, go to ADHD support group).

16. Complete a re-administration of objective tests of ADD as a means of assessing treatment outcome. (26)

17. Complete a survey to assess the degree of satisfaction with treatment. (27)

—. _____
   _____

—. _____
   _____

—. _____
   _____

25. Provide the family members with information about ADHD (e.g., *You Mean I'm Not Lazy, Stupid, or Crazy?* by Kelly and Ramundo).

26. Assess the outcome of treatment by re-administering to the client objective tests of ADD; evaluate the results and provide feedback to the client.

27. Administer a survey to assess the client's degree of satisfaction with treatment.

—. _____
   _____

—. _____
   _____

—. _____
   _____

DIAGNOSTIC SUGGESTIONS:

Axis I:

	315.9	Learning Disorder NOS
	314.01	Attention-Deficit/Hyperactivity Disorder, Combined Type
	314.00	Attention-Deficit/Hyperactivity Disorder, Predominantly Inattentive Type
	314.9	Attention-Deficit/Hyperactivity Disorder NOS
	312.8	Conduct Disorder
	313.81	Oppositional-Defiant Disorder
	312.9	Disruptive Behavior Disorder NOS
	312.30	Impulse Control Disorder NOS
	300.4	Dysthymic Disorder

_____   _____

_____   _____

Axis II: 301.7   Antisocial Personality Disorder

_____   _____

_____   _____

BORDERLINE TRAITS

BEHAVIORAL DEFINITIONS

1. Demonstrates extreme emotional reactivity (e.g., anger, anxiety, or depression) under minor stress, which usually does not last beyond a few hours to a few days.
2. Exhibits a pattern of intense, chaotic interpersonal relationships.
3. Presents with marked identity disturbance.
4. Experiences impulsive behaviors that are potentially self-damaging.
5. Reports recurrent suicidal gestures, threats, or self-mutilating behavior.
6. Verbalizes chronic feelings of emptiness or boredom.
7. Demonstrates frequent eruptions of intense, inappropriate anger.
8. Reports feeling that others are treating him/her unfairly or that they can't be trusted.
9. Analyzes most issues in simple terms of right and wrong (black/white, trustworthy/deceitful) without regard for extenuating circumstances or complex situations.
10. Becomes very anxious with any hint of perceived abandonment in a relationship.

—. _____
   _____
   _____
—. _____
   _____
   _____
—. _____
   _____

LONG-TERM GOALS

1. Develop a program of recovery from addiction that reduces the impact of borderline traits on abstinence.

2. Develop and demonstrate coping skills to reduce mood swings and control impulses.
3. Understand how borderline traits can foster a pattern of continued addictive behavior.
4. Reduce the frequency of self-damaging behaviors (e.g., substance abuse, reckless driving, sexual acting out, binge eating, or suicidal behaviors).
5. Terminate dichotomous thinking, unmanaged anger, and/or fear of abandonment.

—. _____

_____

—. _____

_____

—. _____

_____

SHORT-TERM OBJECTIVES

1. Keep a daily record of negative emotions and self-defeating thinking, which leads to failure. (1, 2, 3)

2. Complete psychological testing or objective questionnaires for assessing symptoms associated with borderline personality. (4)

THERAPEUTIC INTERVENTIONS

1. Assign the client to write a daily journal of emotions that he/she experienced, why the feelings developed, and what actions resulted from those feelings.

2. Help the client to differentiate between and to list his/her self-defeating and self-enhancing thoughts; assign him/her to keep a daily record of his/her self-defeating thoughts.

3. Using cognitive therapy techniques, help the client to see how negative, self-defeating thinking leads to negative consequences, both emotionally and behaviorally.

4. Administer to the client psychological instruments designed to objectively assess depression, suicidality, impulsivity, and/or ag-

gression (e.g., The Millon Clinical Multiaxial Inventory [MCMI], Hamilton Depression Rating Scale [HDRS], Beck's Scale for Suicide Ideation [SSI], Aggressive Acts Questionnaire [AAQ], Barratt Impulsiveness Scale-11 [BIS-11]); give the client feedback regarding the results of the assessment.

3. Practice replacing self-defeating thoughts with self-enhancing, realistic thoughts. (5, 6)

5. Assist the client in building a list of positive reinforcing statements to use daily for self-enhancement.

6. Using cognitive therapy techniques, help the client replace self-derogatory, distorted thinking with positive, self-enhancing statements.

4. Verbalize reasons why borderline traits make recovery from addictive behavior more difficult. (7, 8)

7. Assist the client in defining the criteria for borderline traits, identifying each in himself/herself, and how each trait makes recovery from addictive behavior more difficult.

8. Help the client to see how poor impulse control, poor anger management, fear of abandonment, and intense mood swings increase the probability of addictive behavior; explore instances when his/her borderline traits led to addictive behavior.

5. Describe situations in which impulsive, self-damaging behaviors led to negative consequences, and list alternative adaptive behaviors. (9)

9. Review several impulsive, self-damaging behaviors (e.g., gambling, substance abuse, binge eating, explosive anger, sexual acting out, self-mutilation, or suicidal gestures) and their negative consequences; help the client discover what he/she could have done adaptively in each situation.

6. Verbalize a plan to decrease the frequency of sudden mood swings. (10)

10. Help the client to develop a list of coping skills to be used in dealing with sudden dysphoric mood swings (e.g., delaying the reaction to his/her moodiness, writing down his/her feelings and their causes, checking with others as to the rationality of his/her feelings).

7. Practice the impulse control skills of stopping, looking, listening, thinking, and planning before acting. (11, 12, 13, 14)

11. Teach the client how impulsivity leads to negative consequences and how self-control leads to positive consequences.

12. Teach the client self-control strategies (e.g., "stop, look, listen, think, and plan") to control impulses.

13. Using role-playing, behavior rehearsal, and modeling, apply the "stop, look, listen, think, and plan" strategy to the client's daily life situations; assign him/her to implement this technique in his/her daily life.

14. Review the client's impulse control progress; reinforce success and redirect for failure.

8. Verbalize an understanding of how anger toward others or fear of abandonment is expressed in suicidal gestures or self-mutilating behavior. (15)

15. Probe the relationship between the client's feelings of anger and/or fear and suicide gestures or self-mutilating behavior.

9. Identify interpersonal situations that easily trigger feelings of anger or fear of abandonment. (16, 17)

16. Explore childhood as well as more recent experiences that have shaped the client's psyche such that he/she is overly reactive to any hint of abandonment; assist him/her in not generalizing his/her fears to the current relationship.

17. Assist the client in identifying current triggers for his/her feelings of anger or fear of abandonment, and relate these to historical causes rather than current realities.

10. Verbalize the negative social consequences of frequent expressions of untamed anger or extreme dependency. (18)

11. Verbalize and implement alternative, constructive ways to cope with feelings of anger or fear. (19, 20, 21, 22, 23)

18. Help the client to understand the self-defeating, alienating consequences of frequently expressing anger and/or desperately clinging to others.

19. Develop with the client a list of constructive reactions to feelings of anger or fear (e.g., writing about his/her feelings, talking to a counselor, delaying expression for 24 hours, tracing feelings to his or her own background, substituting a physical exercise for outlet, practicing a relaxation exercise) that reduce the impulsive acting out of feelings.

20. Model verbalization of anger in a controlled, respectful manner, delaying the response, if necessary, to gain more control; ask the client to role-play calm anger expression.

21. Help the client make a list of people to call or visit when he/she becomes upset, and then role-play several situations in which he/she discusses a problem calmly.

22. Assign the client the task of talking to someone calmly when feeling angry, fearful, or depressed.

23. Using techniques such as progressive relaxation, biofeedback, or guided imagery, teach the client how to relax; encourage application of this skill to reduce feelings of tension and anger.

12. Meet with the physician to be evaluated for the need for psychopharmacological treatment. (24, 25)

24. Physician is to evaluate if psychopharmacological intervention is warranted.

25. Physician is to prescribe and adjust medication to maximize its effectiveness and to reduce side effects.

13. Take psychotropic medications as prescribed, and report as to their effectiveness and side effects. (26, 27)

14. Practice the healthy communication skills of listening to others, using "I" statements, and sharing feelings. (28, 29)

15. Verbalize feelings of self-acceptance and self-confidence. (30)

16. Verbalize ways in which a higher power can assist in resolving dependency needs. (31)

17. Verbalize an understanding of how dichotomous thinking leads to interpersonal difficulties. (32, 33, 34)

18. Exercise at least three times per week for at least 20 minutes. (35)

19. Write an aftercare program that lists resources that will be used when feeling angry, anxious, abandoned, or depressed, rather than reverting to addictive behavior. (36)

26. Staff administers medications as ordered by physician.

27. Monitor the client's psychotropic medication for compliance, effectiveness, and side effects.

28. Teach the client how to listen, use "I" statements, and share feelings.

29. Assist the client in developing healthy self-talk and good communication skills as a means of increasing his/her feelings of interpersonal safety.

30. Assist the client in resolving feelings of rejection from childhood in order to decrease his/her current feelings of vulnerability.

31. Teach the client about the higher power concept in 12-step recovery programs, and give examples of how he/she can turn problems over to the higher power while in recovery.

32. Teach the client how dichotomous thinking leads to feelings of interpersonal mistrust.

33. Challenge the extremes of the client's thinking as it relates to decisions about good or bad, or trustworthy or deceitful people.

34. Assist the client in reviewing the strengths and weaknesses of his/her friends and family members.

35. Help the client to develop an exercise program that will aid in reducing his/her stress level.

36. Assist the client in developing a structured aftercare program that lists resources he/she can use when feeling angry, anxious, abandoned, or depressed.

20. Family members verbalize what each can do to assist the client in recovery. (37, 38)

37. In a family session, review what each member can do to assist the client in recovery.

38. Provide the family members with information about borderline syndrome and the steps that the client must take to recover successfully.

21. Complete a re-administration of objective tests to assess progress in resolving borderline traits as a means of assessing treatment outcome. (39)

39. Assess the outcome of treatment by re-administering to the client objective tests of progress in resolving borderline traits (e.g., The Millon Clinical Multiaxial Inventory [MCMI], Depression Rating Scale [HDRS], Beck's Scale for Suicide Ideation [SSI], Aggressive Acts Questionnaire [AAQ], Barratt Impulsiveness Scale-11 [BIS-11]); evaluate the results and provide feedback to the client.

22. Complete a survey to assess the degree of client's satisfaction with treatment. (40)

40. Administer a survey to assess the client's degree of satisfaction with treatment.

__. _____

    _____

__. _____

    _____

__. _____

    _____

__. _____

    _____

__. _____

    _____

__. _____

    _____

DIAGNOSTIC SUGGESTIONS:

Axis I:	296.xx	Major Depressive Disorder
	300.4	Dysthymic Disorder
	296.xx	Bipolar I Disorder
	296.89	Bipolar II Disorder
	309.81	Posttraumatic Stress Disorder
	313.82	Identity Problem
	_____	_____
	_____	_____

Axis II:	301.83	Borderline Personality Disorder
	301.50	Histrionic Personality Disorder
	301.22	Schizotypal Personality Disorder
	301.7	Antisocial Personality Disorder
	301.0	Paranoid Personality Disorder
	301.81	Narcissistic Personality Disorder
	301.6	Dependent Personality Disorder
	_____	_____
	_____	_____

CHILDHOOD TRAUMA

BEHAVIORAL DEFINITIONS

1. Reports a history of childhood physical, sexual, or emotional abuse.
2. Unresolved psychological conflicts caused by childhood abuse or neglect.
3. Experiences irrational fears, suppressed rage, low self-esteem, identity conflicts, depression, or anxious insecurity related to painful early life experiences.
4. Uses addiction to escape emotional pain tied to childhood abuse.
5. Verbalizes intrusive memories, guilt, or emotional numbing from early childhood trauma.
6. Has unresolved emotions and maladaptive behavior that is the result of childhood trauma.
7. Demonstrates inability to trust others, bond in relationships, communicate effectively, and maintain healthy interpersonal relationships because of early childhood neglect or abuse.

__. _____
_____
__. _____
_____
__. _____
_____

LONG-TERM GOALS

1. Resolve conflicting feelings that are associated with childhood traumas and terminate addiction, which has been used as a means of coping with those unresolved feelings.
2. Develop an awareness of how childhood issues have affected addiction.

3. Learn how childhood trauma resulted in interpersonal problems and addiction.
4. Maintain a program of recovery free of addiction and the negative effects of childhood trauma.
5. Learn to forgive perpetrators and turn them over to a higher power.
6. Resolve past childhood/family issues, leading to less fear, anger, and depression, and to greater self-esteem and confidence.

—. _____
   _____
   _____

—. _____
   _____
   _____

—. _____
   _____

SHORT-TERM OBJECTIVES

THERAPEUTIC INTERVENTIONS

1. Verbalize powerlessness and unmanageability experienced as a child and directly relate these feelings to addiction. (1)	1. Using an AA First Step exercise, help the client to see the powerlessness and unmanageability that resulted from using addiction to deal with negative feelings associated with childhood trauma.
2. Describe the traumatic experiences that were endured as a child, and the feelings of helplessness, rage, hurt, and sadness that resulted from those experiences. (2)	2. Explore the painful experiences endured in the client's family of origin, and help identify the unhealthy emotional and behavioral patterns that evolved from those experiences.
3. Complete psychological testing or objective questionnaires for assessing childhood trauma. (3)	3. Administer to the client psychological instruments designed to objectively assess childhood trauma (e.g., Childhood Trauma Questionnaire [CTQ], Davidson Trauma Scale [DTS], Beck Depression Inventory-II [BDI-II], Beck Anxiety Inventory [BAI]); give the client feedback regarding the results of the assessment.

4. Identify the unhealthy rules and roles learned in the family of origin. (2, 4)

2. Explore the painful experiences endured in the client's family of origin, and help identify the unhealthy emotional and behavioral patterns that evolved from those experiences.

4. Teach the client about the unhealthy rules and roles that develop in dysfunctional families, and help identify what role he/she played in the family dynamics.

5. Verbalize an understanding of how childhood abandonment, neglect, or abuse led to emotional and social problems. (5)

5. Help the client to understand the relationship between childhood trauma and current problems with trust, anger, self-esteem, or depression.

6. Identify a pattern of abusing substances as a means of escape from psychological pain associated with childhood traumas, and verbalize more constructive means of coping. (6, 7)

6. Explore the client's behavior of addiction as a means of coping with emotional pain, and assist him or her in identifying the self-defeating, negative consequences of this behavior.

7. Teach the client healthier and more constructive means of coping with emotional pain (e.g., sharing pain with others, attending AA meetings, confronting and then forgiving perpetrator, turning issues over to a higher power).

7. Verbalize a plan as to how to fulfill the unmet needs of childhood now that adulthood has been reached. (8, 9)

8. Assist the client in identifying, understanding, and verbalizing unresolved needs, wishes, and wants from the childhood years; then help him/her develop a written plan to meet each unmet need, wish, or want.

9. Have the client read *Healing the Shame that Binds You* by Bradshaw and *Outgrowing the Pain* by Gil; then help him/her identify unresolved feelings, wishes, and wants.

8. List and replace the dysfunctional thoughts, feelings, and behaviors learned during the childhood trauma and/or neglect. (10, 11)

9. Attend group therapy sessions to share thoughts and feelings related to childhood traumas, and how addiction has been used to avoid negative feelings. (6, 12)

10. Implement healthy problem-solving and communication skills. (13, 14)

11. List five ways a higher power can assist in recovery from childhood trauma and addiction. (15)

12. Verbalize an understanding of the power of forgiving perpetrators. (15, 16, 17, 18)

10. Probe the client's childhood trauma and/or neglect and help him/her to relate these events to current feelings, thoughts, and behaviors.

11. Teach the client realistic, positive self-talk, to replace the distorted messages that were learned from childhood experiences.

6. Explore the client's behavior of addiction as a means of coping with emotional pain, and assist him/her in identifying the self-defeating, negative consequences of this behavior.

12. Direct group therapy sessions in which the client is encouraged to share his/her story of childhood trauma, allowing for feedback of empathy, acceptance, and affirmation from group members.

13. Explore the client's family-of-origin maladaptive style of conflict resolution and communication patterns; relate these patterns to the client's current interpersonal skill deficits.

14. Use modeling, role-playing, and behavior rehearsal to teach the client healthy problem-solving and communication skills to use in recovery (e.g., active listening, using "I" messages, cooperation, compromise, and mutual respect).

15. Teach the client about the AA/NA concept of a higher power, and how the higher power can assist him/her in forgiving others and reestablishing self-esteem.

15. Teach the client about the AA/NA concept of a higher power, and how the higher power can assist

him/her in forgiving others and reestablishing self-esteem.

16. Help the client to understand that often perpetrators were wounded children also, and need to be forgiven and turned over to a higher power in order to not harbor rage at them.

17. Recommend the client read books on the topic of forgiveness (e.g., *Forgive and Forget* by Smedes, *When Bad Things Happen to Good People* by Kushner).

18. Teach the client the benefits (e.g., release of hurt and anger, putting the issue in the past, opens door for trust of others) of beginning a process of forgiveness (not necessarily forgetting or fraternizing with) of abusive adults.

13. Write a letter to the perpetrator, detailing the childhood abuse and its effect on one's thoughts, feelings, and behavior. (19, 20)

19. Assign the client to write a letter to his or her perpetrator detailing the emotional trauma that resulted from the abuse.

20. Assign the client to write a forgiveness letter to the perpetrator of the abuse; process the letter.

14. Write a letter to each primary caregiver describing the childhood abuse and current feelings, wishes, and wants. (21)

21. Assist the client in writing a letter to each parent or primary caregiver, detailing his/her childhood abuse and sharing what the client wants from each person in recovery.

15. Learn and demonstrate honesty, openness, and assertiveness in communicating with others. (14, 22, 23, 24)

14. Use modeling, role-playing, and behavior rehearsal to teach the client healthy problem-solving and communication skills to use in recovery (e.g., active listening, using "I" messages, cooperation, compromise, and mutual respect).

22. Assign the client to read *Taking Charge of Your Social Life* by Gambrill and Richey to enhance social communication skills; process concepts in session.

23. Teach the client the healthy communication skills of being honest, asking for wants, and sharing feelings.

24. Using modeling, role-playing, and behavior rehearsal, teach the client healthy assertive skills; then practice these skills in several current problem situations.

16. Identify any patterns of repeating abandonment, neglect, or abuse experienced as a child. (25)

25. Explore the tendency to repeat a pattern of abuse and neglect toward the client's own children when it has been experienced on a regular basis in childhood.

17. Verbalize an understanding of how the home group in AA/NA can provide a substitute for the healthy home the client never experienced. (26)

26. Help the client to see how the new home AA/NA group can help to substitute for a healthy home that he/she never had.

18. Develop and agree to participate in an aftercare program to continue to recover from childhood abuse and addiction. (27)

27. Help the client to develop an aftercare program that includes regular attendance at recovery group meetings and the continued therapy necessary to recover from childhood trauma and addiction.

19. Share with the family the pain of childhood trauma and commit to working with the family in continuing care. (28)

28. Hold a family therapy session in which the client is supported in sharing the pain of childhood trauma with family members; connect the pain of the past with his/her current addictive behavior.

20. List three things each family member can do to assist in recovery. (29)

29. Help the client make a list of three things each family member can do to assist him/her in recovery.

21. Complete a re-administration of objective tests of childhood trauma effects as a means of assessing treatment outcome. (30)

22. Complete a survey to assess the degree of satisfaction with treatment. (31)

30. Assess the outcome of treatment by re-administering to the client objective tests of childhood trauma; evaluate the results and provide feedback to the client.

31. Administer a survey to assess the client's degree of satisfaction with treatment.

—. _____
   _____

—. _____
   _____

—. _____
   _____

—. _____
   _____

—. _____
   _____

—. _____
   _____

DIAGNOSTIC SUGGESTIONS:

Axis I:	300.4	Dysthymic Disorder
	296.xx	Major Depressive Disorder
	300.02	Generalized Anxiety Disorder
	309.81	Posttraumatic Stress Disorder
	300.14	Dissociative Identity Disorder
	V61.21	Sexual Abuse of a Child (995.5, Victim)
	V61.21	Physical Abuse of a Child (995.5, Victim)
	V61.21	Neglect of Child (995.5, Victim)
	_____	_____
	_____	_____
Axis II:	301.7	Antisocial Personality Disorder
	301.83	Borderline Personality Disorder
	_____	_____
	_____	_____

CHRONIC PAIN*

BEHAVIORAL DEFINITIONS

1. Uses addictive medications to control pain.
2. Experiences pain beyond the normal healing process (6 months or more) and uses addictive medications as a primary coping skill.
3. Complains of generalized pain in many joints, muscles, and bones that debilitates normal functioning.
4. Overuse or use of increased amounts of medications with little, if any, pain relief.
5. Experiences tension, migraine, cluster, or chronic daily headaches of unknown origin.
6. Complains of chronic neck or back pain.
7. Experiences intermittent pain related to a physical disease.
8. Decreased or terminated activities (e.g., work, household chores, socializing, exercise, sex, or other pleasurable activities) because of pain and subsequent substance abuse.
9. Exhibits signs and symptoms of depression related to chronic pain syndrome.

—. _____
_____
_____

—. _____
_____
_____

—. _____
_____

*Most of the content of this chapter (with slight revisions) originates from A. E. Jongsma and L. M. Peterson, *The Complete Adult Psychotherapy Treatment Planner, Third Edition* (New York: Wiley, 2003). Copyright © 2003 by A. E. Jongsma and L. M. Peterson. Reprinted with permission.

LONG-TERM GOALS

1. Discontinue opioid abuse and begin a program of recovery, using the 12-steps process as well as necessary pain management skills.
2. Regulate pain without addictive medications.
3. Find relief from pain and build renewed contentment and joy in performing activities of life.
4. Develop healthy options to deal with chronic pain.
5. Practice a program of recovery, including 12-step involvement and pain management skills.
6. Less daily suffering from pain and from substance abuse.

—. _____
   _____
   _____
—. _____
   _____
   _____
—. _____
   _____

SHORT-TERM OBJECTIVES	THERAPEUTIC INTERVENTIONS
1. Describe the nature, history, impact of, and understood causes for chronic pain and substance abuse. (1, 2)	1. Gather a history and current status of the client's chronic pain and substance abuse.
	2. Explore the changes in the client's mood, attitude, and social, vocational, and familial/marital roles that have occurred in response to pain and substance abuse.
2. Cooperate with a thorough medical examination to rule out any alternative causes for the pain and to explore any new treatment possibilities. (3)	3. Refer the client to a physician or clinic to undergo a thorough examination, so as to rule out any undiagnosed condition and to receive recommendations on any further treatment options.
3. Follow through on a pain management and substance abuse program. (4, 5, 6)	4. Discuss with the physician the use of medications to manage chronic pain and withdrawal from addictive substances.

5. Make a referral to a pain management specialist and substance abuse program of the client's choice and have him/her sign appropriate releases for the therapist to have progress updates from the program and to coordinate services.

6. Elicit from the client a verbal commitment to cooperate with pain management specialists, headache clinic, or rehabilitation program.

4. Complete psychological testing or objective questionnaires for assessing the level of pain. (7)

7. Administer to the client psychological instruments designed to objectively assess chronic pain (e.g., McGill Pain Questionnaire Short Form [MPQ-SF], Psychosocial Pain Inventory [PSPI]); give the client feedback regarding the results of the assessment.

5. Complete a thorough medication review by a physician who is a specialist in dealing with chronic pain and substance abuse. (8)

8. Ask the client to complete a medication review with a physician, including a discussion of the use of methadone, and buprenorphine for pain management and opioid withdrawal.

6. Verbalize a statement of ownership of the pain and the addiction. (9, 10)

9. Assist the client in working through the defenses that prevent him/her from owning the pain and the substance abuse as his/hers.

10. Elicit from the client statements of ownership of the pain and the addiction.

7. Verbalize an increased understanding of pain. (11, 12)

11. Teach the client key concepts of rehabilitation versus biological healing, conservative versus aggressive medical interventions, acute versus chronic pain, benign versus non-benign pain, cure versus management, appropriate use of medication, role of exercise and self-regulation techniques.

12. Assign the client to read books about causes for and management of chronic pain; process key concepts/insights gained from the reading.

8. Identify specific pain triggers. (13, 14)

13. Ask the client to read the chapter on "Identifying Pain Triggers" from *Making Peace With Chronic Pain* by Hunter; then ask him/her to make a list of the triggers that apply to his/her condition; process the list content.

14. Ask the client to keep a pain journal which records the time of day, where and what he/she was doing, the severity, and what was done to alleviate the pain; process the journal with the client to increase insight into the nature of the pain, its trigger, and what intervention seems to offer the most consistent relief.

9. Identify causes for and triggers of pain. (14, 15)

14. Ask the client to keep a pain journal which records the time of day, where and what he/she was doing, the severity, and what was done to alleviate the pain; process the journal with the client to increase insight into the nature of the pain, its trigger, and what intervention seems to offer the most consistent relief.

15. Assign reading the chapter on "Causes and Triggers" in *Taking Control of Your Headaches* by Duckro, Richardson, and Marshall or similar information obtained from the National Headache Foundation (800-255-2243).

10. Identify the steps of the "dance of pain" in his/her life. (16)

16. Develop with the client the metaphor of pain as a dance (see *Making Peace With Chronic Pain* by Hunter), working to identify

the particular steps of the dance as it moves through his/her daily life; challenge the client to either alter the steps of his/her present dance or to design a completely new dance.

11. Verbalize an increased awareness of the mind-body connection. (17, 18)

17. Ask the client to read *Peace, Love, and Healing* by Siegel, *The Mind/Body Effect* by Benson, or attend a seminar related to holistic healing for insight into the mind-body connection.

18. Assist the client in beginning to see the connection between chronic pain, substance abuse, and chronic stress.

12. Implement the use of relaxation techniques to reduce muscle tension and severity of pain. (19, 20, 21)

19. Teach the client relaxation techniques (e.g., breathing exercises, using a focus word or phrase, progressive muscle relaxation, creating a safe place, and positive imagery).

20. Encourage the client to use relaxation tapes and/or videos on a daily basis.

21. Refer for or conduct biofeedback training with the client to increase relaxation skills.

13. Utilize spirituality to reduce tension and pain. (22, 23)

22. Teach the client about prayer and meditation and then assist him/her in implementing meditation into daily life.

23. Visit with a member of the clergy and learn how to turn things over to a higher power.

14. Incorporate physical exercise into daily routine. (24, 25)

24. Assist the client in recognizing his/her need for regular exercise; encourage him/her to implement exercise into daily life; monitor results and offer ongoing encouragement to stay with the regime.

25. Refer the client to a physical therapist to develop an individually tailored exercise program that is approved by his/her personal physician.

15. Identify dysfunctional attitudes about pain that are a foundation for pain and substance abuse being the focus of life. (26, 27)

26. Assign Chapter 6 ("The Power of Mind") and Chapter 7 ("Adopting Healthy Attitudes") from the book *Managing Pain Before It Manages You* by Caudill; process key concepts gathered from the reading and exercises.

27. Ask the client to gather feedback from several friends and relatives in terms of negative attitudes they see in the client; process the feedback and identify possible changes he/she could make.

16. Verbalize new, healthier attitudes about pain and substance abuse. (28, 29)

28. Confront the client's negative attitudes about pain and substance abuse and assist him/her in replacing them with more positive, constructive attitudes.

29. Assist the client in becoming capable of seeing humor in more of his/her daily life; promote this expansion with the use of humorous teaching tapes, Dr. Seuss books, telling jokes, and assigning the client to watch one or two comedy movies each week.

17. Investigate the use of alternative pain remedies to reduce doctor visits and/or dependence on medication. (30)

30. Explore the client's alternatives to doctors and medications to remove or reduce his/her pain.

18. Make changes in diet that will promote health and fitness. (31)

31. Refer the client to a dietitian for consultation about eating and nutritional patterns; process the results of the consultation, identifying changes he/she can make, and how he/she might start implementing these changes.

19. Increase the frequency of identified pleasurable activities, including 12-step involvement. (32)

20. Increase the frequency of assertive behaviors in becoming more active in managing his/her life. (33)

21. Identify and replace negative self-talk that promotes help-lessness, anger, and depression. (34, 35, 36)

22. Identify sources of and coping mechanisms for stress in daily life. (37, 38)

32. Ask the client to create a list of recovery activities that are pleasurable (see Inventory of Rewarding Activities by Birchler and Weiss); process the list and develop a plan for increasing the frequency of the selected pleasurable activities.

33. Provide assertiveness training or refer the client to a group that will educate and facilitate assertiveness skills via lectures and assignments.

34. Assign the chapter in *The Feeling Good Handbook* by Burns entitled "You Can Change the Way You Feel" to assist the client in identifying his/her distorted, automatic thoughts that promote depression, helplessness, and/or anger.

35. Assign the client to complete the written exercises in Step 2: "You Feel the Way You Think" from *Ten Days to Self-Esteem!* by Burns; process exercises when completed.

36. Assist the client in replacing negative, distorted thoughts with positive, reality-based thoughts.

37. Educate the client about various types of stressors, then ask him/her to list the stressors he/she experiences in daily life; process the list.

38. Assist the client in identifying specific ways to cope effectively with the major internal, external, and family stressors (e.g., relaxation techniques, problem-solving skills, assertiveness skills, reframing techniques, replacing distorted cognitions).

23. Write a thorough relapse-prevention plan. (39, 40)

39. Assist the client in developing a written relapse-prevention plan that has a special emphasis on pain- and stress-trigger identification and specific ways to handle each, strengthening areas that are weak or lack an adequate level of thought or planning.

40. Assign the client to share his/her relapse-prevention plan with those who are going to be supportive, so they might help with implementation, support, and feedback of the plan.

24. Complete a re-administration of objective tests of chronic pain and substance abuse as a means of assessing treatment outcome. (41)

41. Assess the outcome of treatment by re-administering to the client objective tests of chronic pain and substance abuse; evaluate the results and provide feedback to the client.

25. Complete a survey to assess the degree of satisfaction with treatment. (42)

42. Administer a survey to assess the client's degree of satisfaction with treatment.

—. _____
_____

—. _____
_____

—. _____
_____

—. _____
_____

—. _____
_____

—. _____
_____

DIAGNOSTIC SUGGESTIONS:

Axis I:	307.89	Pain Disorder Associated with Both Psychological Factors and an Axis III Disorder
	307.80	Pain Disorder Associated with Psychological Factors
	300.81	Somatization Disorder
	300.11	Conversion Disorder
	296.3x	Major Depressive Disorder, Recurrent

300.3	Obsessive-Compulsive Disorder
302.70	Sexual Dysfunction NOS
304.10	Sedative, Hypnotic, or Anxiolytic Dependence
304.80	Polysubstance Dependence
_____	_____
_____	_____

DANGEROUSNESS/LETHALITY

BEHAVIORAL DEFINITIONS

1. Exhibits low frustration tolerance and poor impulse control, with a history of violence.
2. Abuses mood-altering substances, in spite of many negative consequences, including dangerous effects to self.
3. Uses substance abuse to cope with negative emotions such as anger, hurt, embarrassment, or frustration.
4. Demonstrates poor anger management skills.
5. Acts aggressively and is uncooperative with staff and peers.
6. Refuses to listen to parents or authority figures.
7. Has attempted suicide or homicide.
8. Makes threats of physical harm to self or others.
9. Danger of violence escalates under the influence of mood-altering substances.

—. _____

_____

—. _____

_____

—. _____

_____

LONG-TERM GOALS

1. Develop a program of recovery, free from substance abuse and dangerous/lethal behaviors.
2. Terminate all acts that are dangerous to self or others.
3. Verbalize the core conflicts that lead to dangerous/lethal behaviors.

4. Recognize the first signs of anger and use behavioral techniques to control it.
5. Increase self-esteem, purpose for living, and the importance of helping others in recovery.
6. Maintain appropriate parent-child boundaries, setting firm limits when the client acts dangerous to self or others.

—. _____

   _____

—. _____

   _____

—. _____

   _____

SHORT-TERM OBJECTIVES

THERAPEUTIC INTERVENTIONS

1. Sign a contract agreeing to not harm self or others and to obey all rules while in treatment. (1, 2)

1. Request that the client sign a no-harm contract detailing that he/she will not harm himself/herself; ask client to promise to tell a staff member if he/she feels an urge to be harmful to self or others.

2. Read the client the rules of treatment and ask him/her to sign an agreement that he/she will abide by all of the rules.

2. Cooperate with a referral for a medical evaluation. (3, 4)

3. Refer the client to be examined by a physician and/or psychiatrist for a medical evaluation; encourage an assessment for substance abuse effects, organic or neurological basis for violence, and the need for psychotropic medication.

4. Monitor the client for medication compliance, effectiveness, and side effects.

3. Cooperate with a biopsychosocial examination. (5, 6)

5. Complete a biopsychosocial evaluation (e.g., family history

of violence and substance abuse, childhood history of violence, chemical dependence, social relationships).

6. Meet with family members to obtain their perspective on the client's substance abuse and violence.

4. Complete psychological testing or objective questionnaires for assessing violence toward self and others. (7)

7. Administer to the client psychological instruments designed to objectively assess violence toward self or others (e.g., Beck Scale for Suicide Ideation [BSS], Domestic Violence Inventory [DVI]); give the client feedback regarding the results of the assessment.

5. Identify three somatic sensations that occur with building hurt, fear, or anger. (8)

8. Assist the client in identifying three somatic feelings that accompany feelings of hurt, fear, and anger; assess how the client copes with these feelings.

6. Identify the current degree of threat that exists to self or others. (9, 10)

9. Assess the client for his/her degree of urge to harm self, degree of plan development, access to means of harm, history of previous attempts, degree of hopelessness or hurt related to relationship dissolution, and any other factors that increase suicide risk; consider inpatient treatment if indicated.

10. Assess the client for his/her degree of urge to harm others, degree of plan development, history of violence, threats made, relationship conflict, possessiveness or stalking of victim, criminal history, history of restraining orders, use of substance abuse to cope with anger, hurt, or depression; consider the duty to warn if risk is significant.

7. List five things the client can do when angry to cope with feelings. (11)

11. Help the client to make a list of five things he/she can do when feeling angry to cope with angry feelings.

8. Keep an anger journal describing the situations that cause anger. (12, 13)

12. Teach the client how to keep an anger journal, using subjective units of distress as a measurement of the intensity of the dangerous/lethal feelings, giving the anger a subjective unit of distress score from 1 (as little anger as possible) to 100 (as much anger as possible).

13. Review the client's anger journal and process situations that stimulate strong anger, suggesting coping behaviors.

9. Practice relaxation skills twice each day for 10 to 20 minutes. (14)

14. Using progressive relaxation techniques, teach the client how to relax; ask the client to rate the extent of relaxation achieved on a scale of 1 to 10.

10. Participate in physical exercise each day. (15)

15. Encourage the client to participate in exercise for at least 20 minutes each day; monitor implementation, reinforcing success, and redirecting for failure.

11. Identify the possible causes of dangerous lethal behaviors. (16)

16. Explore with the client his/her family-of-origin-issues that may have led to dangerous lethal behaviors (e.g., physical abuse, abandonment, sexual abuse, gang affiliation, parental chemical dependence, etc.).

12. List five ways dangerous and lethal behaviors contribute to substance abuse and vice versa. (17, 18)

17. Help the client to make a list of five ways that dangerous lethal behaviors have contributed to substance abuse, and have the client share this list in group.

18. Assist the client in listing five ways that substance abuse contributes to lethal behaviors (e.g.,

deepens depression and shame, reduces inhibition to reason with self or others).

13. Verbalize acceptance of powerlessness and unmanageability of substance abuse and dangerous lethal behaviors. (19)

14. Verbalize an understanding of AA's steps Two and Three and list three ways a higher power can assist in recovery. (20)

15. Complete an AA Step Four and Step Five exercise that includes a history of past assets and liabilities, discussing the exact nature of wrongs. (21, 22)

16. Parents verbalize an understanding of their child's aggressiveness and its interaction with substance abuse. (23, 24)

17. Sign a behavior contract that lists all behavior expected in recovery and the consequences of failing to meet these contractual obligations. (25)

18. Complete a re-administration of objective tests of violence toward self and others as a means of assessing treatment outcome. (26)

19. Discuss the meaning of powerlessness and unmanageability in the recovery program and show how this step can be used to manage dangerous lethal behaviors.

20. Teach the client about steps Two and Three of AA, then show three ways a higher power can assist him/her in recovery.

21. Have the client complete a Fourth Step inventory of who are the targets of anger and resentment, why they are resented, and how this has affected the client.

22. As part of a Fifth Step, ask the client to share how he/she has wronged others.

23. Meet with family members and discuss dangerousness and lethal behaviors and substance abuse, talking about what the client is going to do differently in recovery.

24. Assign the parents to read *Parenting Your-Out-of-Control Teenager* by Sells and discuss with them measures to reestablish control over their child.

25. Develop with the family a behavior contract that outlines what the client will do in recovery and the consequences of failing to meet these contractual obligations.

26. Assess the outcome of treatment by re-administering to the client objective tests of violence toward self and others; evaluate the results and provide feedback to the client.

19. Complete a survey to assess
the degree of satisfaction with
treatment. (27)

—. _____
   _____

—. _____
   _____

—. _____
   _____

27. Administer a survey to assess the
client's degree of satisfaction with
treatment.

—. _____
   _____

—. _____
   _____

—. _____
   _____

DIAGNOSTIC SUGGESTIONS:

Axis I:

312.8	Conduct Disorder
313.81	Oppositional Defiant Disorder
296.xx	Bipolar I Disorder
296.89	Bipolar II Disorder
312.34	Intermittent Explosive Disorder
309.4	Adjustment Disorder with Mixed Disturbance of Emotions and Conduct
296.xx	Major Depressive Disorder
V71.01	Adult Antisocial Behavior
_____	_____
_____	_____

Axis II:

301.0	Paranoid Personality Disorder
301.83	Borderline Personality Disorder
301.9	Personality Disorder NOS
301.81	Narcissistic Personality Disorder
_____	_____
_____	_____

DEPENDENT TRAITS

BEHAVIORAL DEFINITIONS

1. Passively submits to the wishes, wants, and needs of others; too eager to please others.
2. Dependent traits have fostered engagement in addictive behavior.
3. Chronically fears interpersonal abandonment and desperately clings to destructive relationships.
4. Goes to excessive lengths to gain acceptance from others to the point of volunteering to do unpleasant things.
5. Has a history of being anxious about making decisions without an excessive amount of advice and support from others.
6. Lacks ability to trust own judgment about everyday life decisions.
7. Persistently feels worthless and believes rejection is inevitable.
8. Needs others to assume responsibility and make decisions for most major areas of life.
9. Fears group situations unless certain of being accepted.
10. Chronically feels alienation from others.

—. _____
_____
_____

—. _____
_____
_____

—. _____
_____

LONG-TERM GOALS

1. Recovery from substance abuse, which reduces the impact of dependent traits on addiction-free living.
2. Demonstrate increased independence and self-confidence through au-

tonomous decision making, honest expression of feelings and ideas, and reduced fear of rejection.

3. Decrease dependence on relationships while beginning to meet own needs, build confidence, and practice assertiveness.
4. Demonstrate healthy communication that is honest, open, and self-disclosing.
5. Reduce the frequency of behaviors exclusively designed to please others.
6. Reduce feelings of alienation by learning similarity to others who were raised in a more normal home.

—. _____

_____

_____

—. _____

_____

_____

—. _____

_____

SHORT-TERM OBJECTIVES	THERAPEUTIC INTERVENTIONS
1. Acknowledge the feelings of powerlessness and unmanageability that result from dependent traits and addictive behavior. (1)	1. Probe the feelings of powerlessness that the client experienced as a child and how these feelings are similar to how he/she feels when engaging in addictive behavior.
2. Complete psychological testing or objective questionnaires for assessing dependent traits. (2)	2. Administer to the client psychological instruments designed to objectively assess dependent traits and addictive behavior (e.g., Millon Clinical Multiaxial Inventory-III [MMCI-III]); give the client feedback regarding the results of the assessment.
3. Identify at least two dynamics of early family life that contributed to developing dependent traits. (3, 4, 5, 6)	3. Educate the client about the childhood etiology of his/her fear of making decisions and how this is not appropriate as an adult.
	4. Explore how the dysfunctional family's inconsistent rules led to the client's fear of failure.

5. Assist the client in understanding how his/her early childhood experiences led to a fear of abandonment, rejection, and neglect, and the assumption of a childlike role that is detrimental to intimate adult relationships.

6. Teach the client about how low self-esteem and fear of making the wrong choice resulted from being raised in a home where family members were overly controlling and critical.

4. Identify incidents in which dependent traits were used to avoid the anxiety of making decisions that could have resulted in failure. (7, 8, 9)

7. Explore the influence that the client's fear and shame had on choosing a life-style of dependent traits and addictive behavior.

8. Ask the client to identify at least five instances in which he/she avoided decisions out of fear of failure or rejection.

9. Probe the client's inability to trust his/her own judgment; raise his/her awareness of this tendency and explore its origins.

5. Verbalize an understanding of how dependent traits contributed to addictive behavior. (10)

10. Discuss the relationship between the client's dependent traits and his/her addictive behavior; explore how dependency has fostered addictive behavior.

6. Identify abandonment experiences in the family of origin, and how this has influenced current relationships. (5, 11, 12)

5. Assist the client in understanding how his/her early childhood experiences led to a fear of abandonment, rejection, and neglect, and the assumption of a child-like role that is detrimental to intimate adult relationships.

11. Raise the client's awareness of his/her tendency to take over the child role in relationships; explore causes for this pattern in the client's childhood abandonment and rejection experiences.

7. Share the feeling of worthlessness that was learned in the family and relate this feeling to addictive behavior as a coping mechanism. (13)

8. Report three incidents per week in which relaxation skills were implemented to counteract anxiety in interpersonal situations. (14, 15)

9. Openly share thoughts, feelings, and problems in each therapy session. (16, 17)

10. Report two incidents per week of telling the truth rather than only saying what the other person wanted to hear. (18, 19)

12. Explore the client's childhood experiences of abandonment and neglect; relate these to his/her dependent traits and addictive behavior.

13. Assist the client in identifying a pattern of using addictive behavior as an escape from feelings of anxiety and worthlessness.

14. Teach the client relaxation procedures (e.g., deep muscle release, rhythmic deep breathing, positive imagery) as a coping technique for anxiety.

15. Role-play instances in which the client could implement relaxation techniques as a healthy escape from anxiety; monitor and reinforce implementation of this skill in daily life.

16. Explore how the client's family responded to expressions of feelings, wishes, and wants, and why the client became anxious when he/she expressed a choice, feeling, or decision.

17. Educate the client about healthy interpersonal relationships based on openness, respect, and honesty, and explain the necessity of sharing feelings to build trust and mutual understanding.

18. Teach the client about how the behavior of telling other people what we think they want to hear—rather than the truth—is based on a fear of rejection, learned in the family; use behavior rehearsal to teach the client more honest communication skills.

11. Verbalize an understanding of how dependent traits contributed to choosing partners and friends who were controlling. (20)

12. Implement decision-making skills in at least three situations per week; document and report on the process and feelings associated with the experience. (21, 22, 23)

13. Discuss fears related to attendance at recovery group meetings and verbalize specific plans to deal with each fear. (24, 25)

19. Teach the client the assertive formula of "I feel … When you … I would prefer it if … ," role-playing several applications to his/her life; have the client journal one assertive situation each day.

20. Review the client's choice of friends and intimate partners; relate his/her dependency traits to selection of controlling people.

21. Teach problem-solving skills (e.g., identify the problem, brainstorm alternate solutions, examine the advantages and disadvantages of each option, select an option, implement a course of action, and evaluate the result); role-play solving a problem drawn from the client's life experience.

22. Educate the client about how the fear of making decisions is based in low self-esteem and need for acceptance.

23. Assign the client to implement decision-making skills at least three times per week, and record the process and feelings; review, reinforce, and redirect when necessary.

24. Teach the client how becoming actively involved in a 12-step recovery group can aid in building trust in others and confidence in self.

25. Probe the relationship between the client's dependent traits and fear of attending recovery group meetings; assist the client in identifying coping skills (e.g., relaxation techniques, going to meetings with a sponsor, positive self-talk, assertiveness skills) to overcome fears.

14. List reasons why regular attendance at recovery group meetings is necessary in arresting dependent traits and addictions. (26, 27)

26. Assist the client in developing an aftercare plan centered on regular attendance at a 12-step recovery group meeting.

27. Discuss how the 12-step home group can be like the healthy family the client never had; help the client list reasons why he/she needs such a group to recover (e.g., "I need love and support from people in recovery," "I want a new family to help me," "I need brothers and sisters in recovery to keep me in recovery").

15. Report on successfully contacting a sponsor within the 12-step community. (28)

28. Educate the client about the importance of sponsorship within the 12-step community and facilitate his/her establishment of a relationship with a temporary sponsor.

16. List ways that belief in an interaction with a higher power can reduce fears and aid in recovery. (29)

29. Teach the client about the positive ways that faith in a higher power can aid in recovery and arrest the fear associated with dependent traits and addiction (e.g., regular attendance at worship services, daily prayer, and meditation).

17. Verbalize a feeling of serenity that results from turning problems that are out of one's own control over to a higher power. (30)

30. Review and reinforce the client's enactment of faith in a higher power in his/her daily life.

18. Read portions of recovery literature 6 days per week and share insights obtained with others. (31)

31. Assign the client to read recovery literature (e.g., Alcoholic Anonymous *Big Book*) and process the material in an individual or group therapy session.

19. Practice assertiveness skills and keep a daily journal of the times the skills were used in interpersonal conflict. (19, 32)

19. Teach the client the assertive formula of "I feel ... When you ... I would prefer it if ... ," role-playing several applications to his/her life; have the client journal one assertive situation each day.

20. Complete a re-administration of objective tests of dependent traits as a means of assessing treatment outcome. (33)

21. Complete a survey to assess the degree of satisfaction with treatment. (34)

—. _____
   _____
—. _____
   _____
—. _____
   _____

32. Use modeling, behavior rehearsal, and role-playing to teach the client healthy assertiveness skills; then assign the application of these skills to several current problem situations.

33. Assess the outcome of treatment by re-administering to the client objective tests of dependent traits; evaluate the results and provide feedback to the client.

34. Administer a survey to assess the client's degree of satisfaction with treatment.

—. _____
   _____
—. _____
   _____
—. _____
   _____

DIAGNOSTIC SUGGESTIONS:

Axis I:		
	300.00	Anxiety Disorder NOS
	300.02	Generalized Anxiety Disorder
	300.23	Social Phobia
	300.21	Panic Disorder with Agoraphobia
	309.81	Posttraumatic Stress Disorder
	V61.20	Parent-Child Relational Problem
	_____	_____
	_____	_____

Axis II:		
	301.82	Avoidant Personality Disorder
	301.6	Dependent Personality Disorder
	301.50	Histrionic Personality Disorder
	301.9	Personality Disorder NOS
	_____	_____
	_____	_____

DEPRESSION

BEHAVIORAL DEFINITIONS

1. Feels sad or down most of the days of the week.
2. Engages in addictive behavior as a means of escaping from feelings of sadness, worthlessness, and helplessness.
3. Presents with vegetative symptoms (e.g., sleep disturbance, appetite disturbance, anhedonia, lack of energy, weight change).
4. Verbalizes persistent feelings of helplessness, hopelessness, worthlessness, and/or guilt.
5. Lacks energy and has excessive fatigue.
6. Reports poor concentration, indecisiveness.
7. Demonstrates low self-esteem.
8. Experiences mood-congruent hallucinations or delusions.
9. Reports suicidal thoughts.
10. Expresses a wish to die without a suicidal thought or plan.

—. _____
_____
—. _____
_____
—. _____
_____

LONG-TERM GOALS

1. Elevate mood and develop a program of recovery free from addiction.
2. Decrease dysfunctional thinking and increase positive, self-enhancing self-talk.
3. Understand affective disorders and how these symptoms increase vulnerability to addiction.

4. Develop a program of recovery that includes healthy exercise, relaxation, and eating and sleeping habits.
5. Improve social skills and attend recovery groups regularly.
6. Resolve grief and guilt issues and increase feelings of self-worth.

—. _____
_____
_____

—. _____
_____
_____

—. _____
_____

SHORT-TERM OBJECTIVES

1. Verbalize the powerlessness and unmanageability that result from using addictive behavior to cope with depression. (1, 2)

2. Describe the signs and symptoms of depression that are experienced. (3, 4)

3. Complete psychological testing or objective questionnaires for assessing depression. (5)

THERAPEUTIC INTERVENTIONS

1. Using a 12-step recovery program's Step One exercise, help the client to admit powerlessness and unmanageability over addictive behavior and depression.

2. Teach the client that addictive behavior results in negative psychological effects and that it is often used to escape from these same psychological symptoms, creating a vicious cycle.

3. Explore how depression is experienced in the client's day-to-day living.

4. Encourage the client's sharing feelings of depression in order to clarify them and gain insight as to its causes.

5. Administer to the client psychological instruments designed to objectively assess depression and addictive behavior (e.g., Beck Depression Inventory-II [BDI-II], Zung's Self-Rating Depression Scale [SDS]); give the client feedback regarding the results of the assessment.

4. Verbally identify, if possible, the source of depressed mood. (6)

5. Identify a pattern of using drug or alcohol abuse as a means of escaping from depression, and verbalize more constructive means of coping. (2, 7, 8)

6. Ask the client to make a list of what he/she is depressed about; process the list with the therapist.

2. Teach the client that addictive behavior results in negative psychological effects, and that it is often used to escape from these same psychological symptoms, creating a vicious cycle.

7. Confront the client's addictive behavior as a means of coping with depression; assist him/her in identifying the self-defeating, negative consequences of this behavior.

8. Process healthier, more constructive means of coping with depression (e.g., sharing pain with others, attending 12-step recovery program meetings, developing positive cognitions, taking medication, turning conflicts over to a higher power).

6. State a desire to live and an end to death wishes. (9, 10)

9. Assess and monitor the client's suicide potential, arranging for suicide precautions, if necessary.

10. Reinforce the client's positive statements regarding his/her life and the future.

7. Verbalize an understanding of how depression and addictive behavior lead to a condition that a 12-step recovery program calls *insane*. (2, 11)

2. Teach the client that addictive behavior results in negative psychological effects, and that it is often used to escape from these same psychological symptoms, creating a vicious cycle.

11. Teach the client about the 12-step recovery program's concept of *insanity*, and relate this concept to his/her addiction and depression.

8. List five ways in which a higher power can be useful in recovery

12. Teach the client about the 12-step recovery program's concept of

from addiction and depression. (12)

a higher power, and the ways in which a higher power can assist in recovery.

9. Keep a daily record of dysfunctional thinking. (13, 14)

13. Assist the client in identifying his/her dysfunctional thoughts that trigger depression.

14. Assign the client to keep a daily record of dysfunctional thinking that includes listing each situation associated with depressed feelings, and the dysfunctional thinking about that situation that triggered depression.

10. Replace negative, self-defeating thinking with positive, accurate, self-enhancing self-talk. (15)

15. Using logic and reality, challenge each of the client's dysfunctional thoughts for accuracy, replacing dysfunctional thinking with positive, accurate thoughts.

11. Learn and demonstrate the ability to use positive conflict resolution skills to resolve interpersonal discord. (16, 17)

16. Teach the client conflict resolution skills (e.g., empathy, active listening, "I" messages, respectful communication, assertiveness without aggression, compromise), use modeling, role-playing, and behavior rehearsal to work through several of his/her current conflicts.

17. In conjoint sessions, help the client apply conflict resolution skills to resolve interpersonal conflicts and problems.

12. Cooperate with a physician evaluation to determine if psychopharmacological intervention is warranted, and take all medication as prescribed. (18)

18. Refer the client to a physician to examine him/her, and order medications as appropriate; titrate them, and monitor him/her for side effects.

13. Report as to the effectiveness and side effects of psychotropic medications that have been prescribed. (19, 20)

19. Direct the medical staff to administer medications as prescribed by the physician and to monitor for side effects and effectiveness.

14. Verbalize unresolved grief and make a written plan to recover from grief issues. (21, 22, 23, 24)

15. Write a plan to develop social relationships. (25)

16. Write an autobiography detailing the exact nature of wrongs, and turn past misbehavior over to a higher power. (26)

17. Read aloud positive, self-enhancing statements each morning. (27)

18. Encourage someone in recovery each day. (28, 29)

20. Monitor the client's psychotropic medications for effectiveness and for side effects.

21. Help the client identify grief issues and develop a written plan for resolving grief (e.g., visit the grave, write a goodbye letter, attend a support group, begin social activities, volunteer to help others).

22. Verify the positive and negative elements of the relationship with the deceased individual.

23. Encourage the client to share his/her feelings of anger and resentment felt toward the significant other for leaving.

24. Probe the client's grief and help him/her to say goodbye in a letter to the person who has died or broken a relationship.

25. Help the client to develop a plan for increasing social relationships (e.g., through 12-step recovery program meetings, work relationships, church acquaintances, school, or special group contacts).

26. Using a 12-step recovery program's Step Four inventory, assign the client to write an autobiography that details exactly how he/she has hurt others; help him/her turn over past misbehavior to a higher power.

27. Help the client to develop a list of 10 accurate, self-enhancing statements to read each morning.

28. Help the client to understand that he/she is needed in a 12-step recovery program to help others; discuss specific ways to help others, and how this builds the client's self-esteem and self-worth.

19. Write a plan and express hope for the future. (30)

20. Implement an exercise program. (31)

21. Write down five things each night for which gratitude is felt. (32)

22. Attend group therapy sessions to share thoughts and feelings that are related to depression, and how addictive behavior has been used to avoid these negative feelings. (33)

23. Write an aftercare program. (34)

24. Family members verbalize a connection between depression and addictive behavior. (35)

25. Family members verbalize what each can do to assist the client in recovery. (36, 37)

29. Teach the client the importance of helping others to build their own sense of self-worth and self-esteem; assign the client to encourage someone in the 12-step recovery program each day and to record this in a journal.

30. Assist the client in developing future plans, and show that these plans create new hope for tomorrow; list future plans in writing.

31. Using current physical fitness levels, increase the client's exercise by 10 percent each week until the client is exercising at a training heart rate for at least 20 minutes, three times per week; consult with his/her physician, if indicated.

32. Teach the client about the 12-step recovery program's concept of *an attitude of gratitude*; assign him/ her to write down five things for which he/she is grateful each day.

33. Direct or refer the client to group therapy sessions in which he/she is encouraged to share feelings of depression, allowing for feedback of empathy, acceptance, and affirmation from group members.

34. Help the client to develop a written aftercare program that includes regular attendance at 12-step recovery groups and any other therapy that the client needs to improve his/her health.

35. Discuss with family members the connection between depression and addictive behavior.

36. In a family session, review what each member can do to assist the client in recovery.

37. Provide the family members with information about depression (e.g., recommend reading *What to Do When Someone You Love is Depressed* by Golant or *When Someone You Love is Depressed* by Rosen and Amador) and the steps that the client must take to recover successfully.

26. Complete a re-administration of objective tests of depression as a means of assessing treatment outcome. (38)

38. Assess the outcome of treatment by re-administering to the client objective tests of depression; evaluate the results and provide feedback to the client.

27. Complete a survey to assess the degree of satisfaction with treatment. (39)

39. Administer a survey to assess the client's degree of satisfaction with treatment.

—. _____
   _____

—. _____
   _____

—. _____
   _____

—. _____
   _____

—. _____
   _____

—. _____
   _____

DIAGNOSTIC SUGGESTIONS:

Axis I:	309.0	Adjustment Disorder with Depressed Mood
	309.28	Adjustment Disorder with Mixed Anxiety and Depressed Mood
	311	Depressive Disorder NOS
	296.xx	Bipolar I Disorder
	296.89	Bipolar II Disorder
	300.4	Dysthymic Disorder
	301.13	Cyclothymic Disorder
	296.2x	Major Depressive Disorder, Single Episode
	296.3x	Major Depressive Disorder, Recurrent
	295.70	Schizoaffective Disorder

	310.1	Personality Change Due to (Axis III Disorder)
	V62.82	Bereavement
	_____	_____
	_____	_____

Axis II:

	301.83	Borderline Personality Disorder
	301.9	Personality Disorder NOS
	_____	_____
	_____	_____

EATING DISORDERS

BEHAVIORAL DEFINITIONS

1. Expresses a fear of loss of control over eating; feels that eating cannot be stopped and/or the amount of food consumed cannot be controlled.
2. Has intense fear of gaining weight or becoming fat.
3. Presents with marked body image disturbance: perceives self as overweight, even when thin.
4. Engages in intermittent starving, gorging, purging, use of laxatives and/or enemas, excessive exercise, or other dysfunctional behaviors aimed at weight control.
5. Reports chronic feelings of depression revolving around the belief that one is fat.
6. Reports frequent, unsuccessful attempts to bring the abnormal eating behavior under control.
7. Uses food consumption as a means of relaxation or escape from stress.
8. Verbalizes that self-evaluation is unduly influenced by body shape and weight.
9. Becomes very anxious when thinking of body weight, food, or eating.
10. Uses addictive behavior to cope with anxiety.

—. _____
_____

—. _____
_____

—. _____
_____

LONG-TERM GOALS

1. Eat nutritionally and develop healthy, realistic attitudes about body image and weight.
2. Terminate overeating, purging, use of laxatives, enemas, and/or excessive exercise.
3. Terminate addictive behavior.
4. Develop the ability to control the impulse to overeat.
5. Learn and demonstrate constructive strategies to cope with dysphoric moods.
6. Replace negative, self-defeating addictive thinking about food and body image with more realistic, self-enhancing self-talk.

—. _____

_____

—. _____

_____

—. _____

_____

SHORT-TERM OBJECTIVES	THERAPEUTIC INTERVENTIONS
1. Describe the history and current status of dysfunctional eating patterns. (1, 2)	1. Explore the client's history and current status of his/her eating disorder.
	2. Confront client's minimization and denial of the eating disorder behavior and its related, distorted thinking.
2. Complete psychological testing or objective questionnaires for assessing eating disorders. (3)	3. Administer to the client psychological instruments designed to objectively assess eating disorders (e.g., Eating Inventory, Stirling Eating Disorders Scales, Eating Disorders Inventory [EDI]); give the client feedback regarding the results of the assessment.
3. List five occasions when the eating disorder has been triggered. (4, 5, 6)	4. Help the client see how negative feelings increase the probability of dysfunctional eating and addictive behavior.

5. Explore the specific circumstances that increase the probability of the client's eating disorder behaviors being triggered.

6. Review several eating disorder behaviors (e.g., gorging, purging, use of laxatives, excessive exercise) that occurred under stress, and help the client discover what he/she could have done to cope more effectively, rather than to use food dysfunctionally in each situation.

4. Keep a daily feelings journal. (7)

7. Assign the client to write a daily journal of what emotions were experienced, why the feelings developed, and what actions resulted from the feelings.

5. Identify distorted, negative thoughts that lead to eating-disordered behavior. (8, 9, 10)

8. Help the client to differentiate between distorted, self-defeating thoughts and self-enhancing, realistic thinking.

9. Use cognitive techniques to help the client identify his/her negative, self-defeating thoughts and how they lead to eating disorders and other addictive behavior.

10. Assign the client to keep a daily record of distorted, self-defeating thoughts.

6. Implement self-enhancing, realistic thoughts to replace distorted, self-defeated thinking. (11, 12)

11. Assist the client in building a list of 10 positive, reinforcing statements to use daily for self-enhancement.

12. Use cognitive techniques to help the client correct self-defeating thinking, and replace self-derogatory thinking with positive, self-enhancing statements.

7. Draw an outline of one's own body and ask for feedback about the accuracy of one's body image. (13)

13. Teach the client about his/her distorted, negative body image and ask him/her to draw an outline of his/her body; give feedback as to

8. Develop a written plan to decrease the frequency of impulsive eating or addiction behavior related to dysphoric moods. (4, 6, 14, 15, 16)

the accuracy or distortion of the drawing.

4. Help the client see how negative feelings increase the probability of dysfunctional eating and addictive behavior.

6. Review several eating disorder behaviors (e.g., gorging, purging, use of laxatives, excessive exercise) that occurred under stress, and help the client discover what he/she could have done to cope more effectively, rather than to dysfunctionally use food or addictive behavior in each situation.

14. Help the client develop and practice coping skills to deal with dysphoric moods, rather than engaging in disordered eating or addiction behavior.

15. Teach the client how negative thinking, feeling, and acting lead to negative consequences; teach how positive thinking leads to positive consequences.

16. Teach the client self-control strategies (e.g., "stop, look, listen, and think") to control the impulse to engage in eating disorders and other addictive behavior.

9. Verbalize an understanding of how fear of abandonment is expressed in eating disorders and addictive behavior. (17, 18)

17. Probe the relationship between the client's feelings of anger, sadness, or fear of abandonment and the eating disorder and other addictive behaviors.

18. Assist the client in identifying triggers for fear of abandonment, and possible historical causes for these feelings being so predominant.

10. Identify situations that easily trigger feelings of fear about weight and body image. (19)

19. Assist the client in identifying situations that trigger fear regarding weight and body image;

process more adaptive messages to counteract the fear response.

11. Verbalize five negative consequences of eating disorder behavior. (20)

12. Verbalize alternative, constructive ways to cope with feelings of anger, sadness, or fear. (12, 16, 21, 22, 23)

20. Help the client understand the self-defeating, alienating consequences of being obsessed with weight.

12. Use cognitive techniques to help the client correct self-defeating thinking, and replace self-derogatory thinking with positive, self-enhancing statements.

16. Teach the client self-control strategies (e.g., "stop, look, listen, and think") to control the impulse to engage in eating disorders and other addictive behavior.

21. Develop with the client a list of constructive reactions to feelings of anger or fear (e.g., writing about feelings, talking to counselor, delaying expression for 24 hours, tracing feelings to one's own background, substituting physical exercise for outlet, practicing a relaxation exercise) that reduce impulsive acting out of feelings.

22. Use role-playing and modeling to teach the client to verbalize anger in a controlled, respectful manner, delaying the response, if necessary, to gain more control.

23. Help the client make a list of the people to call or visit when he/she becomes upset; role-play several situations where the client discusses a problem calmly.

13. Five times this week, talk calmly to someone while feeling upset. (24)

24. Assign the client the task of talking to someone calmly while feeling sad, angry, fearful, or depressed.

14. Cooperate with a complete physical exam. (25, 26)

25. Refer the client to a physician for a complete physical exam.

26. Stay in close consultation with physician as to the client's medical condition and nutritional habits.

15. Submit to a dental exam. (27)

27. Refer the client to dentist for a dental exam.

16. Cooperate with admission to inpatient treatment if a fragile medical condition necessitates such treatment. (28)

28. Refer the client for hospitalization, as necessary, if his/her weight loss becomes severe and physical health is jeopardized.

17. Attain and maintain balanced fluids and electrolytes, as well as resumption of reproductive functions. (29, 30, 31)

29. Establish a minimum daily caloric intake for the client; solicit the client's agreement to consume these calories daily and to record this in a journal.

30. Assist the client in meal planning.

31. Refer the client back to physician at regular intervals if fluids and electrolytes need monitoring due to poor nutritional habits.

18. Meet with a physician to be evaluated for the need for pharmacological treatment. (32)

32. Refer the client to a physician to evaluate if psychopharmacological intervention is warranted.

19. Take medications as prescribed and report any side effects to appropriate professionals. (33, 34)

33. Monitor the client's response as the physician prescribes and adjusts medication to maximize effectiveness and reduce side effects.

34. Direct the staff to administer medications to the client as ordered by physician and monitor for compliance, effectiveness, and side effects.

20. Practice the healthy communication skills of listening to others, the use of "I statements," and sharing feelings. (35)

35. Teach the client how to listen, use "I statements," and share feelings; assign him/her to implement listening skills and "I message" communication in daily life, and then monitor, review, reinforce, and redirect as indicated.

21. Acknowledge how perfection-ism leads to fear of rejection. (36, 37)

36. Assist the client in understanding how the need to be perfect leads to feelings of inadequacy; help him/her see positive and negative traits in himself/herself.

37. Challenge the extremes of the client's thinking about how he/she needs to be perfect to be loved.

22. Make a list of 10 positive body characteristics. (38)

38. Assign the client the task of list-ing 10 positive characteristics of his/her body; process the list.

23. Practice relaxation techniques two times a day for 10 to 20 minutes per session. (39)

39. Teach the client relaxation techniques (e.g., progressive relaxation, deep breathing, and/or guided imagery); urge implemen-tation of relaxation techniques as a substitute for eating disorder or addictive behaviors during times of anxiety or stress.

24. Complete a re-administration of objective tests of eating dis-orders as a means of assessing treatment outcome. (40)

40. Assess the outcome of treatment by re-administering to the client objective tests of eating disorders; evaluate the results and provide feedback to the client.

25. Complete a survey to assess the degree of satisfaction with treatment. (41)

41. Administer a survey to assess the client's degree of satisfaction with treatment.

—. _____
   _____

—. _____
   _____

—. _____
   _____

—. _____
   _____

—. _____
   _____

—. _____
   _____

DIAGNOSTIC SUGGESTIONS:

Axis I:	307.1	Anorexia Nervosa
	307.51	Bulimia Nervosa
	307.50	Eating Disorder NOS

296.xx   Major Depressive Disorder
300.4   Dysthymic Disorder
309.81   Posttraumatic Stress Disorder

_____   _____

_____   _____

Axis II: 301.83   Borderline Personality Disorder
301.50   Histrionic Personality Disorder
301.81   Narcissistic Personality Disorder
301.6   Dependent Personality Disorder
300.3   Obsessive-Compulsive Disorder

_____   _____

_____   _____

FAMILY CONFLICTS

BEHAVIORAL DEFINITIONS

1. Exhibits a pattern of family conflicts leading to dysfunctional relationships and addiction.
2. Describes a family that engages in repeated physical fights, verbal arguments, and/or unresolved disputes.
3. Demonstrates poor communication skills, leading to an inability to solve family problems.
4. Admits to physical or verbal abuse of family members.
5. Uses addiction to cope with feelings of anger, alienation, or depression related to conflict within the family.
6. The family has a history of unresolved intrafamily conflicts leading to distrust and alienation.
7. Experiences long periods of non-communication with family members due to unresolved conflicts.
8. Describes a family that is not supportive to recovery.
9. Has a history of addiction in family members, leading to a poor recovery environment.

__. _____
_____
__. _____
_____
__. _____
_____

LONG-TERM GOALS

1. Maintain a program of recovery that is free of addiction and family conflict.

2. Learn and demonstrate healthy communication and conflict resolution skills, leading to harmony within the family and the cessation of addiction.
3. Forgive family members' past misdeeds and begin a life of harmony with each family member.
4. Terminate addiction and implement more healthy coping behaviors to deal with conflicts within the family.
5. Begin to emancipate from the parents in a healthy way by making reasonable arrangements for independent living.

—. _____

_____

—. _____

_____

—. _____

_____

SHORT-TERM OBJECTIVES

THERAPEUTIC INTERVENTIONS

1. Verbalize the powerlessness and unmanageability that have resulted from using addictive behavior to cope with family conflicts. (1, 2)

1. Help the client to see the powerlessness and unmanageability that have resulted from using addiction to cope with family conflicts.

2. Assist the client in understanding the vicious cycle that results from reacting to family conflicts with addictive behaviors.

2. Identify the nature and history of current family conflicts. (3)

3. Explore the client's history to identify the nature of and causes for the current family conflicts.

3. Complete or give permission for a significant other to complete a survey of the client's family. (4)

4. Administer to the client or a significant other an objective survey (e.g., Family Environment Scale [FES] by Moos and Moos, Family Relationship Inventory [FRI] by Michaelson, Bascom, Nash, Morrison, and Taylor, or Family System Test [FAST] by Gehring) to assess the client's family; give the client feedback regarding the results of the assessment.

4. Verbalize how current family conflicts relate to conflicts in the family of origin, which were experienced as a child. (5)

5. Help the client to see the relationship between the family of origin childhood conflicts and current family conflicts; assign him/her to write a detailed account of how the two are related.

5. Acknowledge that attempts to seize power and control within the family lead to unhealthy interpersonal relationships. (6, 7)

6. Assist the client in identifying how he/she has attempted to seize power and control within the family.

7. Teach the client about respect for independence and autonomy in a healthy family, and help the client to see how power struggles led to unresolved family conflicts.

6. Family members give individual perspectives on current conflicts. (8)

8. In a family session make a list of current family conflicts from each member's perspective.

7. Family members identify and implement changes that each one must make to reduce conflict. (9, 10, 11)

9. Assist each family member in identifying what he/she could do to reduce family conflicts and heal wounds of the past.

10. Develop a written contract that outlines what each family member will do to resolve family conflicts.

11. Review the family members' implementation of changes to reduce conflict; reinforce success, confront projection, and redirect for failures.

8. In a family session, verbalize how addiction fosters misunderstanding and conflict and how conflict fosters addiction. (12)

12. Help the family members understand how family conflict increases the probability of addictive behavior and how addictive behavior increases the probability of family conflict.

9. Write a letter to each family member taking responsibility for past misdeeds, stating remorseful feelings, and asking for support from each member during recovery. (13, 14)

13. Help the client write a letter to each family member, taking responsibility for problems in the past, sharing his/her feelings, and asking for what he/she would like from each family member to support his/her recovery.

10. Family members read letters sharing how they feel and stating what behavior they would like from the client during his/her recovery. (15)

11. List and implement conflict resolution skills to be used during a family argument. (16, 17)

12. List the ways in which a higher power can assist in recovery from family conflicts and addiction. (18)

13. List instances when feelings, wishes, and wants were shared calmly in a respectful manner. (19, 20)

14. Confront the client when he/she blames others and does not accept responsibility for his/her own role in the family conflict.

15. Help each family member write a letter to the client stating how they feel, and asking for what they would like from him/her during recovery; ask each member to read the letter to the client in a family session.

16. Using modeling, role-playing and behavior rehearsal, teach the client what to do when he/she is in a family conflict (e.g., call someone, go to a meeting, use "I" messages, accept the responsibility for his/her own behavior, don't blame, turn it over to a higher power, stop, look, listen, think, and plan before acting).

17. Review the client's implementation of conflict resolution skills; reinforce success, confront the projection of blame, and redirect him/her for failure.

18. Teach the client about the 12-step recovery group's concept of a higher power, and how this power can be used to assist in resolving family conflicts and addiction (e.g., attend worship services with family members, pray at meals, have family devotions where the family prays together).

19. Teach the client the assertive communication formula "I feel ... When you ... I would prefer it if ... ;" practice the formula five times in role-playing current family conflict situations.

14. Verbalize the negative effects of passive or aggressive behaviors, and list the positive effects of using assertive skills. (21)

15. Increase the level of independent functioning. (22, 23, 24)

16. Agree to continue to work on family conflict and addiction issues by regularly attending recovery groups and family therapy in aftercare. (25)

17. Complete or give permission to a significant other to complete a re-administration of a survey of the client's family as a means of assessing treatment outcome. (26)

20. Using modeling, role-playing, and behavior rehearsal, teach the client how to share feelings, wishes, and wants calmly in several difficult situations; assign implementation of this communication style with family members.

21. Teach the client the difference between passive, aggressive, and assertive behavior; assign him/her to list the positive and negative effects of passivity and aggression and the positive effects of assertiveness.

22. Probe the client's fears surrounding emancipation; process these fears to resolution.

23. Confront the client's emotional dependence and his/her avoidance of economic responsibility, which promote a continuing pattern of dependently living off of others.

24. Develop a structured written plan for the client's emancipation that includes steady employment, paying his/her own expenses, and independent housing.

25. Help the client develop an aftercare program that includes regular attendance at recovery groups and the family therapy that is necessary to resolve family conflicts and maintain abstinence from addictive behavior.

26. Assess the outcome of treatment by re-administering to the client or a significant other an objective survey of the client's family conflict; give the client feedback regarding the results of the assessment.

18. Complete a survey to assess the degree of satisfaction with treatment. (27)

27. Administer a survey to assess the client's degree of satisfaction with treatment.

___. _____
   _____

___. _____
   _____

___. _____
   _____

___. _____
   _____

___. _____
   _____

___. _____
   _____

DIAGNOSTIC SUGGESTIONS:

Axis I:

313.81	Oppositional Defiant Disorder
312.8	Conduct Disorder
V61.20	Parent-Child Relational Problem
V61.1	Partner Relational Problem
V61.8	Sibling Relational Problem
V71.01	Adult Antisocial Behavior

_____ _____

_____ _____

Axis II:

301.83	Borderline Personality Disorder
301.7	Antisocial Personality Disorder
301.6	Dependent Personality Disorder

_____ _____

_____ _____

GAMBLING

BEHAVIORAL DEFINITIONS

1. Reports a history of repeated unsuccessful attempts to stop or cut down on gambling, despite the verbalized desire to do so and the many negative consequences of continued gambling.
2. Denies that gambling is a problem, despite feedback from significant others that gambling is negatively affecting them and others.
3. Maintains a distorted belief that more gambling will certainly result in a financial windfall.
4. Experiences persistent physical, legal, financial, vocational, social, and/or relationship problems that are directly caused by gambling.
5. Has suspended important social, recreational, and/or occupational activities because they interfere with gambling.
6. Exhibits restlessness and irritability when attempting to stop gambling.
7. Reports frequent loss of time when gambling.
8. Demonstrates physical withdrawal symptoms (e.g., shaking, nausea, headaches, sweating, anxiety, insomnia, and/or depression) when going without gambling for any length of time.
9. Has a history of arrests for gambling-related offenses (e.g., bad checks, forgery, embezzlement, theft).
10. Invests large amounts of money, time, and activities to gamble.
11. Gambles greater amounts of money and for a longer time than intended.
12. Substance abuse accompanies gambling behavior.

—. _____
   _____

—. _____
   _____

—. _____
   _____

LONG-TERM GOALS

1. Accept the powerlessness and unmanageability over gambling and participate in a recovery-based program.
2. Accept the problem with gambling and begin to actively participate in a recovery program.
3. Withdraw from gambling emotionally and learn a new program of recovery, free from excessive stress and addictive behavior.
4. Acquire the necessary skills to maintain long-term abstinence from gambling.
5. Develop financial planning that will allow repayment of losses and established financial stability.

—. _____
_____

—. _____
_____

—. _____
_____

SHORT-TERM OBJECTIVES	THERAPEUTIC INTERVENTIONS
1. Provide honest and complete information regarding gambling history. (1)	1. Complete a thorough family and personal biopsychosocial history that has a focus on the client's gambling.
2. Complete psychological testing or objective questionnaires for assessing problem gambling. (2)	2. Administer to the client psychological instruments designed to objectively assess problem gambling (e.g., Maroondah Assessment Profile for Problem Gambling [G-MAP] by Loughman, Pierce, and Sagris-Desmond, South Oaks Gambling Screen [SOGS]); give the client feedback regarding the results of the assessment.
3. Verbalize an increased knowledge of addiction and the process of recovery. (3, 4, 5, 6)	3. Assign the client to attend a gambling didactic series to increase knowledge of the patterns and effects of gambling.

4. Attend group therapy sessions to share thoughts and feelings associated with reasons for, consequences of, feelings about, and alternatives to gambling. (7, 8)

5. List 10 negative consequences resulting from or exacerbated by gambling. (9)

6. Verbally admit to powerlessness over gambling. (10)

7. Verbalize a recognition that gambling was used as the primary coping mechanism to escape from stress or emotional pain, and resulted in negative consequences. (11, 12, 13)

4. Ask the client to identify several key points attained from attending each didactic; process these points.

5. Teach the client about cross-tolerance (i.e., one drug or addictive behavior causes tolerance to develop for another); apply this to the client's situation.

6. Require the client to read the Gambler's Anonymous (GA) *Combo Book* and gather five key points; process the points in session.

7. Assign the client to attend group therapy that is focused on gambling and other addictions.

8. Direct group therapy that facilitates the sharing of causes for, consequences of, feelings about, and alternatives to gambling.

9. Ask the client to make a list of the ways gambling has negatively impacted his/her life and to process the list with the therapist or group.

10. Assign the client to complete a GA first-step paper admitting to powerlessness over gambling behavior and any other addictions, and present it in group therapy or to therapist for feedback.

11. Assess the client's history for depression, abuse, neglect, or other traumas that contribute to underlying emotional pain.

12. Explore how gambling was used to escape from stress, emotional pain, and/or boredom; highlight the negative consequences of this pattern of escapism.

8. Develop a list of the social, emotional, and family factors that contributed to gambling. (1, 14)

13. Probe the client's sense of shame, guilt, and low self-worth that has resulted from gambling and its consequences.

1. Complete a thorough family and personal biopsychosocial history that has a focus on the client's gambling.

14. Using the biopsychosocial history, assist the client in understanding the familial, emotional, and social factors that contributed to the development of problem gambling.

9. List 10 reasons to work on a plan for recovery from gambling. (15)

15. Assign the client to write a list of 10 reasons to be abstinent from gambling.

10. List 10 lies used to hide gambling behavior. (16)

16. Help the client to see the dishonesty that goes along with gambling; have him/her list 10 lies he/she told to hide gambling, teaching the client why honesty is essential to recovery.

11. Practice turning problems over to a higher power each day. Record each event and share it with primary therapist. (17, 18)

17. Teach the client about the GA concept of a higher power and how this can assist in recovery.

18. Using a GA Step Three exercise, teach the client about the GA concept of *turning it over*, then assign turning over problems to a higher power each day; have the client record the event and discuss the results.

12. Apply problem-solving skills to gambling-related problems. (19)

19. Using modeling, role-playing and behavior rehearsal, teach the client how to solve problems in an organized fashion (e.g., write the problem, list the options of action, evaluate alternatives, act, monitor results); apply this technique to problems caused by gambling.

13. Identify underlying emotional issues that contributed to gambling as an escape behavior. (12, 20, 21)

14. Follow through on obtaining treatment for underlying emotional issues. (22, 23, 24)

15. Verbalize that there are options to gambling in dealing with stress and in finding pleasure or excitement in life. (25, 26, 27)

12. Explore how gambling was used to escape from stress, emotional pain, and/or boredom; highlight the negative consequences of this pattern of escapism.

20. Assist the client in clarifying why he/she was gambling, and help him/her identify healthier ways to satisfy these needs.

21. Assess the depth of the client's underlying depression, and whether the depression predates the gambling problem.

22. Refer the client to a physician for an evaluation of the need for antidepressant medication.

23. Monitor the client for medication prescription compliance, effectiveness, and side effects.

24. Recommend to the client that he/she obtain counseling to resolve underlying emotional issues that contribute to gambling behavior; make referrals, if necessary.

25. Assign the client to list the pleasurable activities he/she plans to use in recovery to take the place of gambling.

26. Using progressive relaxation, guided imagery, or biofeedback, teach the client how to relax; assign him/her to relax twice a day for 10 to 20 minutes per session.

27. Considering the client's current physical fitness levels (clear strenuous exercise with the client's physician), direct him/her to exercise three times a week, then increase the exercise by 10 percent a week, until he/she is exercising at a training heart rate for at least 20 minutes at least three times a week.

16. Complete a fourth-step inventory and share with a member of the clergy or someone else in the GA program. (28)

17. List the triggers that may precipitate a relapse into gambling. (29)

18. Make a written plan to cope with each high-risk or trigger situation. (30, 31)

19. Write a personal recovery plan that includes regular attendance at recovery group meetings, aftercare, getting a sponsor, and helping others in recovery. (32)

20. Family members verbalize an understanding of their role in the gambling problem and the process of recovery. (33, 34, 35)

21. Family members decrease the frequency of enabling the gambler after verbally identifying their enabling behaviors. (36)

22. Acknowledge the abuse of mood-altering drugs and/or

28. Assign the client to complete a fourth-step inventory, then make arrangements for him/her to share this with a member of the clergy or someone else in recovery.

29. Using a GA relapse prevention exercise, help the client to uncover his/her triggers for relapse into gambling.

30. Teach the client about high-risk situations (i.e., negative emotions, social pressure, interpersonal conflict, positive emotions, test personal control); assist him/her in making a written plan to cope with each high-risk situation.

31. Using modeling, role-playing, and behavior rehearsal, teach the client how to say no to gambling and other addictive behaviors; also, practice saying no in high-risk situations.

32. Help the client to develop a personal recovery plan that includes regular attendance at recovery group meetings, aftercare, getting a sponsor, and helping others in recovery.

33. Direct the client's family to attend GA meetings.

34. Educate the client's family in the dynamics of enabling and tough love.

35. Ask the client's family to attend the family education component of the treatment program.

36. Monitor the client's family for enabling behaviors; assist the client's family members in implementing persistent tough-love techniques.

37. Explore the client's use and abuse of mood-altering drugs and alco-

alcohol and the role substance abuse plays in gambling behavior. (37)

hol; assess the role of substance abuse in reinforcing gambling behavior.

23. Complete a re-administration of objective tests of problem gambling as a means of assessing treatment outcome. (38)

38. Assess the outcome of treatment by re-administering to the client objective tests of problem gambling; evaluate the results and provide feedback to the client.

24. Complete a survey to assess the degree of satisfaction with treatment. (39)

39. Administer a survey to assess the client's degree of satisfaction with treatment.

__. _____

__. _____

__. _____

__. _____

__. _____

__. _____

DIAGNOSTIC SUGGESTIONS:

Axis I:	312.31	Pathological Gambling
	312.30	Impulse-Control Disorder NOS
	296.xx	Bipolar I Disorder
	296.3x	Major Depressive Disorder, Recurrent
	296.89	Bipolar II Disorder

_____   _____

_____   _____

GRIEF/LOSS UNRESOLVED

BEHAVIORAL DEFINITIONS

1. Presents with unresolved bereavement and engaging in addictive behavior to cope with the grief.
2. Reports constant thoughts of the lost loved one, to the point of inability to move forward in life to other plans or relationships.
3. Verbalizes excessive and unreasonable feelings of responsibility for the loss of a significant other, including believing that he/she did not do enough to prevent the person's death.
4. Expresses feelings of guilt about being a survivor when loved ones have died.
5. Lacks ability to talk about the death of a loved one on anything more than a superficial level.
6. Demonstrates vegetative symptoms of depression (e.g., lack of appetite, weight loss, sleep disturbance, anhedonia, lack of energy).
7. Talking or thinking about the deceased loved one results in overwhelming sadness.

—. _____

_____

—. _____

_____

—. _____

_____

LONG-TERM GOALS

1. Resolve feelings of anger, sadness, guilt, and/or abandonment surrounding the loss of the loved one, and make plans for the future.
2. Accept the loss of the loved one and increase social contact with others.

3. Develop a plan for life, renewing old relationships and making new ones.
4. Maintain a program of recovery free from addiction and unresolved grief.

—. _____
   _____
   _____

—. _____
   _____
   _____

—. _____
   _____

SHORT-TERM OBJECTIVES

THERAPEUTIC INTERVENTIONS

1. Tell the story of the lost relationship. (1, 2)

   1. Encourage the client to share the entire story of the relationship with the lost person, possibly using pictures or mementos connected to the deceased loved one.

   2. Ask the client to elaborate in an autobiography the circumstances, feelings, and effects of the loss or losses in his/her life.

2. Complete psychological testing or objective questionnaires for assessing the depth of grief. (3)

   3. Administer to the client psychological instruments designed to objectively assess the depth of grief and depression (e.g., Beck Depression Inventory-II [BDI-II], Grief Experience Inventory [GEI]); give the client feedback regarding the results of the assessment.

3. Discuss the positive and negative aspects of the lost relationship. (4)

   4. Help the client to see both the positive and negative aspects of the lost relationship, keeping him/her from over-idealizing the relationship.

4. Read books on the topic of grief to better understand the

   5. Ask the client to read books on grief and loss (e.g., *Getting to the*

loss experience and to increase a sense of hope. (5, 6)

5. Identify what stages of grief have been experienced along the continuum of the grieving process. (7, 8)

6. Verbalize the feelings of anger, guilt, sadness, and/or abandonment felt because of the loss. (9)

7. Verbalize how the loss of the loved one led to addiction in order to avoid painful feelings. (10, 11)

8. List several negative consequences that resulted from using addiction to cope with grief and loss. (12)

9. Verbalize a resolution of guilt about the loss. (13, 14)

Other Side of Grief: Overcoming the Loss of a Spouse by Zonnebelt-Smeenge and DeVries, *How Can It Be All Right When Everything Is All Wrong* by Smedes, *How to Survive the Loss of a Love* by Colgrove, Bloomfield, and McWilliams, *When Bad Things Happen to Good People* by Kushner); process the content.

6. Ask the parents of a deceased child to read a book on coping with their loss (e.g., *The Bereaved Parent* by Schiff); process the key themes gleaned from the reading.

7. Educate the client on the stages of the grieving process and answer any questions he/she may have.

8. Assist the client in identifying the stages of grief that he/she has experienced and which stage he/she is presently working through.

9. Help the client to identify the feelings of hurt, loss, abandonment, and anger felt because of the loss; trace and resolve the cause of these strong feelings.

10. Teach the client how the loss of the loved one led to addiction so as to cope with the pain.

11. Teach the client how chemical use has led to an avoidance of working through the loss.

12. Assist the client in identifying how addiction has led to more pain and unresolved feelings.

13. Explore the client's feelings of guilt and blame surrounding the loss.

10. Terminate the blame of others for the loss. (15)

11. Verbalize an understanding of how dependence on the lost person and dependence on addictive behavior are similar. (16)

12. Express thoughts and feelings about the deceased that went unexpressed while the deceased was alive. (17, 18, 19, 20)

13. Make a written plan to increase independence and social interaction. (21, 22, 23)

14. Using logic and reasoning, help the client to see that he/she is not responsible for the loss.

15. Teach the client about the destructive consequences of holding on to anger and blaming others for the loss.

16. Help the client to see the common elements in the dependency on the deceased individual and on addictive behavior.

17. Conduct an empty chair exercise with the client, where he/she focuses on expressing to the lost loved one, imagined in the chair, what he/she never said while that loved one was alive.

18. Assign the client to visit the grave of the loved one to "talk to" the deceased and ventilate his/her feelings.

19. Ask the client to write a letter to the lost person describing his/her fond memories, painful and/or regretful memories, and how he/she currently feels; process the letter in session.

20. Assign the client to write to the deceased loved one, with a special focus on his/her feelings associated with the last meaningful contact with that person.

21. Help the client to make a written plan to help him/her to live a more active and independent life (e.g., make plans for social life, hobbies, financial security, job, recovery, contact sponsor, a grief group, a singles' group).

22. Assign the client to write a plan to improve social contact with old friends and to make new ones.

23. Teach the client about the importance of regularly attending recovery groups, getting a sponsor, and helping others in recovery.

14. Attend a grief/loss support group. (24)

24. Ask the client to attend a grief/loss support group and report to the therapist how he/she felt about attending.

15. List ways in which a higher power can assist in recovery from grief and addiction. (25, 26, 27)

25. Teach the client about the 12-step recovery program's concept of a higher power, and help him/her to see how this can assist in recovery from grief and addiction (e.g., talk to the higher power about the grief/loss, imagine the higher power healing the pain, ask the higher power to direct you to other friends and family who can provide support).

26. Assign the client to read page 449 in the Alcoholics Anonymous *Big Book*, and discuss how the loss of a loved one could be a part of the higher power's plan.

27. Using a 12-step recovery program's Step Eleven exercise, teach the client how to pray and meditate; then assign them to contact his/her higher power each day about his/her grief.

16. Write a letter of goodbye to the lost loved one, sharing feelings and thoughts. (9, 13, 28)

9. Help the client to identify the feelings of hurt, loss, abandonment, and anger felt because of the loss; trace and resolve the cause of these strong feelings.

13. Explore the client's feelings of guilt and blame surrounding the loss.

28. Assign the client to write a letter to the lost individual, sharing the unresolved feelings; process the letter in group or individual session.

17. Make contact with a 12-step recovery program temporary sponsor and share plans for recovery. (23, 29)

23. Teach the client about the importance of regularly attending recovery groups, getting a sponsor, and helping others in recovery.

29. Assign the client to make contact with a 12-step recovery program's temporary sponsor and discuss recovery plans.

18. Identify the positive characteristics of the deceased loved one, the positive aspects of the relationship with the deceased loved one, and how these things may be remembered. (30, 31)

30. Ask the client to list the most positive aspects of and memories about his/her relationship with the lost loved one.

31. Assist the client in developing rituals (e.g., placing memoriam in newspaper on anniversary of death, volunteering time to a favorite cause of the deceased person) that will celebrate the memorable aspects of the loved one and his/her life.

19. Encourage at least one person in recovery each day. (32)

32. To improve self-worth and self-esteem, assign the client to encourage one person in recovery each day.

20. Develop a written aftercare plan to resolve addiction and grief. (33)

33. Help the client to develop a written aftercare plan that specifically outlines a recovery plan (e.g., attend 12-step recovery program meetings, aftercare sessions, continued therapy, contact sponsor, turn it over daily, pray and meditate).

21. Family members verbalize a connection between unresolved grief/loss and addictive behavior. (34, 35)

34. Discuss with family members the connection between grief and addictive behavior.

22. Complete a re-administration of objective tests of depth of grief and depression as a means of assessing treatment outcome. (36)

23. Complete a survey to assess the degree of satisfaction with treatment. (37)

—. _____
  _____

—. _____
  _____

—. _____
  _____

35. In a family session, review what each member can do to assist the client in recovery.

36. Assess the outcome of treatment by re-administering to the client objective tests of depth of grief and depression; evaluate the results and provide feedback to the client.

37. Administer a survey to assess the client's degree of satisfaction with treatment.

—. _____
  _____

—. _____
  _____

—. _____
  _____

DIAGNOSTIC SUGGESTIONS:

Axis I:	296.2x	Major Depressive Disorder, Single Episode
	296.3x	Major Depressive Disorder, Recurrent
	311	Depressive Disorder NOS
	308.3	Acute Stress Disorder
	V62.82	Bereavement
	309.0	Adjustment Disorder with Depressed Mood
	309.3	Adjustment Disorder with Disturbance of Conduct
	309.28	Adjustment Disorder with Mixed Anxiety and Depressed Mood
	309.4	Adjustment Disorder with Mixed Disturbance of Emotions and Conduct

_____   _____

_____   _____

IMPULSIVITY

BEHAVIORAL DEFINITIONS

1. Exhibits a tendency to act too quickly on impulses without careful deliberation, resulting in numerous negative consequences.
2. Demonstrates difficulty with patience, particularly while waiting for someone or waiting in line.
3. Impulsivity facilitates a self-defeating pattern of addiction behavior.
4. Reports loss of control over aggressive impulses, resulting in assault, self-destructive behavior, and/or damage to property.
5. Desires everything immediately—demonstrates a decreased ability to delay pleasure or gratification.
6. Has a history of acting out in at least two areas that are potentially self-damaging, (e.g., spending money, sexual activity, reckless driving, addiction).
7. Overreacts to mildly aversive or pleasure-oriented stimulation.
8. Experiences a sense of tension or affective arousal before engaging in the impulsive behavior (e.g., kleptomania or pyromania).
9. Senses pleasure, gratification, or release at the time of committing the ego-dystonic act.

—. _____
   _____
—. _____
   _____
—. _____
   _____

LONG-TERM GOALS

1. Maintain a program of recovery, free from impulsive behavior and addiction.
2. Reduce the frequency of impulsive behavior and increase the frequency of behavior that is carefully thought out.
3. Learn the techniques necessary to decrease impulsive thoughts, feelings, and behaviors, and develop a program of recovery consistent with thoughtful behavior and abstinence.
4. Learn to stop, think, and plan before acting.

__. _____
   _____
__. _____
   _____
__. _____
   _____

SHORT-TERM OBJECTIVES

1. Verbalize an understanding of the powerlessness and unmanageability that results from impulsivity and addiction. (1)

2. Identify specific instances of impulsivity. (2)

3. Complete psychological testing or objective questionnaires for assessing impulsivity. (3)

THERAPEUTIC INTERVENTIONS

1. Using a 12-step recovery program's Step One exercise, help the client to understand how impulsivity and addictive behavior led to powerlessness and unmanageability.

2. Review the client's behavior pattern to assist him/her in clearly identifying, without minimization, denial, or projection of blame, his/her pattern of impulsivity.

3. Administer to the client psychological instruments designed to objectively assess impulsivity (e.g., Barratt Impulsiveness Scale [BIS], Conners' Adult ADHD Rating Scales [CARRS]); give the client feedback regarding the results of the assessment.

4. Discuss how impulsivity and addiction meet the 12-step recovery program's criteria for *insanity*. (4)

4. Using a 12-step recovery program's Step Two exercise, help the client to see that doing the same things over and over again and expecting different results meets the 12-step recovery program's definition of *insanity*.

5. Identify the negative consequences that are caused by impulsivity. (5, 6, 7)

5. Assist client in making connections between his/her impulsivity and the negative consequences for himself/herself and others resulting from it.

6. Assign the client to write a list of negative consequences that occurred because of impulsivity.

7. Help the client to see how dangerous it is to act impulsively (e.g., you don't have time to think, you can't plan effectively).

6. Verbally identify several times when impulsive action led to addictive behavior and subsequent negative consequences. (8)

8. Explore times when the client acted too quickly on impulses, resulting in addictive behavior.

7. Increase the frequency of reviewing behavioral decisions with a trusted friend or family member for feedback regarding consequences before the decision is enacted. (9, 10)

9. Conduct a session with spouse, significant other, sponsor, or family member and client to develop a contract for the client to receive feedback prior to his/her engaging in impulsive acts.

10. Review the client's implementation of reviewing with significant others decisions to act before engaging in impulsive actions; reinforce success and redirect for failure.

8. Verbalize the biopsychosocial elements that cause or exacerbate impulsivity and addictive behavior. (11)

11. Probe the client's biopsychosocial history and help the client to see the contributing factors to his/her impulsivity and addictive behavior (e.g., family models of impulsiv-

9. Comply with a physician's evaluation regarding the necessity for psychopharmacological intervention. (12)

10. Take all medications as prescribed and report as to effectiveness and side effects. (13, 14)

11. Identify the thoughts that trigger impulsive behavior, and then replace each thought with a thought that is more accurate. (15, 16)

12. List the inappropriate behaviors that are displayed when feeling anxious and uncomfortable, and replace each behavior with an action that is positive and adaptive. (2, 17)

ity or addictive behavior, anxiety that energizes impulsivity, failure to learn delay of gratification in childhood).

12. Refer the client to a physician to examine him/her, order medications as indicated, titrate medications, and monitor for side effects and effectiveness.

13. Direct the staff to administer the medications as ordered by the physician.

14. Monitor the client's psychotropic medication for effectiveness as well as side effects.

15. Help the client to uncover dysfunctional thoughts that lead to impulsivity; assist him/her in replacing each dysfunctional thought with a thought that is more accurate, positive, self-enhancing and adaptive.

16. Help the client to develop a list of positive, accurate, self-enhancing thoughts to read to himself/herself each day, particularly when feeling upset, anxious, or uncomfortable.

2. Review the client's behavior pattern to assist him/her in clearly identifying, without minimization, denial, or projection of blame, his/her pattern of impulsivity.

17. Probe the client's anxious, impulsive behaviors, and then use modeling, role-playing, and behavior rehearsal to teach him/her new behaviors that are positive and adaptive (e.g., talking to someone about the problem, taking a time out, calling the sponsor, going to a meeting, exercising, relaxing).

13. Implement relaxation procedure when feeling upset or uncomfortable. (18)

18. Teach the client relaxation techniques (e.g., progressive relaxation, self-hypnosis, biofeedback); assign him/her to relax whenever he/she feels uncomfortable.

14. Practice stopping, looking, listening, thinking, and planning before acting. (19, 20)

19. Using modeling, role-playing and behavior rehearsal, show the client how to use "stop, look, listen, think, and plan before acting" in various current situations.

20. Review the client's use of "stop, look, listen, think, and plan" in day-to-day living, and identify the positive consequences.

15. Verbalize an understanding of a 12-step recovery program's Step Three regarding the role of a higher power, and how this step can be used in recovery from impulsivity and addiction. (21, 22)

21. Teach the client about the 12-step recovery program's concept of a higher power, and discuss how he/she can use a higher power effectively in recovery (e.g., practice stopping and asking a higher power for strength and direction, practice daily prayer and meditation).

22. Using a 12-step recovery program's Step Three exercise, teach the client how to turn his/her will and life over to the care of a higher power.

16. Relate how each wrong behavior identified in a 12-step recovery program's Step Four exercise can be related to impulsivity and addiction. (23, 24)

23. Using a 12-step recovery program's Step Four exercise, assign the client to write an autobiography of the exact nature of his/her wrongs, and relate these wrongs to impulsivity and addictive behavior.

24. Assist the client in acknowledging the relationship between the wrongful behavior identified in a Step Four exercise and his/her impulsivity and addictive behavior.

17. Develop and write a continuing care program that includes the recovery group meetings and any further therapy that is necessary for recovery. (25)

18. Family members verbalize a connection between impulsivity and addictive behavior. (26, 27, 28)

19. Complete a re-administration of objective tests of impulsivity as a means of assessing treatment outcome. (29)

20. Complete a survey to assess the degree of satisfaction with treatment. (30)

___. _____

_____

___. _____

_____

___. _____

_____

25. Help the client to develop an aftercare plan that includes regular recovery groups, getting a sponsor, and any further therapy necessary to recover from impulsivity and addiction.

26. Encourage the client to share with family members the journey through impulsivity, addiction, and recovery.

27. Discuss with family members the connection between impulsive behavior and addictive behavior.

28. In a family session, review what each member can do to assist the client in recovery.

29. Assess the outcome of treatment by re-administering to the client objective tests of impulsivity; evaluate the results and provide feedback to the client.

30. Administer a survey to assess the client's degree of satisfaction with treatment.

___. _____

_____

___. _____

_____

___. _____

_____

DIAGNOSTIC SUGGESTIONS:

Axis I:	312.8	Conduct Disorder
	313.81	Oppositional Defiant Disorder
	296.4x	Bipolar I Disorder, Most Recent Episode Manic
	301.13	Cyclothymic Disorder
	296.89	Bipolar II Disorder

312.34   Intermittent Explosive Disorder
314   Attention Deficit Hyperactivity Disorder
321.30   Impulse Control Disorder NOS

_____   _____

_____   _____

Axis II: 301.7   Antisocial Personality Disorder
               301.83   Borderline Personality Disorder
               301.81   Narcissistic Personality Disorder

_____   _____

_____   _____

LEGAL PROBLEMS

BEHAVIORAL DEFINITIONS

1. Presents with legal charges pending adjudication.
2. Has a history of repeated violations of the law, many occurring while under the influence of drugs or alcohol.
3. Unresolved legal problems are complicating recovery from addiction.
4. Expresses fear of the legal system adjudicating current problems.
5. Has a history of repeated violations of the law related to buying, selling, or using illegal substances.
6. Is under a court order to seek treatment for addiction.
7. Expresses feelings of anger, resentment, and fear of abandonment associated with impending divorce.
8. Chemical dependency has resulted in several arrests.
9. Fears loss of freedom due to current legal charges.

—. _____
   _____
   _____
—. _____
   _____
   _____
—. _____
   _____

LONG-TERM GOALS

1. Maintain a program of recovery free from addiction and legal conflicts.
2. Accept the responsibility for legal problems without blaming others.
3. Consult with legal authorities (e.g., attorney, probation officer, police, court official) to make plans for adjudicating legal conflicts.

4. Understand the need to maintain abstinence to remain free of negative consequences, which include legal problems.

—. _____

_____

—. _____

_____

—. _____

_____

SHORT-TERM OBJECTIVES

THERAPEUTIC INTERVENTIONS

1. Verbalize the powerlessness and unmanageability that results from legal conflicts and addiction. (1)

1. Help the client to understand the relationship between addictive behavior and legal conflicts, and how these problems result in powerlessness and unmanageability.

2. Identify the nature and history of legal problems. (2)

2. Gather a history of the client's illegal behavior and his/her experience with the legal system.

3. Complete psychological testing or objective questionnaires for assessing antisocial traits and propensity for illegal behavior. (3)

3. Administer to the client psychological instruments designed to objectively assess antisocial traits and propensity for illegal behavior (e.g., Millon Clinical Multiaxial Inventory-III [MCMI-III] Jesness Behavior Checklist]; give the client feedback regarding the results of the assessment.

4. Verbalize an acceptance of the responsibility for addiction and legal problems without blaming others. (4, 5)

4. Help the client to identify and accept responsibility for the many decisions that he/she made that resulted in addiction and legal problems without blaming others.

5. Confront the client for avoidance of his/her responsibility for legal problems.

5. Acknowledge the connection between legal problems and addictive behavior. (6, 7)

6. Teach the client the relationship between his/her legal problems and his/her addictive behavior; so-

licit the client's acknowledgment of this relationship.

7. Assign the client to write how each legal conflict has been related to addictive behavior.

6. Write a plan that outlines the changes needed in behavior, attitude, and associates to protect self from harmful legal consequences. (8)

8. Teach the client the difference between antisocial and prosocial behaviors, helping to identify his/her antisocial behaviors and attitudes; help develop prosocial plans for changes to be made in recovery (e.g., respect for the law, helping others, honesty, reliability, regular attendance at work, recovery groups, aftercare, halfway house).

7. Replace distorted thoughts with realistic, positive cognitions. (9, 10)

9. Probe the client's distorted thoughts and feelings that surround addictive behavior and legal problems.

10. Assist the client in identifying positive, realistic thoughts to replace dysfunctional thinking that leads to addictive and illegal behaviors.

8. Meet with an attorney to make plans for resolving legal conflicts. (11)

11. Encourage and facilitate the client to meet with an attorney to discuss plans for resolving legal conflicts.

9. Contact the probation or parole officer and agree in writing to meet the conditions of probation or parole. (12)

12. Encourage and facilitate the client to meet with his/her probation or parole officer, and assign him/her to agree in writing to meet all conditions of probation or parole.

10. Verbalize ways to meet social, emotional, and financial needs in recovery without illegal activity or addiction. (13)

13. Help the client to develop a plan to meet social, emotional, and financial needs in recovery without resorting to criminal activity or addictive behavior.

11. Verbalize the importance of obeying the laws of society to maintain abstinence and work a program of recovery. (8, 14)

8. Teach the client the difference between antisocial and prosocial behaviors, helping to identify his/her antisocial behaviors and

attitudes; help develop prosocial plans for changes to be made in recovery (e.g., respect for the law, helping others, honesty, reliability, regular attendance at work, recovery groups, aftercare, halfway house).

14. Help the client to understand why he/she needs to obey the law in order to maintain abstinence from addictive behavior.

12. Identify and replace the criminal thinking that led to legal conflicts and addiction. (15, 16)

15. Teach the client about criminal thinking (e.g., rationalization, denial, superoptimism, blaming others); assist him/her in identifying his/her criminal thinking, correcting each criminal thought with a thought that is honest and respectful of others.

16. Help the client to understand the importance of helping others in recovery in order to replace a criminal attitude of taking and entitlement with an attitude of giving and self-sacrifice.

13. Verbalize the importance of a higher power in recovery, and list five ways in which a higher power can assist in recovery. (17)

17. Teach the client about the 12-step recovery program's concept of a higher power and how a higher power can assist in recovery from legal conflicts and addiction (e.g., practice trusting a higher power to help with legal problems, practice daily prayer and meditation).

14. Develop an aftercare program that includes regular attendance at recovery groups and any other necessary therapy. (18)

18. Help the client to develop an aftercare program that has all of the elements necessary to maintain abstinence and resolve legal conflicts.

15. Verbalize the importance of resolving legal issues honestly. (19)

19. Help the client to understand the importance of resolving legal conflicts honestly and legally; teach that honesty is the basis for trust.

16. Family members verbalize what each can do to assist the client in recovery. (20, 21)

17. Complete a re-administration of objective tests of legal problems and antisocial behavior as a means of assessing treatment outcome. (22)

18. Complete a survey to assess the degree of satisfaction with treatment. (23)

—. _____
   _____

—. _____
   _____

—. _____
   _____

20. Discuss with family members the connection between legal problems and addictive behavior.

21. In a family session, review what each member can do to assist the client in recovery.

22. Assess the outcome of treatment by re-administering to the client objective tests of antisocial traits and propensity for illegal behavior; evaluate the results and provide feedback to the client.

23. Administer a survey to assess the client's degree of satisfaction with treatment.

—. _____
   _____

—. _____
   _____

—. _____
   _____

DIAGNOSTIC SUGGESTIONS:

Axis I:	312.8	Conduct Disorder
	313.81	Oppositional Defiant Disorder
	309.3	Adjustment Disorder with Disturbance of Conduct
	312.34	Intermittent Explosive Disorder
	V71.01	Adult Antisocial Behavior
	_____	_____
	_____	_____
Axis II:	301.7	Antisocial Personality Disorder
	301.83	Borderline Personality Disorder
	301.81	Narcissistic Personality Disorder
	_____	_____
	_____	_____

LIVING ENVIRONMENT DEFICIENCY

BEHAVIORAL DEFINITIONS

1. Lives in an environment in which there is a high risk for relapse.
2. Lives with an individual who is a regular user/abuser of alcohol and/or drugs.
3. Experiencing significant social isolation, withdrawal from social life.
4. Lives in an environment in which there is a high risk of physical, sexual, or emotional abuse.
5. Has many friends or relatives who are addicted.
6. Reports that family is angry or negative toward the addict and not supportive of a recovery program.
7. Presents as financially destitute and in need of assistance for adequate food and shelter.
8. Associates with peer group members who are regular users/abusers of alcohol and/or drugs.
9. Lives in a neighborhood that has a high incidence of alcohol and drug addiction as well as crime.

—. _____
   _____
—. _____
   _____
—. _____
   _____

LONG-TERM GOALS

1. Maintain a program of recovery free from addiction and the negative impact of the deficient environment.

144

2. Improve the social, occupational, financial, and living situation sufficiently to increase the probability of a successful recovery from addiction.
3. Understand the negative impact of the current environment on addiction recovery.
4. Develop a peer group that is supportive of recovery.
5. Family members support the client's recovery.
6. Accept the importance of working a program of recovery that necessitates attendance at recovery groups and helping others.

—. _____

  _____

—. _____

  _____

—. _____

  _____

SHORT-TERM OBJECTIVES

1. Verbalize the sense of power-lessness and unmanageability that results from a deficient environment and addiction. (1)

2. Identify specific living environment problems and how they negatively affect recovery. (2, 3)

3. Complete psychological testing or objective questionnaires for assessing perception of social and family environment. (4)

THERAPEUTIC INTERVENTIONS

1. Using a 12-step recovery program's Step One exercise, help the client to see the powerlessness and unmanageability that results from addiction and a deficient environment.

2. Help the client identify problems with his/her living environment and the negative impact that they have on recovery.

3. Help the client to list specific instances when the high-risk social and/or family environment led to negative consequences and addiction.

4. Administer to the client psychological instruments designed to objectively assess the client's perception of his/her social and family environment (e.g., Quality of Life Inventory [QOLI] by Frish, Family Environment Scale

[FES] by Moos and Moos); give the client feedback regarding the results of the assessment.

4. Make a written plan to address each living environment problem in recovery. (5)

5. Help the client to develop a written plan for addressing each living environment problem in recovery.

5. List alternatives to living in the current high-risk environment. (6)

6. Discuss the alternatives that are available for moving out of the current living situation, which promotes ongoing addiction.

6. Identify current social, occupational, and financial needs, and make a plan to meet each need in recovery. (7, 8)

7. Help the client to identify his/her social, occupational, and financial needs, and make a written plan to meet each need in recovery.

8. Teach the importance of a supportive peer group, and assign the client to list 10 reasons why he/she needs a new peer group to maintain abstinence.

7. Write a personal recovery plan detailing the recovery groups, aftercare, social relationships, and further treatment that will be needed in recovery. (9, 10, 11, 12)

9. Facilitate the client meeting with a 12-step recovery program contact person, and encourage him/her to discuss recovery plans.

10. Help the client to develop a personal recovery plan that has all of the elements necessary to recover from addictive behavior and the deficient living environment.

11. Encourage the client's attendance at 12-step recovery program meetings as a means of developing a supportive peer group.

12. Assign the client to write at least five steps that he/she will take to initiate new relationships with recovering people.

8. Implement turning over to a higher power the living environmental problems and the urge to engage in addictive behavior. (13, 14, 15)

13. Teach the client about the 12-step recovery program's concept of a higher power, and show him/her how a higher power can assist in recovery (e.g., by learning how

to turn problems over to a higher power, practicing regular prayer and meditation).

14. Using a 12-step recovery program's Step Three exercise, teach the client how to turn his/her will and life over to a higher power.

15. Monitor the client's implementation of a 12-step recovery program's Step Three exercise; reinforce his/her success and redirect for failure.

9. Verbalize a plan to continue spiritual growth within a community of believers. (16)

16. Assist the client in developing a plan to continue his/her spiritual growth (e.g., church, recovery groups, counseling, meeting with a pastor, spiritual reading material).

10. Implement refusal behavior in high-risk situations. (17, 18, 19, 20)

17. Using modeling, role-playing, and behavior rehearsal, teach the client refusal to engage in addictive behavior, then practice refusal in the high-risk situations for relapse (e.g., negative emotions, social pressure, interpersonal conflict, positive emotions, and testing personal control).

18. Using a 12-step recovery program's Step Four inventory, assign the client to write an autobiography detailing the exact nature of his/her wrongs, and how these relate to the negative peer group and addictive behavior.

19. Clarify the distinction between passive, aggressive, and assertive behavior.

20. Have the client role-play assertive responses to situations he/she is currently facing in his/her life; assign the client to practice assertive expression of feelings, thoughts, and desires to others during the week.

11. Write a letter to each significant other, discussing problems with the living environment, and share plans for recovery. (21, 22)

21. Help the client to write a letter to each significant other sharing his/her problem with addiction, how the living environment has fostered the addiction, and the plan for recovery.

22. Meet with family members to teach them about addiction, discuss the living environment deficiencies, and make plans for support of the client's recovery.

12. Develop a written plan as to how to react to family members who are addicted. (20, 23)

20. Have the client role-play assertive responses to situations he/she is currently facing in his/her life; assign the client to practice assertive expression of feelings, thoughts, and desires to others during the week.

23. Help the client to develop a plan as to how to deal with family members who are addicted.

13. Family members verbalize what each can do to assist the client in recovery. (24, 25)

24. Discuss with family members the connection between living environment deficiencies and addictive behavior.

25. In a family session, review what each member can do to assist the client in recovery.

14. Complete a re-administration of objective tests of perception of social and family environment as a means of assessing treatment outcome. (26)

26. Assess the outcome of treatment by re-administering to the client objective tests of the client's perception of his/her social and family environment; evaluate the results and provide feedback to the client.

15. Complete a survey to assess the degree of satisfaction with treatment. (27)

27. Administer a survey to assess the client's degree of satisfaction with treatment.

__. _____

__. _____

_____

_____

___. _____   ___. _____
    _____   _____
___. _____   ___. _____
    _____   _____

DIAGNOSTIC SUGGESTIONS:

Axis I:

	V61.20	Parent-Child Relational Problem
	V61.1	Partner Relational Problem
	V61.8	Sibling Relational Problem
	V62.81	Relational Problem NOS
	V61.21	Physical Abuse of Child
	V61.21	Sexual Abuse of Child
	V61.21	Neglect of Child
	V61.10	Physical Abuse of Adult
	V61.10	Sexual Abuse of Adult
	V62.20	Occupational Problem
	V62.89	Religious or Spiritual Problem
	V62.40	Acculturation Problem
	995.54	Physical Abuse of Child Focus on Victim
	995.5	Neglect of Child Focus on Victim

_____   _____

_____   _____

MANIA/HYPOMANIA

BEHAVIORAL DEFINITIONS

1. Experiences a distinct period of persistently elevated or irritable mood lasting at least four days.
2. Has an inflated sense of self-esteem and an exaggerated, euphoric belief in capabilities that denies any self-limitations or realistic obstacles, but sees others as standing in the way.
3. Reports decreased need for sleep.
4. Is more talkative than normal—pressured speech.
5. Experiences racing thoughts.
6. Has short attention span and is susceptible to distraction.
7. Initiates projects at home, work, or school, but without completion of tasks.
8. Engages in impulsive activities that are potentially self-damaging (e.g., buying sprees, sexual acting out, foolish business investments).
9. Impulsively uses drugs or alcohol without regard of the negative consequences.
10. Demonstrates verbal and/or physical aggression coupled with tantrum-like behavior (e.g., breaking things explosively) if wishes are blocked, which is in contrast to an earlier pattern of restraint.

—. _____
   _____
   _____
—. _____
   _____
—. _____
   _____

LONG-TERM GOALS

1. Maintain a program of recovery, free of manic/hypomanic behavior and addiction.

2. Increase control over impulses, reduce energy level, and stabilize mood.
3. Reduce agitation, irritability, and pressured speech, while increasing rational thinking and behavior.
4. Understand the biopsychosocial aspects of manic/hypomanic states and addiction, and accept the need for continued treatment, including medication.
5. Understand the relationship between manic/hypomanic states and addiction.
6. Terminate addiction and take medications for mania on a consistent basis.

—. _____
_____
—. _____
_____
—. _____
_____

SHORT-TERM OBJECTIVES	THERAPEUTIC INTERVENTIONS
1. Verbalize an acceptance of the sense of powerlessness and unmanageability that results from mania/hypomania and using addiction to cope with impulsivity and mood swings. (1)	1. Using a 12-step recovery program's Step One exercise, help the client to see the powerlessness and unmanageability that result from mania/hypomania and the use of addictive behavior to cope with these symptoms.
2. Identify manic behavior patterns and list several specific instances in which manic/hypomanic states led to addiction. (2, 3, 4)	2. Teach the client about the signs and symptoms of mania/hypomania, and how it can foster addictive behavior.
	3. Explore the client's pattern of manic/hypomanic behavior.
	4. Explore the client's addictive behavior history, and identify instances in which manic/hypomanic states led to addictive behavior.
3. Complete psychological testing or objective questionnaires for assessing mania/hypomania. (5)	5. Administer to the client psychological instruments designed to objectively assess mania/hypoma-

nia (e.g., Minnesota Multiphasic Personality Inventory-2 [MMPI-2], Personality Assessment Inventory [PAI] by Morey); give the client feedback regarding the results of the assessment.

4. Verbalize an understanding of the biopsychosocial correlates of mania/hypomania and addiction. (6)

6. Teach the client about the biopsychosocial correlates of mania/hypomania and addictive behavior.

5. List several negative consequences that resulted from untreated mania/hypomania and addiction. (7)

7. Help the client to identify the negative consequences of mania/hypomania and addictive behavior; emphasize the need for consistent treatment with medication and psychotherapy.

6. Turn over at least one problem to a higher power each day. (8, 9, 10)

8. Teach the client about the 12-step recovery program's concept of a higher power, and how a higher power can help restore him/her to sanity (e.g., attend worship services and practice daily prayer and meditation).

9. Using a 12-step recovery program's Step Three exercise, teach the client how to turn problems over to a higher power.

10. Assign the client to turn over one problem each day to a higher power; review the client's implementation, reinforcing success and redirect for failure.

7. Meet with the physician to see if psychopharmacological intervention is warranted, and take all medication as directed. (11)

11. Refer the client to a physician for an examination and to order psychotropic medications as indicated, titrate medications, and monitor for effectiveness and side effects.

8. Verbalize an acceptance of the necessity for continued medical treatment of manic/hypomanic symptoms. (12, 13)

12. Direct the staff to administer psychotropic medications as ordered by the physician and monitor for effectiveness and side effects.

9. Achieve mood stability by becoming slower to react with anger, less expansive, and more socially appropriate and sensitive. (13, 14, 15)

13. Monitor the client's use of prescribed psychotropic medication for effectiveness as well as side effects; emphasize the importance of consistent medical management of manic/hypomanic illness.

13. Monitor the client's use of prescribed psychotropic medication for effectiveness as well as side effects; emphasize the importance of consistent medical management of manic/hypomanic illness.

14. Confront gently but firmly the client's grandiosity and demandingness.

15. Reinforce the client's increased mood stability, social appropriateness, and reduced impulsivity.

10. Terminate self-destructive impulsive behaviors. (16, 17, 18)

16. Focus repeatedly on the negative consequences of impulsive behavior, to increase thoughtfulness.

17. Facilitate the client's impulse control by using role-play, behavior rehearsal, and role reversal to increase sensitivity to the consequences of manic/hypomanic behavior.

18. Set limits on the client's manipulation or acting out by making rules and establishing clear consequences for breaking them.

11. Speak more slowly and be more subject-focused. (13, 19, 20)

13. Monitor the client's use of prescribed psychotropic medication for effectiveness as well as side effects; emphasize the importance of consistent medical management of manic/hypomanic illness.

19. Provide structure and focus for the client's thoughts and actions by regulating the direction of conversation and by establishing plans for behavior.

12. Dress and groom in a less attention-seeking manner. (17, 21)

13. Identify positive traits and behaviors that build genuine self-esteem. (22)

14. Develop a personal recovery plan that includes all of the elements necessary to control mania/hypomania and to recover from addiction. (23, 24)

15. Write a 12-step program's fourth-step inventory, and share with someone in recovery. (25)

16. Verbalize the importance of consistently attending recovery groups and of helping others in recovery. (26, 27)

20. Verbally reinforce slower speech and more deliberate thought processes.

17. Facilitate the client's impulse control by using role-play, behavior rehearsal, and role reversal to increase sensitivity to the consequences of manic/hypomanic behavior.

21. Encourage and reinforce appropriate dress and grooming.

22. Assist the client in identifying strengths and assets in order to build self-esteem and confidence.

23. Outline with the client the essential components for managing manic/hypomanic states and addiction (e.g., taking medication, complying with medical monitoring, continuing therapy, attending recovery groups regularly, using a higher power, getting a sponsor, helping others in recovery).

24. Help the client to decide what environment he/she needs in early recovery to stabilize mood and maintain abstinence.

25. Using a 12-step recovery program's fourth-step inventory, assign the client to write an autobiography and then to share it with someone in recovery.

26. Teach the client the importance of working a program of recovery that includes attending recovery group meetings regularly and helping others.

27. Arrange for the client to meet a 12-step program contact person, and assign him/her to talk about manic/hypomanic states and addictive behavior.

17. Family members meet with a physician to discuss medication and its side effects. (28)

18. Family members verbalize a connection between mania/hypomania and addictive behavior. (29, 30)

28. Refer the family to a physician to discuss the client's medication and side effects.

29. Provide the family members with information about mania/hypomania and its connection to addictive behavior; review the steps that the client must take to recover successfully.

30. In a family session, review what each member can do to assist the client in recovery.

19. Complete a re-administration of objective tests of mania/hypomania as a means of assessing treatment outcome. (31)

20. Complete a survey to assess the degree of satisfaction with treatment. (32)

31. Assess the outcome of treatment by re-administering to the client objective tests of mania/hypomania; evaluate the results and provide feedback to the client.

32. Administer a survey to assess the client's degree of satisfaction with treatment.

__. _____
_____

__. _____
_____

__. _____
_____

__. _____
_____

__. _____
_____

__. _____
_____

DIAGNOSTIC SUGGESTIONS:

Axis I: 296.xx   Bipolar I Disorder
296.89   Bipolar II Disorder
301.13   Cyclothymic Disorder
295.70   Schizoaffective Disorder
296.80   Bipolar Disorder NOS
301.1   Personality Change Due to (Axis III Disorder)

_____ _____

_____ _____

MEDICAL ISSUES

BEHAVIORAL DEFINITIONS

1. Has been diagnosed with medical problems that complicate recovery from addiction.
2. Presents with medical problems that require medical monitoring of medications or assistance with mobility.
3. Has organic brain syndrome that compromises learning, as a result of use of mood-altering chemicals.
4. Demonstrates inability to self-administer prescribed medications.
5. Suffers from chronic pain syndrome, which places the client at high risk for relapse.
6. Has medical problems that require medical/nursing assistance.
7. Self-medicates medical problems through use of mood-altering chemicals.
8. Reports negative emotions concerning medical illness that led to addiction.
9. Demonstrates a compromised ability to concentrate on recovery due to the severity of medical problems.

—. _____

_____

—. _____

_____

—. _____

_____

LONG-TERM GOALS

1. Maintain a program of recovery, free of addiction and the negative effects of medical issues.
2. Resolve medical problems and return to a normal level of functioning.
3. Understand the relationship between medical issues and addiction.

4. Reduce the impact of medical problems on recovery and relapse potential.
5. Improve coping skills with organic brain syndrome, to allow for a self-directed program of recovery.
6. Understand and participate in the medical management of physical health problems.

—. _____
_____
—. _____
_____
—. _____
_____

SHORT-TERM OBJECTIVES	THERAPEUTIC INTERVENTIONS
1. Verbalize an acceptance of the powerlessness and unmanageability that results from using addictive behavior to cope with medical problems. (1)	1. Using a 12-step recovery program's Step One exercise, help the client to see the powerlessness and unmanageability that result from medical issues and addiction.
2. Identify medical problems and how these relate to addiction. (2)	2. Explore the client's medical history and help him/her to see the relationship between his/her medical problems and addictive behavior.
3. Complete psychological testing or objective questionnaires for assessing coping with medical problems. (3)	3. Administer to the client psychological instruments designed to objectively assess coping with medical problems (e.g., Beck Depression Inventory-FastScreen for Medical Patients [BDI-FastScreen], Coping with Health, Injuries, and Problems [CHIP]); give the client feedback regarding the results of the assessment.
4. Verbalize an acceptance of the seriousness of medical problems and addictive behavior. (4)	4. Teach the client about the medical issues and addiction, and how each of these illnesses poses a serious risk to his/her welfare.

5. List the negative consequences that resulted from using addiction to cope with medical problems. (2, 5, 6)

2. Explore the client's medical history and help him/her to see the relationship between his/her medical problems and addictive behavior.

5. Help the client to develop a list of negative consequences that occurred because of using addictive behavior to cope with medical problems.

6. Educate the client regarding the negative impact of addictive behavior on bodily functioning and systems.

6. Visit with a physician for examination of the medical condition and addiction, and cooperate with treatment plan. (7, 8)

7. Physician to examine the client and to make recommendations as indicated to treat the medical condition and alleviate symptoms.

8. Monitor the client's compliance with the treatment plan as ordered by the physician; redirect the client as needed.

7. Verbalize an understanding of the medical condition, the treatment options, and prognosis. (9, 10, 11, 12)

9. Help the client to understand his/her medical problem and the need to cooperate with medical management.

10. Provide the client with references to literature of other informational resources regarding his/her medical condition.

11. Facilitate the medical personnel's teaching the client about his/her medical condition and discussing the treatment plan and prognosis.

12. Help the client to understand the importance of medical management and follow-up in aftercare.

8. Participate in decisions regarding the medical management of biomedical problems. (7, 13)

7. Physician to examine the client and to make recommendations as indicated to treat the medical condition and alleviate symptoms.

13. Teach the client assertiveness skills, and encourage the implementation of assertiveness in obtaining information about and becoming involved in the management of his/her medical treatment.

9. List 10 things to do to improve physical functioning. (14)

14. After a consultation with the medical staff, help the client to list 10 actions that he/she can take to improve physical functioning (e.g., take medications, maintain abstinence, practice relaxation, implement proper diet, rest and exercise, keep regular follow-up appointments with the physician).

10. Implement relaxation exercises as a pain management technique. (15)

15. Teach deep muscle relaxation and guided imagery, to be used by the client in pain management.

11. Accept and follow through on a referral to a pain management clinic. (16)

16. Refer the client to a pain clinic for medical and psychological management of pain.

12. Discuss with family members the medical problems and addiction, and make plans for family members to obtain supportive services. (17)

17. In a family session, discuss the medical issues and addiction, and make recommendations for family members to obtain supportive services (e.g., Alanon, Alateen, medical support group).

13. List ways in which a higher power can assist in recovery from medical issues and addictive behavior. (18, 19)

18. Teach the client the 12-step recovery program's concept of a higher power, and help him/her to see how a higher power can be helpful in recovery (e.g., pray for assistance with medical problems, practice regular meditation, attend religious activities to gain support).

19. Teach the client about the 12-step recovery program's Step Eleven, and how this step can be used in daily recovery.

14. Write a personal recovery plan that includes regular attendance at recovery groups and any medical treatment necessary to control medical issues and addiction. (20)

20. Help the client to develop a personal recovery plan that details what he/she is going to do in recovery to remain abstinent and to treat biomedical issues (e.g., attend recovery groups regularly, make medical visits regularly, take medication as indicated, get a sponsor, attend aftercare, help others).

15. Family members verbalize what each can do to assist the client in recovery. (21, 22)

21. Discuss with family members the connection between the client's medical issues and his/her addictive behavior; review the steps that the client must take to recover successfully.

22. In a family session, review what each member can do to assist the client in recovery.

16. Complete a re-administration of objective tests of coping with medical problems as a means of assessing treatment outcome. (23)

23. Assess the outcome of treatment by re-administering to the client objective tests of coping with medical problems; evaluate the results and provide feedback to the client.

17. Complete a survey to assess the degree of satisfaction with treatment. (24)

24. Administer a survey to assess the client's degree of satisfaction with treatment.

—. _____
_____
—. _____
_____
—. _____
_____

—. _____
_____
—. _____
_____
—. _____
_____

DIAGNOSTIC SUGGESTIONS:

Axis I: 307.89   Pain Disorder Associated with Psychological Factors and Axis III Disorder

307.80	Pain Disorder Associated with Psychological Factors
300.7	Hypochondriasis
300.81	Somatization Disorder
316	Personality Traits Affecting (Axis III Disorder)
316	Maladaptive Health Behaviors Affecting (Axis III Disorder)
316	Psychological Symptoms Affecting (Axis III Disorder)
294.9	Cognitive Disorder NOS
309.24	Adjustment Disorder with Anxiety
309.0	Adjustment Disorder with Depressed Mood
309.3	Adjustment Disorder with Disturbance of Conduct

_____   _____

_____   _____

NARCISSISTIC TRAITS

BEHAVIORAL DEFINITIONS

1. Displays a grandiose sense of self-importance and self-worth.
2. Reports fantasies about unlimited power, success, intelligence, or beauty.
3. Verbalizes a belief in being a special person who is appreciated by other special people.
4. Demonstrates a powerful need to be recognized, admired, and adored.
5. Becomes angry and resentful when wishes, wants, and needs are not met immediately by others.
6. Demonstrates a lack of empathy for others.
7. Verbalizes unreasonable expectations of others in relationships, with little concern for the other person.
8. Verbalizes envy of others or feeling others are envious of them.
9. Brags about achievements, exaggerated abilities, and body image.
10. Is interpersonally manipulative and exploitive.

—. _____
_____
_____
—. _____
_____
—. _____
_____

LONG-TERM GOALS

1. Maintain a program of recovery, free of addiction and the negative effects of narcissistic traits.
2. Develop a realistic sense of self, without narcissistic grandiosity, exaggeration, or sense of entitlement.
3. Understand the relationship between narcissistic traits and addiction.

4. Understand narcissistic traits and how the sense of omnipotence places the client at high risk for relapse.
5. Develop empathy for other people, particularly victims of his/her narcissism.
6. Learn and demonstrate healthy impulse-control skills.

__. _____
   _____
   _____
__. _____
   _____
   _____
__. _____
   _____

SHORT-TERM OBJECTIVES

THERAPEUTIC INTERVENTIONS

1. Verbalize the powerlessness and unmanageability that results from narcissistic traits and addiction. (1)

1. Using a 12-step recovery program's Step One exercise, help the client to see that narcissistic traits and addictive behavior lead to a state of powerlessness and unmanageability.

2. Verbalize an identification of several narcissistic traits and describe how they contribute to addictive behavior. (2, 3)

2. Assist the client in identifying his/her narcissistic traits, and how they can lead to addictive behavior.

3. Help the client to identify times when narcissistic traits and addictive behavior led to negative consequences.

3. Complete psychological testing or objective questionnaires for assessing narcissistic traits. (4)

4. Administer to the client psychological instruments designed to objectively assess narcissistic traits (e.g., Millon Clinical Multiaxial Inventory [MCMI]); give the client feedback regarding the results of the assessment.

4. Verbalize a commitment to honesty and humility that can form the basis for a program of recovery. (5, 6, 7)

5. Teach the client how a 12-step recovery program can assist in recovery from narcissistic traits and addiction.

5. List 10 lies that were told to exaggerate accomplishments and to seek acceptance and recognition. (8)

6. Teach the client that honesty is essential for real intimacy, and explain how lies lead to interpersonal frustration and loneliness.

7. Discuss why resolution of narcissistic traits, especially the tendency toward dishonesty and feeling superior and all-powerful, is essential in maintaining abstinence.

8. Assign the client to list common lies told to exaggerate accomplishments and bolster self-image; show why the self-defeating lies eventually led to the rejection from others that he/she feared.

6. List several narcissistic strategies used to manipulate others in relationships. (9)

9. Assist the client in listing ways in which he/she can use narcissistic traits to control and manipulate others; explain how narcissistic behaviors are counterproductive to interpersonal acceptance and respect.

7. Identify with the vulnerable revelations of other people by sharing similar experiences, feelings, and thoughts. (10, 11)

10. Conduct or refer the client for group therapy sessions that focus on developing empathy, by asking him/her to share with the group members his/her similar vulnerable, anxious experiences, feelings, and/or thoughts.

11. Use role-playing, modeling, and behavior rehearsal to teach the client self-disclosure of feelings of vulnerability.

8. Verbalize how the dynamics of the family of origin led to a poor self-image and a sense of rejection and failure. (12)

12. Probe the client's family of origin for experiences of criticism, emotional abandonment or rejection, and abuse or neglect that led to feelings of low self-esteem masked by narcissism.

9. Identify a pattern of narcissism (e.g., anxious, fearful thoughts followed the exaggerated thoughts of power and importance) and replace that pattern with confident but realistic self-talk. (13, 14)

13. Probe the client's narcissistic thoughts (e.g., grandiosity, sense of entitlement, tendency to blame others, need to exaggerate achievements in search of acceptance); show the client how these thoughts are based in low self-esteem and an expectation of rejection, then replace this pattern with confident, realistic self-talk.

14. Teach the client to replace cognitive messages of low self-esteem and fear of rejection with more realistic, healthy, and adaptive self-talk.

10. Acknowledge that low self-esteem and fear of failure or rejection are felt internally, in spite of the external façade of braggadocio. (15, 16)

15. Confront expressions of entitlement and braggadocio, interpreting them as a cover for feelings of fear and low self-esteem.

16. Reinforce the client's social interactions that are characterized by humility, empathy, honesty, and compassion.

11. List ways in which a higher power can assist in recovery from narcissistic traits and addiction. (17, 18)

17. Teach the client about the 12-step recovery program's concept of a higher power and how this can be used in recovery (e.g., see God, not self, as the higher power, trust God to help with temptations, help others in recovery, and practice regular prayer and meditation).

18. Using the 12-step recovery program's Step Three exercise, teach the client how to turn over problems to a higher power.

12. Verbalize a commitment to helping others as essential to recovery from narcissistic traits and addictive behavior. (16, 19)

16. Reinforce the client's social interactions that are characterized by humility, empathy, honesty, and compassion.

19. Teach the client that helping others will give him/her a genuine sense of self-worth, which is essential to working a good program of recovery.

13. Practice honesty and realistic humility in communication with others. (16, 20, 21)

16. Reinforce the client's social interactions that are characterized by humility, empathy, honesty, and compassion.

20. Using modeling, role-playing, and behavior rehearsal, teach the client the impulse control skills of stopping, looking, listening, thinking, and planning before acting without regard for others' feelings.

21. Using modeling, role-playing, and behavior rehearsal, teach the client healthy interpersonal communication skills (e.g., honesty, ask for what you want, share how you feel, care about what the other person wants, active listening, and the use of "I" messages).

14. Write a personal recovery plan that details the regular attendance at recovery groups and further treatment that are needed to recover from narcissistic traits and addictive behavior. (22)

22. Help the client to develop a personal recovery plan that will detail what he/she is going to do for further treatment in recovery (e.g., regular attendance at recovery groups, get a sponsor, further treatment or therapy).

15. Family members verbalize what each can do to assist the client in recovery. (23, 24, 25)

23. Discuss with family members the connection between narcissistic traits and addictive behavior.

24. In a family session, review what each member can do to assist the client in recovery.

25. Provide family members with information about narcissistic traits and the steps that the client must take to recover successfully.

16. Complete a re-administration of objective tests of narcissistic traits as a means of assessing treatment outcome. (26)

17. Complete a survey to assess the degree of satisfaction with treatment. (27)

—. _____
   _____

—. _____
   _____

—. _____
   _____

26. Assess the outcome of treatment by re-administering to the client objective tests of narcissistic traits; evaluate the results and provide feedback to the client.

27. Administer a survey to assess the client's degree of satisfaction with treatment.

—. _____
   _____

—. _____
   _____

—. _____
   _____

DIAGNOSTIC SUGGESTIONS:

Axis I:
296.xx	Bipolar I Disorder
296.89	Bipolar II Disorder
301.13	Cyclothymic Disorder
310.1	Personality Change Due to (Axis III Disorder)

_____   _____

_____   _____

Axis II:
301.81	Narcissistic Personality Disorder
301.83	Borderline Personality Disorder
301.50	Histrionic Personality Disorder

_____   _____

_____   _____

NICOTINE ABUSE/DEPENDENCE

BEHAVIORAL DEFINITIONS

1. Demonstrates a maladaptive pattern of tobacco use, manifested by increased tolerance and withdrawal.
2. Is unable to stop or cut down use of tobacco once started, despite the verbalized desire to do so and the negative consequences continued use brings.
3. Exhibits physical indicators (chronic obstructive lung disease, bronchitis, lung cancer, oral cancers, etc.) that reflect the results of a pattern of heavy tobacco use.
4. Denies that nicotine dependence is a problem, despite feedback from significant others that the use of tobacco is negatively affecting them and others.
5. Continues tobacco use despite knowledge of experiencing persistent physical, financial, vocational, social, and/or relationship problems that are directly caused by the use of nicotine.
6. Presents with physical withdrawal symptoms (e.g., nicotine craving, anxiety, insomnia, irritability, depression) when going without nicotine for any length of time.
7. Consumes tobacco in greater amounts than intended.
8. Continues to use mood-altering chemicals after being told by a physician that using is causing health problems.
9. Nicotine dependence is concurrent with other addictive behaviors, and their practice reinforces one another.

—. _____

_____

—. _____

_____

—. _____

_____

LONG-TERM GOALS

1. Accept the powerlessness and unmanageability over tobacco, and participate in a recovery-based program of abstinence.
2. Accept chemical dependence on tobacco and begin to actively participate in a recovery program.
3. Withdraw from tobacco, stabilize physically and emotionally, and then establish a supportive recovery plan.
4. Establish and maintain total abstinence from tobacco products while increasing knowledge of the addiction and the process of recovery.
5. Acquire the necessary skills to maintain long-term sobriety from all mood-altering substances.

—. _____
   _____
   _____
—. _____
   _____
   _____
—. _____
   _____

SHORT-TERM OBJECTIVES

THERAPEUTIC INTERVENTIONS

1. Cooperate with a medical assessment and an evaluation of the necessity for pharmacological intervention, taking medications as directed. (1, 2)

1. Refer the client to a physician to perform a physical exam and write treatment orders, including, if necessary, prescribing medications, monitoring the effectiveness and side effects of medication, and titrating as necessary.

2. Direct the staff to administer prescribed medications to the client and monitor for effectiveness and side effects.

2. Complete psychological testing or objective questionnaires for assessing nicotine abuse/dependence. (3)

3. Administer to the client psychological instruments designed to objectively assess nicotine abuse/dependence (e.g., Addiction Severity Index [ASI], Substance Abuse Subtle Screening Inventory-3 [SASSI-3], Fagerstrom Test for

3. Report acute withdrawal symptoms to the staff. (4)

4. Provide honest and complete information for a chemical dependence biopsychosocial history. (5)

5. Attend didactic sessions and read assigned material in order to increase knowledge of tobacco abuse and the process of recovery. (6, 7, 8)

6. Attend group therapy sessions to share thoughts and feelings associated with reasons for, consequences of, feelings about, and alternatives to nicotine abuse. (9, 10)

7. List the negative consequences resulting from or exacerbated by nicotine dependence. (11)

Nicotine Dependence [FTND]); give the client feedback regarding the results of the assessment.

4. Direct the staff to assess and monitor the client's condition during withdrawal.

5. Complete a thorough family and personal biopsychosocial history that has a focus on nicotine abuse and any other addictions.

6. Assign the client to attend a nicotine dependence didactic series to increase knowledge of the patterns and effects of nicotine dependence.

7. Require the client to attend all nicotine dependence didactics; ask him/her to identify several key points attained from each didactic, and process these points with the therapist.

8. Ask the client to read literature of nicotine dependence etiology and its negative social, emotional, and medical consequences; process with the therapist five key points gained from the reading.

9. Assign the client to attend group therapy that focuses on nicotine dependence recovery issues.

10. Direct group therapy that facilitates the sharing of causes for, consequences of, feelings about, and alternatives to nicotine dependence.

11. Ask the client to make a list of the ways in which nicotine dependence has negatively impacted his/her life; process the list with the therapist or group.

8. Verbally admit to powerlessness over nicotine. (12)

9. Verbalize a recognition that nicotine was used as the primary coping mechanism to escape from stress or pain, and resulted in negative consequences. (13)

10. List the negative emotions that were caused by or exacerbated by nicotine dependence. (14)

11. Develop a list of social, emotional, and family factors that contributed to nicotine dependence. (5, 15)

12. List 10 reasons to work on a plan for recovery from nicotine use. (12, 14, 16)

12. Assign the client to complete a 12-step program's first-step paper admitting to powerlessness over nicotine, and present it in group therapy or to the therapist for feedback.

13. Explore how nicotine abuse was used to escape from stress, physical and emotional pain, and boredom; confront the negative consequences of this pattern.

14. Probe the sense of powerlessness, shame, guilt, and low self-worth that has resulted from nicotine abuse and its consequences.

5. Complete a thorough family and personal biopsychosocial history that has a focus on nicotine abuse and any other addictions.

15. Using the biopsychosocial history, assist the client in understanding the familial, emotional, and social factors that contributed to the development of nicotine dependence (e.g., modeling effects of older adults, peer pressure and anxiety).

12. Assign the client to complete a 12-step program's first-step paper admitting to powerlessness over nicotine, and present it in group therapy or to the therapist for feedback.

14. Probe the sense of powerlessness, shame, guilt, and low self-worth that has resulted from nicotine abuse and its consequences.

16. Assign the client to write a list of 10 reasons to be abstinent from nicotine dependence.

13. List 10 lies used to hide nicotine abuse. (17)

17. Help the client see the dishonesty that accompanies nicotine dependence; have him/her list 10 lies they told to hide tobacco use, and then teach him/her why honesty is essential to recovery.

14. Report success in practicing turning problems over to a higher power each day. (18, 19)

18. Teach the client about the concept of a higher power and how this can assist in recovery (e.g., God's power can assist in resisting temptation, regular prayer and meditation can reduce craving and stress).

19. Using a recovery program's Step Three exercise, teach the client about the concept of "turning it over," then assign turning over problems to a higher power each day; have the client record the event and discuss the results.

15. Practice health communication skills to reduce interpersonal stress and increase positive social interaction. (20, 21)

20. Teach the client healthy communication skills (e.g., using "I" messages, reflecting, active listening, empathy, being reinforcing, sharing).

21. Refer the client for or teach him/her social interaction skills to reduce the interpersonal anxiety that triggered nicotine use.

16. Practice problem-solving skills. (22)

22. Using modeling, role-playing, and behavior rehearsal, teach the client how to solve problems in an organized fashion (i.e., write the problem, think accurately, list the options of action, evaluate alternatives, act, monitor, and evaluate results).

17. List the reasons for nicotine use and the ways the same things can be attained in an adaptive manner. (23, 24)

23. Using progressive relaxation or biofeedback, teach the client how to relax; assign him/her to relax twice a day for 10 to 20 minutes.

18. Practice stress management and relaxation skills to reduce overall stress levels and attain a feeling of relaxation and comfort. (23, 25)

19. Make a written plan to cope with each high-risk trigger situation that may precipitate relapse. (13, 26, 27, 28)

20. Identify rewards for nicotine abstinence. (29)

24. Assist the client in clarifying why he/she was using nicotine, and help him/her to identify adaptive ways to obtain the sought-after result (e.g., relaxation).

23. Using progressive relaxation or biofeedback, teach the client how to relax; assign him/her to relax twice a day for 10 to 20 minutes.

25. Using current physical fitness levels, urge the client to exercise three times a week; increase the exercise by ten percent a week, until he/she is exercising at a training heart rate for at least 20 minutes at least three times a week.

13. Explore how nicotine abuse was used to escape from stress, physical and emotional pain, and boredom; confront the negative consequences of this pattern.

26. Using a relapse prevention exercise, help the client uncover his/her triggers for relapse into nicotine dependence.

27. Teach the client about high-risk situations (e.g., negative emotions, social pressure, interpersonal conflict, positive emotions, testing personal control); assist the client in making a written plan to cope with each high-risk situation.

28. Using modeling, role-playing, and behavior rehearsal, teach the client how to say no to nicotine, alcohol, or drugs; practice saying no in high-risk situations.

29. Assist the client in identifying reinforcing events that could be used in rewarding abstinence from nicotine.

21. Implement a structured behavior modification program for nicotine abstinence. (30, 31, 32)

30. Design, with the client, a behavior modification program that targets nicotine abuse and reinforces periods of abstinence.

31. Assign implementation of a behavior modification program that stipulates rewards for nicotine abstinence.

32. Review, process, and redirect the behavior modification to maximize success rates.

22. Complete a re-administration of objective tests of nicotine abuse/dependence as a means of assessing treatment outcome. (33)

33. Assess the outcome of treatment by re-administering to the client objective tests of nicotine abuse/dependence; evaluate the results and provide feedback to the client.

23. Complete a survey to assess the degree of satisfaction with treatment. (34)

34. Administer a survey to assess the client's degree of satisfaction with treatment.

—. _____

_____

—. _____

_____

—. _____

_____

—. _____

_____

—. _____

_____

—. _____

_____

DIAGNOSTIC SUGGESTIONS:

Axis I: 305.10   Nicotine Dependence
292.0   Nicotine Withdrawal
304.90   Other (or Unknown) Substance Dependence

_____   _____

_____   _____

OCCUPATIONAL PROBLEMS

BEHAVIORAL DEFINITIONS

1. Reports feelings of inadequacy, fear, and failure following severe business losses.
2. Has a history of rebellion against and/or conflicts with authority figures in the employment situation.
3. Is underemployed or unemployed due to the negative effects of addictive behavior on work performance and attendance.
4. Reports that work environment is too stressful, leading to addictive behavior to escape.
5. Works with people who are alcohol and/or drug abusers and are supportive of addiction, increasing the risk for relapse.
6. Risks loss of job due to addictive behavior.
7. Lacks employer understanding of addiction or what is required for recovery.
8. Retirement has led to feelings of loneliness, lack of meaning in life, and addictive behavior.
9. Experiences anxiety related to perceived or actual job jeopardy.

__. _____
_____

__. _____
_____

__. _____
_____

LONG-TERM GOALS

1. Maintain a program of recovery, free of addiction and occupational problems.

2. Educate employers and coworkers to be supportive of recovery.
3. Fill life with new interests, so retirement can be appreciated.
4. Understand the relationship between the stress of occupational problems and addiction.
5. Arrange for onsite drug and/or alcohol testing and monitoring of recovery.
6. Make a contract with management that details the recovery plan and consequences of relapse.

—. _____
_____
_____

—. _____
_____
_____

—. _____
_____

SHORT-TERM OBJECTIVES

1. Identify occupational problems and how they relate to addiction. (1, 2)

2. Complete psychological testing or objective questionnaires for assessing occupational problems. (3)

3. Identify own role in the conflict with coworkers or supervisor. (4, 5, 6)

THERAPEUTIC INTERVENTIONS

1. Take a history of the client's occupational problems; explore what employment patterns were modeled in the family of origin.

2. Teach the client how his/her occupational problems led to his/her addiction.

3. Administer to the client psychological instruments designed to objectively assess occupational problems (e.g., 16 PF); give the client feedback regarding the results of the assessment.

4. Confront projection of responsibility for the client's behavior and feelings onto others.

5. Assist the client in identifying his/her patterns of interpersonal conflict that occur beyond the work setting; relate these patterns to current occupational problems.

4. Identify own behavioral changes that would help resolve conflict with coworkers or supervisors. (7, 8)

6. Probe family-of-origin history for how the client may have learned dysfunctional relationship patterns; relate these patterns to current coworker/supervisor conflicts.

7. Assist the client in listing behavioral changes that he/she could make to resolve conflicts with coworkers and supervisors; assign implementation of these changes.

8. Review the client's attempts to implement behavioral changes at work; reinforce success and redirect for failure.

5. Acknowledge the interaction between occupational problems and addictive behavior. (9, 10)

9. Help the client to list times when addictive behavior led to problems at work.

10. Assign the client to list times that occupational problems led to addictive behavior.

6. Verbalize why current employment increases the risk for relapse. (10, 11)

10. Assign the client to list times that occupational problems led to addictive behavior.

11. Help the client to see why his/her current employment is a high risk for relapse (e.g., coworker's addictions, job dissatisfaction, supervisor conflict, work hours too long, absence from his/her family due to travel, ethical conflicts).

7. Verbalize feelings of fear, anger, and helplessness associated with the vocational stress. (12)

12. Probe and clarify emotions regarding the client's vocational situation.

8. Identify distorted cognitive messages associated with perception of job stress. (13, 14)

13. Assess and make the client aware of his/her distorted, negative cognitive messages and the schema that is connected with vocational stress.

14. Confront the client's catastrophizing the situation, leading to immobilizing anxiety.

9. Develop healthier, more real-istic cognitive messages that promote harmony with others, self-acceptance, and self-confidence. (15)

10. Develop a written plan to resolve occupational problems and maximize chances for recovery in the workplace. (16, 17, 18)

11. Implement the assertiveness skills that are necessary to be honest with coworkers about addiction and recovery. (19, 20)

12. List the skills or changes that will help in coping with the stress of the current occupation. (21)

15. Teach the client more realistic, healthy cognitive messages that relieve anxiety and depression.

16. Help the client develop a writ-ten plan to resolve occupational problems and maximize recovery (e.g., regular attendance at recov-ery groups, regular drug testing, management monitors recovery plan, honesty with management and coworkers).

17. Meet with the client and his/her employer to educate the employer about addiction and to gain sup-port for treatment and recovery.

18. Help the client to learn the skills necessary to remain abstinent in his/her current work environment (e.g., honesty with management and coworkers, regular attendance at recovery group meetings, using a sponsor, eliciting the support of management, continued treat-ment).

19. Using modeling, role–playing, and behavior rehearsal, have the client practice telling his/her coworkers and employer the truth about his/her addictive behavior and plans for recovery.

20. Use role-playing, behavior re-hearsal, and modeling to teach the client assertiveness skills.

21. Help the client to develop skills to reduce job stress and improve em-ployment satisfaction (e.g., time management; relaxation; exercise; assertiveness; reducing responsi-bilities, work hours, and/or travel

13. List five ways in which working a program of recovery will improve occupational problems. (18, 22)

time; realistic expectations of work performance).

18. Help the client to learn the skills necessary to remain abstinent in his/her current work environment (e.g., honesty with management and coworkers, regular attendance at recovery group meetings, using a sponsor, eliciting the support of management, continued treatment).

22. Teach the client how working a 12-step recovery program will improve occupational problems.

14. Make written plans to change employment to a job that will be supportive to recovery. (23)

23. Help the client to accept the need to change jobs, to employment that will be more supportive to recovery.

15. Turn the stress of occupational problems and the urge for addictive behavior over to a higher power at least once a day. (24, 25)

24. Teach the client about the 12-step recovery program's concept of a higher power and how this can assist in recovery (e.g., ____, ____, ____).

25. Using a 12-step recovery program's Step Three exercise, teach the client how to turn problems over to a higher power; assign him/her to practice turning problems over to a higher power at least once a day.

16. Honestly acknowledge the negative impact that addiction has had on work performance. (9, 26)

9. Help the client to list times when addictive behavior led to problems at work.

26. Help the client to be honest with himself/herself, coworkers, and management about the negative impact of addictive behavior on job performance; list the negative consequences of addictive behavior on employment.

17. Discuss the grief over retirement, and make written plans to replace addictive behavior with specific constructive activities. (27, 28)

27. Explore and resolve the client's feelings associated with retirement.

28. Assist the client in making plans to engage in constructive activities (e.g., volunteering, hobbies, exercise, social contacts, special-interest groups, 12-step recovery program meetings, continuing education, religious involvement).

18. Family members verbalize what each can do to assist the client in recovery. (29, 30)

29. Discuss with family members the connection between occupational problems and addictive behavior.

30. In a family session, review what each member can do to assist the client in recovery.

19. Complete a re-administration of objective tests of occupational problems as a means of assessing treatment outcome. (31)

31. Assess the outcome of treatment by re-administering to the client objective tests of occupational problems; evaluate the results and provide feedback to the client.

20. Complete a survey to assess the degree of satisfaction with treatment. (32)

32. Administer a survey to assess the client's degree of satisfaction with treatment.

—. _____

—. _____

—. _____

—. _____

—. _____

—. _____

DIAGNOSTIC SUGGESTIONS:

Axis I:	V62.81	Relational Problem NOS
	V62.2	Occupational Problem
	V62.89	Phase of Life Problem
	300.02	Generalized Anxiety Disorder
	311	Depressive Disorder NOS

309.0	Adjustment Disorder with Depressed Mood
309.24	Adjustment Disorder with Anxiety

_____   _____

_____   _____

Axis II:

301.7	Antisocial Personality Disorder
301.0	Paranoid Personality Disorder

_____   _____

_____   _____

OPIOID DEPENDENCE

BEHAVIORAL DEFINITIONS

1. Demonstrates a pattern of opioid use leading to clinically significant impairment or distress.
2. Reports a need for markedly increased amounts of opioids to achieve the desired effect.
3. Presents with withdrawal symptoms characteristic of opioid dependence.
4. Verbalizes a persistent desire to cut down or control opioid use.
5. Spends a great deal of time trying to obtain opioids and recover from use.
6. Gives up important social, occupational, or recreational activities because of opioid use.
7. Engages in illegal activity to financially support the opioid habit.
8. Opioid abuse continues despite significant negative financial, legal, social, vocational, medical, familial, and self-esteem consequences.
9. Abuses opioids in a maladaptive response to pain management.

—. _____
   _____
   _____

—. _____
   _____
   _____

—. _____
   _____

LONG-TERM GOALS

1. Accept the powerlessness and unmanageability over opioids, and participate in a recovery-based program.
2. Withdraw from mood-altering substance, stabilize physically and emotionally, and then establish a supportive recovery plan.

3. Establish a sustained recovery, free from the use of all mood-altering substances.
4. Establish and maintain total abstinence while increasing knowledge of the disease and the process of recovery.
5. Acquire the necessary skills to maintain long-term abstinence from all mood-altering substances and live a life free of chemicals.

—. _____
_____
—. _____
_____
—. _____
_____

SHORT-TERM OBJECTIVES

1. Cooperate with medical assessment and an evaluation of the necessity for pharmacological intervention. (1, 2)

2. Take prescribed medications as directed by the physician. (3, 4)

3. Report acute withdrawal symptoms to the staff. (5)

THERAPEUTIC INTERVENTIONS

1. Refer the client to a physician to perform a physical examination (include tests for HIV, hepatitis, and sexually transmitted diseases) and discuss the use of methadone, buprenorphine, and the abstinence-based model of opioid treatment.

2. Refer the client to a pharmacology-based maintenance/withdrawal program (e.g., methadone, buprenorphine).

3. Physician will monitor the effectiveness and side effects of medication, titrating as necessary.

4. Staff will administer prescribed medications and monitor for effectiveness and side effects.

5. Assess and monitor the client's condition during withdrawal, using a standardized procedure (e.g., Narcotic Withdrawal Scale) as needed.

4. Complete psychological testing or objective questionnaires for assessing opioid dependence. (6)

6. Administer to the client psychological instruments designed to objectively assess opioid dependence (e.g., Substance Use Disorders Diagnostic Schedule-IV [SUDDS-IV], Substance Abuse Subtle Screen Inventory-3 [SASS-3]); give the client feedback regarding the results of the assessment.

5. Provide honest and complete information for a chemical dependence biopsychosocial history. (7)

7. Complete a thorough family and personal biopsychosocial history that has a focus on addiction (e.g., family history of addiction and treatment, other substances used, progression of substance abuse, consequences of abuse).

6. Attend didactic sessions and read assigned material in order to increase knowledge of addiction and the process of recovery. (8, 9, 10, 11)

8. Assign the client to attend a chemical dependence didactic series to increase his/her knowledge of the patterns and effects of chemical dependence.

9. Require the client to attend all chemical dependence didactics; ask him/her to identify several key points attained from each didactic and process these points with the therapist.

10. Assign the client to read material on addiction (e.g., *Willpower's Not Enough* by Washton, *The Addiction Workbook* by Fanning, or *Alcoholics Anonymous*); and process key points gained from the reading.

11. Require the client to read the book *Narcotics Anonymous* and gather five key points from it to process with the therapist.

7. Attend group therapy sessions to share thoughts and feelings associated with, reasons for, consequences of, feelings

12. Assign the client to attend group therapy.

13. Direct group therapy that facilitates the client sharing of causes for,

about, and alternatives to addiction. (12, 13)

8. Verbally admit to powerlessness over mood-altering substances. (14)

9. List 10 negative consequences resulting from or exacerbated by substance dependence. (15, 16, 17)

10. Verbalize recognition that mood-altering chemicals were used as the primary coping mechanism to escape from stress or pain, and resulted in negative consequences. (18)

11. List the negative emotions that were caused by or exacerbated by substance dependence. (19)

12. List 10 reasons to work on a plan for recovery from addiction. (20)

13. List 10 lies used to hide substance dependence. (21, 22)

consequences of, feelings about, and alternatives to addiction.

14. Assign the client to complete a Narcotics Anonymous (NA) First Step paper admitting to powerlessness over mood-altering chemicals, and present it in group therapy or to therapist for feedback.

15. Ask the client to make a list of the ways chemical use has negatively impacted his/her life; process the list in individual or group sessions.

16. Confront the client's use of denial to minimize the severity of and negative consequences of opioid abuse.

17. Using the biopsychosocial history and the client's list of negative consequences of opioid abuse, assist him/her in understanding the need to stay in treatment.

18. Explore how addiction was used to escape from stress, physical and emotional pain, and boredom; confront the negative consequences of this pattern.

19. Probe the client's sense of shame, guilt, and low self-worth that has resulted from addiction and its consequences.

20. Assign the client to write a list of 10 reasons to be abstinent from addiction.

21. Help the client see the dishonesty that goes along with addiction; ask him/her to list 10 lies told to hide substance use.

22. Teach the client why honesty is essential to recovery.

14. Verbalize ways a higher power can assist in recovery. (23)

15. Implement pain management techniques in order to cope with pain without opioid use. (24, 25, 26)

16. Identify distorted, self-defeating automatic thoughts that trigger debilitating emotional responses to pain or other sources of stress. (27, 28)

17. Increase the use of positive self-talk in response to daily pain or other sources of stress. (29, 30)

23. Teach the client about the AA concept of a higher power and how this can assist in recovery (e.g., God can help with chronic pain or craving, regular prayer and meditation can reduce stress).

24. Teach the client 10 healthy pain management skills (e.g., bio-feedback, progressive relaxation, transcutaneous nerve stimulation (TENS) units, regular exercise, acupuncture).

25. Assist the client in obtaining verbal and written information about causes and management of chronic pain (e.g., *Learning to Master Your Chronic Pain* by Jamison, *The Chronic Pain Control Workbook* by Catalano, or *Free Yourself from Pain* by Bresler).

26. Teach the client behavioral sleep techniques (e.g., use relaxation techniques, eliminate naps, establish a pre-sleep ritual).

27. Teach the client how negative, distorted cognitions (e.g., over-generalization, catastrophizing, all-or-none thinking) can mediate (or exaggerate) a dysfunctional emotional, behavioral, and/or psychological response to pain and stress.

28. Assist the client in identifying negative, automatic thoughts that precipitate depression, tension, and/or exacerbated pain.

29. Teach and reinforce the client's use of positive, realistic, cognitive self-talk as a means of coping with pain and depression.

30. Train the client in comprehending and using the cognitive tech-

18. Practice problem-solving skills. (31)

19. List the reasons for substance use and the ways the same things can be attained in an adaptive manner. (32)

20. Verbalize that there are options to substance use in dealing with stress and in finding pleasure or excitement in life. (33, 34, 35)

21. Verbalize the results of turning problems over to God each day. (36)

22. Practice stress-management skills to reduce overall stress levels and attain a feeling of relaxation and comfort. (27, 28, 29, 30, 37)

niques of focused attention and visualization as tools for psycho-physiological self-regulation.

31. Using modeling, role-playing, and behavior rehearsal, teach the client how to problem-solve in an organized fashion (e.g., write the problem, think accurately, list the options of action, evaluate alternatives, act, monitor results).

32. Assist the client in clarifying why he/she began using substances, and help to identify adaptive ways to get the same result.

33. Teach the client the importance of getting pleasure out of life without using mood-altering substances.

34. Assign the client in developing a list of pleasurable activities (see *Inventory of Rewarding Activities* by Birchler and Weiss); assign engagement in selected activities daily.

35. Encourage the client to establish a daily routine of physical exercise to build body stamina, self-esteem, and reduce depression (see *Exercising Your Way to Better Mental Health* by Leith).

36. Using a Step Three exercise, teach the client about the recovery concept of "turning it over;" then assign turning over problems to a higher power each day; ask the client to record the event and discuss the results.

27. Teach the client how negative, distorted cognitions (e.g., over-generalization, catastrophizing, all-or-none thinking) can mediate (or exaggerate) a dysfunctional

emotional, behavioral, and/or psychological response to pain and stress.

28. Assist the client in identifying negative, automatic thoughts that precipitate depression, tension, and/or exacerbated pain.

29. Teach and reinforce the client's use of positive, realistic, cognitive self-talk as a means of coping with pain and depression.

30. Train the client in comprehending and using the cognitive techniques of focused attention and visualization as tools for psycho-physiological self-regulation.

37. Using progressive relaxation or biofeedback, teach the client how to relax, then assign him/her to relax twice a day for 10–20 minutes.

23. Complete a re-administration of objective tests of opioid abuse as a means of assessing treatment outcome. (38)

38. Assess the outcome of treatment by re-administering to the client objective tests of opioid dependence; evaluate the results and provide feedback to the client.

24. Complete a survey to assess the degree of satisfaction with treatment. (39)

39. Administer a survey to assess the client's degree of satisfaction with treatment.

__. _____

_____

__. _____

_____

__. _____

_____

__. _____

_____

__. _____

_____

__. _____

_____

DIAGNOSTIC SUGGESTIONS:

Axis I: 304.00   Opioid Dependence
               305.50   Opioid Abuse

304.80	Polysubstance Dependence
292.89	Opioid Intoxication
292.0	Opioid Withdrawal
292.9	Opioid-Related Disorder NOS
_____	_____
_____	_____

OPPOSITIONAL DEFIANT BEHAVIOR

BEHAVIORAL DEFINITIONS

1. Has a history of explosive, aggressive outbursts.
2. Often argues with authority figures over requests or rules.
3. Deliberately annoys people as a means of gaining control.
4. Blames others rather than accept responsibility for own problems.
5. Displays angry overreaction to perceived disapproval, rejection, or criticism.
6. Passively withholds feelings and then explodes in a violent rage.
7. Abuses substances to cope with feelings of anger and alienation.
8. Has a persistent pattern of challenging or disrespecting authority figures.
9. Demonstrates body language of tense muscles (e.g., clenched fists or jaw, glaring looks, or refusal to make eye contact).
10. Verbalizes a view of aggression as a means to achieve needed power and control.
11. Uses verbally abusive language.
12. Expresses deep resentment toward authority figures.

—. _____
_____

—. _____
_____

—. _____
_____

LONG-TERM GOALS

1. Maintain a program of recovery, free of addiction and oppositional defiant behavior.

2. Decrease the frequency of occurrence of angry thoughts, feelings, and behaviors.
3. Follow rules established by authority figures, without opposition or complaint.
4. Stop blaming others for problems and begin to accept responsibility for own feelings, thoughts, and behaviors.
5. Learn and implement stress management skills, to reduce the level of stress and the irritability that accompanies it.
6. Understand the relationship between angry feelings and the feelings of hurtfulness and worthlessness experienced in the family of origin.

—. _____

_____

_____

—. _____

_____

—. _____

_____

SHORT-TERM OBJECTIVES

THERAPEUTIC INTERVENTIONS

1. Acknowledge feelings of anger and identify trigger situations. (1, 2)

1. Explore the client's angry feelings and assist him/her in identifying sources for his/her anger.

2. Assign the client to keep a daily anger log, writing down each situation that produced angry feelings and the thoughts associated with the situation; then rate the level of anger on a scale from 1 to 100; process the anger log, and assist in uncovering the dysfunctional thoughts that trigger anger.

2. Complete psychological testing or objective questionnaires for assessing defiance of authority. (3)

3. Administer to the client psychological instruments designed to objectively assess traits of oppositional defiance (e.g., Adolescent Psychopathology Scale-Short Form [APS-SF], Millon Adolescent Clinical Inventory [MACI]); give the client feedback regarding the results of the assessment.

3. Identify and verbalize the pain and hurt of past and current life that fuels oppositional defiant behavior. (4, 5)

4. Assign the client to list experiences of life that have hurt and have led to oppositional defiant behavior.

5. Probe the family dynamics that led to the oppositional defiant behavior.

4. Verbalize an understanding of how anger covers feelings of hurt, guilt, or hopelessness. (6)

6. Teach the client how anger blocks the awareness of pain, discharges uncomfortable feelings, erases guilt, and places the blame for problems on someone else.

5. Increase the frequency of assertive behaviors while reducing the frequency of aggressive behaviors. (7, 8)

7. Teach the client the impulse control skill of "stop, look, listen, think, and plan" before acting.

8. Teach assertiveness and its benefits through role-playing and modeling, assigning appropriate reading material (e.g., *Your Perfect Right* by Alberti and Emmons) or participating in an assertiveness training group.

6. Verbalize regret and remorse for harmful consequences of oppositional defiant behavior, as well as the steps that are necessary to forgive self and to react more constructively. (9)

9. Use modeling and role reversal to make client more aware of the negative consequences his/her oppositional defiant behavior has had on others, who have been the target of or witness to the oppositional defiant behavior.

7. Decrease the frequency of blaming others, and increase the frequency of positive, self-enhancing self-talk. (10, 11)

10. Help the client develop a list of positive, self-enhancing statements to use daily in building a positive and accurate self-image; use role-playing and modeling to demonstrate implementation of positive self-talk.

11. Probe the patterns of violence, anger, and suspicion in the family of origin; help the client to see how these problems lead to a tendency to see people and situations as dangerous and threatening.

8. Report a termination of assuming to know the negative thoughts, intentions, and feelings of others, and start asking others for more information. (12)

9. Verbalize an understanding of the need for and process of forgiving others, to reduce oppositional defiant behavior. (4, 11, 13)

10. Verbalize an understanding of how angry thoughts and feelings can lead to an increased risk of addiction. (14, 15, 16)

12. Teach the client about the tendency to read malicious intent into the words and actions of others; use modeling, role-playing, and behavior rehearsal to show the client how to ask other people what they think and feel.

4. Assign the client to list experiences of life that have hurt and have led to oppositional defiant behavior.

11. Probe the patterns of violence, anger, and suspicion in the family of origin; help the client to see how these problems lead to a tendency to see people and situations as dangerous and threatening.

13. Assist the client in identifying who he/she needs to forgive, and educate him/her as to the long-term process involved in forgiveness, versus a magical single event; recommend reading material on forgiveness (e.g., *Forgive and Forget* by Smedes).

14. Educate the client about his/her tendency to use addictive behavior as a means of relieving uncomfortable feelings; develop a list of several instances of this occurrence.

15. Teach the client about the high-risk situations of strong negative emotions, social pressure, interpersonal conflict, strong positive emotions, and testing personal control; discuss how anger, as a strong negative emotion, places him/her at high risk for addictive behavior.

16. Assist the client in identifying reasons why anger increases the risk of relapse.

11. Make a list of thoughts that trigger hurt or angry feelings, and replace each thought with a more positive and accurate thought that is supportive of self and recovery. (2, 17)

2. Assign the client to keep a daily anger log, writing down each situation that produced angry feelings and the thoughts associated with the situation; then rate the level of anger on a scale from 1 to 100; process the anger log, and assist in uncovering the dysfunctional thoughts that trigger anger.

17. Assist the client in identifying his/her distorted thoughts that trigger anger; teach him/her to replace these thoughts with realistic, positive thoughts.

12. Report instances of the implementation of stress management skills. (18, 19, 20, 21)

18. Teach the client how to turn perpetrators of pain over to his/her higher power for judgment and punishment.

19. Teach the client progressive relaxation skills, and encourage their utilization twice a day for 10 to 20 minutes.

20. Teach the client the stress management skills of regular exercise and positive self-talk, and their benefits.

21. Teach the client the stress-reducing value of actively attending Alcoholics Anonymous/Narcotics Anonymous (AA/NA) meetings, getting a sponsor, reinforcing people around his/her sharing feelings, and developing pleasurable leisure activities.

13. Implement proactive steps to meet the needs of self without expecting other people to meet those needs, and then angrily blaming them when they fail to do so. (8, 22)

8. Teach assertiveness and its benefits through role-playing and modeling, assigning appropriate reading material (e.g., *Your Perfect Right* by Alberti and Emmons) or participating in an assertiveness training group.

14. Report implementation of stopping the impulsive, angry reaction: opening the hands, relaxing the muscles, using reassuring self-talk, and speaking in a soft voice when feeling angry. (23)

15. Parents verbalize an understanding of positive and negative rewards, and use them effectively in setting rules. (24)

16. Parents write a plan for dealing with the client's suicidal threats, violent behavior, running away, and poor academic performance. (25)

17. Parents develop a written plan for nurturing each family member through positive interaction and positive events each week. (26)

18. Develop an aftercare program that details what to do when feeling angry or frustrated. (27)

19. Complete a re-administration of objective tests of defiance of authority as a means of assessing treatment outcome. (28)

22. Assist the client in developing a list of his/her own needs and wishes and the personal actions that are necessary to attain these, rather than being angry with others for not meeting his/her needs and wishes.

23. Using modeling, role-playing, and behavior rehearsal, show the client how to stop the impulse to react with anger: relax the muscles, use positive, comforting self-talk, and speak softly in frustrating, threatening, or hurtful situations.

24. Using modeling and behavior rehearsal, help the parents to role-play their response to oppositional defiant behavior; teach them the use of positive and negative consequences, as well as consistent rule enforcement.

25. Teach the parents how to deal with suicidal threats, violent behavior, running away, and poor academic performance; role-play each situation.

26. Help the parents to develop a written plan for how to nurture family members by doing positive things with each child each week.

27. Help the client to develop a list of what adaptive action he/she is going to take when he/she feels angry in recovery (e.g., calling a sponsor, being assertive rather than aggressive, taking a time out, praying to a higher power) to avoid relapse.

28. Assess the outcome of treatment by re-administering to the client objective tests of oppositional defiant behavior; evaluate the re-

sults and provide feedback to the client.

20. Complete a survey to assess the degree of satisfaction with treatment. (29)

29. Administer a survey to assess the client's degree of satisfaction with treatment.

—. _____   —. _____
   _____   _____
—. _____   —. _____
   _____   _____
—. _____   —. _____
   _____   _____

DIAGNOSTIC SUGGESTIONS:

Axis I:		
	313.81	Oppositional Defiant Disorder
	312.8	Conduct Disorder
	296.xx	Bipolar I Disorder
	296.89	Bipolar II Disorder
	312.34	Intermittent Explosive Disorder
	312.30	Impulse-Control Disorder NOS
	309.4	Adjustment Disorder with Mixed Disturbance of Emotions and Conduct
	V71.02	Child or Adolescent Antisocial Behavior
	_____	_____
	_____	_____

Axis II:		
	301.7	Antisocial Personality Disorder
	V71.09	No Diagnosis

PARENT-CHILD RELATIONAL PROBLEM

BEHAVIORAL DEFINITIONS

1. Expresses parent-child relationship stress that provides an excuse for addiction and addictive behavior, which exacerbates relationship conflicts.
2. Lack of communication between parent and child.
3. Refuses to obey parent's rules or accept their limits.
4. Exhibits poor communication skills between parent and child.
5. Demonstrates a pattern of addiction and dishonesty, leading to parent-child anger and resentments.
6. Frequent arguing and a feeling of emotional distance between parent and child.
7. Has a history of substance abuse, leading to social isolation and withdrawal.
8. Displays a pattern of verbal or physical abuse by the parent toward the child.
9. Becomes involved in a peer group to the exclusion of parents and family members.
10. Lacks ability to establish and maintain meaningful, intimate family relationships.

—. _____
   _____
   _____
—. _____
   _____
   _____
—. _____
   _____

LONG-TERM GOALS

1. Maintain a program of recovery, free of addiction and parent-child conflicts.

2. Terminate addictive behavior and resolve parent-child relationship conflicts.
3. Understand the relationship between addictive behavior and parent-child conflicts.
4. Learn and demonstrate healthy communication skills.
5. Decrease parent-child conflict and increase mutually supportive interaction.

—. _____
_____
_____

—. _____
_____
_____

—. _____
_____

SHORT-TERM OBJECTIVES

1. Describe the nature and history of the parent-child conflicts. (1)

2. Verbalize the powerlessness and unmanageability that result from parent-child conflicts and addiction. (2)

3. Complete psychological testing or objective questionnaires for assessing parent-child conflict. (3)

4. List times when addictive behavior led to parent-child relational conflicts. (4, 5)

THERAPEUTIC INTERVENTIONS

1. Explore in family and individual sessions the nature and history of the client's parent-child conflicts; compare these to conflicts the parent may have had with his/her parents.

2. Using a 12-step recovery program's Step One exercise, help the client to see how parent-child relational conflicts and addiction led to powerlessness and unmanageability.

3. Administer to the client psychological instruments designed to objectively assess parent-child relational conflict (e.g., Intra and Interpersonal Relations Scale); give the client feedback regarding the results of the assessment.

4. Help the client to see how addiction has caused parent-child conflicts, and how conflicts have precipitated addictive behavior.

5. List occasions when parent-child conflicts triggered addictive behavior. (4, 6)

6. Verbalize an acceptance of responsibility for own role in parent-child relationship problems, and in choosing addictive behavior as a means of coping with relationship conflicts. (6, 7, 8)

7. Acknowledge that the child has been the victim of abuse. (8, 9, 10, 11)

5. Ask the client to list instances when addictive behavior led to parent-child relationship conflicts.

4. Help the client to see how addiction has caused parent-child conflicts, and how conflicts have precipitated addictive behavior.

6. Ask the client to list occasions when parent-child conflicts triggered addictive behavior.

6. Ask the client to list occasions when parent-child conflicts triggered addictive behavior.

7. Help the client to accept the responsibility for his/her role in relationship problems, and for choosing addiction as a reaction to the conflicts.

8. Confront the client's denial of responsibility for the parent-child conflict, and the client's projection of all responsibility onto others.

8. Confront the client's denial of responsibility for the parent-child conflict, and the client's projection of all responsibility onto others.

9. Assess the nature and severity of the client's abusive behaviors toward the child; follow through on mandatory reporting of any child abuse.

10. Facilitate the immediate protection of the child from any further abuse (e.g., notifying legal authorities of the abuse, temporary placement of the child with other family or a friend, removal of the abusive parent from the home).

11. Refer the abusive parent to a domestic violence treatment program.

8. Identify five positive and five negative aspects of the current parent-child relationship. (12)

9. Each family member list the changes that he/she believes each person must make to restore the relationship. (13, 14, 15, 16)

10. Initiate activities that verbally and nonverbally promote intimacy. (17, 18)

11. Learn and demonstrate healthy communication skills. (19, 20, 21)

12. Ask the client to list five positive and five negative aspects of the parent-child relationship.

13. Assist the client and other family members in identifying the causes for past and present conflicts between them.

14. Assign the client the task of listing the behavioral changes that he/she needs to make and the changes that he/she believes each family member needs to make to restore the relationship.

15. Assign each family member the task of listing the behavioral changes that he/she needs to make and the changes that he/she believes the other family members need to make to restore the relationship.

16. In a family session, obtain a written commitment from each member as to what behaviors each will attempt to change.

17. In a family session, facilitate a discussion of parent-child problems, and make plans to improve intimacy, nurturing, and communication.

18. Using modeling, role-playing, and behavior rehearsal, teach the family members how to show verbal and nonverbal affection toward each other (e.g., going for a walk together, sharing feelings, doing fun things together, giving hugs, giving each other compliments and praise).

19. Using modeling, role-playing, and behavior rehearsal, teach the client healthy communication skills

(e.g., active listening, reflecting, sharing feelings, using "I" messages).

12. Make written plans to increase pleasurable activities spent by the parent and child. (22, 23)

20. Facilitate a family session with the focus on teaching and improving communication skills.

21. Assign the client to develop a written plan as to the time, place, and amount of time that will be devoted to private, one-to-one communication with each family member each day.

22. Help the family to make a list of the pleasurable activities that they would like to do together; help them to make plans to become involved in at least one activity each week.

23. Assign the client to write a letter to each family member sharing how he/she feels, and suggesting pleasurable activities that they could engage in together during recovery.

13. Write a plan for meeting social and emotional needs during aftercare. (24)

24. Encourage and support the client in building new social relationships that will meet his/her emotional needs, increase satisfaction with life, replace addictive behavior, and reinforce social skills.

14. Develop a personal recovery plan that includes regular attendance at recovery groups, getting a sponsor, and any other therapy that is necessary to recover from parent-child relational conflicts and addiction. (25, 26)

25. Help the client to develop a written personal recovery plan that includes attending recovery group meetings regularly, getting a sponsor, and any other therapy that is necessary to recover from parent-child relational problems and addiction.

26. Teach the client and the family about 12-step recovery groups (e.g., Alanon, Narcanon, Alateen).

15. Complete a re-administration of objective tests of parent-child conflicts as a means of assessing treatment outcome. (27)

16. Complete a survey to assess the degree of satisfaction with treatment. (28)

27. Assess the outcome of treatment by re-administering to the client objective tests of parent-child relational conflict; evaluate the results and provide feedback to the client.

28. Administer a survey to assess the client's degree of satisfaction with treatment.

—. _____
   _____

—. _____
   _____

—. _____
   _____

—. _____
   _____

—. _____
   _____

—. _____
   _____

DIAGNOSTIC SUGGESTIONS:

Axis I:	313.81	Oppositional Defiant Disorder
	V61.20	Parent-Child Relational Problem
	V62.81	Relational Problem NOS
	V61.21	Physical Abuse of a Child
	V61.21	Sexual Abuse of a Child
	V61.21	Neglect of a Child
	_____	_____
	_____	_____
Axis II:	301.7	Antisocial Personality Disorder
	301.20	Schizoid Personality Disorder
	301.81	Narcissistic Personality Disorder
	_____	_____
	_____	_____

PARTNER RELATIONAL CONFLICTS

BEHAVIORAL DEFINITIONS

1. Expresses relationship stress as an excuse for addiction, which, in turn, exacerbates the relationship conflicts.
2. Lacks communication with spouse or significant other.
3. Separated from partner due to addictive behavior.
4. Reports an impending or recent divorce.
5. Has a pattern of superficial or nonexistent communication, frequent arguing, infrequent sexual enjoyment, and a feeling of emotional distance from partner.
6. Presents with a pattern of substance use leading to social isolation and withdrawal.
7. Reports a pattern of verbal and/or physical abuse present in the relationship.
8. Engages in multiple superficial relationships, often with sexual intercourse, but without commitment or meaningful intimacy.
9. Has not established and maintained meaningful, intimate interpersonal relationships.

—. _____
_____
—. _____
_____
—. _____
_____

LONG-TERM GOALS

1. Maintain a program of recovery, free of addiction and partner relational conflicts.

2. Terminate addiction and resolve the relationship conflicts that increase the risk of relapse.
3. Understand the relationship between addiction and partner relational conflicts.
4. Accept termination of the relationship, and make plans to move forward in life.
5. Develop the skills necessary to maintain open, effective communication, sexual intimacy, and enjoyable time with a partner.

—. _____
   _____
   _____
—. _____
   _____
   _____
—. _____
   _____

SHORT-TERM OBJECTIVES

THERAPEUTIC INTERVENTIONS

1. Verbalize the powerlessness and unmanageability that result from partner relational conflicts and addiction. (1)

1. Using a 12-step recovery program's Step One exercise, help the client to see how partner relational conflicts and addiction lead to powerlessness and unmanageability.

2. Client and partner give their perspective on the nature of and causes for the relational conflicts. (2, 3)

2. Explore the client's perspective on the nature of and causes of conflicts with his/her partner.

3. In an individual or conjoint session, explore the client's partner's perspective on the nature of and causes of the conflicts between them.

3. Complete psychological testing or objective questionnaires for assessing partner relational conflicts. (4)

4. Administer to the client psychological instruments designed to objectively assess partner relational conflicts (e.g., Partner Satisfaction Inventory, Revised); give the client feedback regarding the results of the assessment.

4. List instances when addiction has led to partner relational conflicts. (5, 6)

5. Help the client see how addiction has caused relationship conflicts, and how relationship conflicts have precipitated addiction.

6. Ask the client to list instances when addiction has led to relationship conflict.

5. List occasions when relationship conflicts have led to addiction. (5, 7)

5. Help the client see how addiction has caused relationship conflicts, and how relationship conflicts have precipitated addiction.

7. Ask the client to list occasions when relationship conflicts have led to addiction.

6. Verbalize an acceptance of the responsibility for own role in relationship problems, and in choosing addiction as a means of coping with relationship conflicts. (8)

8. Help the client to accept responsibility for his/her role in the relationship problems, and for choosing addiction as a reaction to the conflicts.

7. Identify the positive and negative aspects of the current relationship. (9)

9. Ask the client to list the positive and negative aspects of the relationship; if possible, ask the partner to also list the positive and negative aspects of the relationship.

8. Develop a plan as to behaviors that each partner will change to improve the relationship. (10, 11, 12)

10. Assign the client the task of listing the behavioral changes he/she needs to make, and the changes he/she believes the spouse or significant other needs to make, to restore the relationship.

11. Assign the spouse or significant other the task of listing the behavioral changes he/she needs to make, and the changes he/she believes the partner needs to make, to restore the relationship.

12. In a conjoint session, obtain a commitment from each partner as to what behaviors each will attempt to change.

9. Discuss the sexual problems that exist in the relationship and demonstrate the ability to show intimacy, verbally and nonverbally. (13, 14)

13. In a conjoint session, facilitate a discussion of the sexual problems, and list those things each partner can do to improve intimacy and communication.

14. Using modeling, role-playing, and behavior rehearsal, teach the partners how to show verbal and nonverbal affection to each other (e.g., going for a walk together, talking intimately, holding hands, hugs, dancing, giving each other compliments and praise).

10. Implement healthy communication skills. (15)

15. Using modeling, role-playing, and behavior rehearsal, teach the client healthy communication skills (e.g., active listening, reflecting, sharing feelings, using "I" messages).

11. Verbalize acceptance of the need for continued therapy to improve the relationship and to maintain gains. (16)

16. Help the couple to see the importance of continued therapy to improve the relationship and maintain gains.

12. Increase the quality and frequency of healthy communication with the partner. (17, 18)

17. Assign the client to develop a written plan as to the time, place, and amount of time that will be devoted to private, one-to-one communication with partner each day.

18. Facilitate a conjoint session with the focus on improving communication skills.

13. Grieve the loss of the relationship and make plans to move forward in life. (19, 20)

19. Encourage the client to share the grief of losing the significant other or spouse, and help him/her make a written plan to increase social interaction and improve old relationships.

20. Encourage and support the client's efforts to build new social relationships.

14. Increase the frequency of pleasurable activities with the partner. (21)

15. Write a plan for meeting social and emotional needs during separation and/or divorce. (22)

16. Develop a personal recovery plan that includes regular attendance at recovery groups, getting a sponsor, and any other therapy necessary to recover from partner relational conflicts and addiction. (23)

17. Complete a re-administration of objective tests of partner relational conflicts as a means of assessing treatment outcome. (24)

18. Complete a survey to assess the degree of satisfaction with treatment. (25)

21. Help the couple to make a list of the pleasurable activities that they would like to do together; solicit a promise from them to become involved in one activity together a week.

22. Assign the client to write a letter to the partner sharing how he/she feels, and suggesting pleasurable activities they could engage in together during recovery.

23. Help the client develop a written personal recovery plan that includes regular attendance at recovery group meetings, getting a sponsor, and any other therapy necessary to recover from partner relational problems and addiction.

24. Assess the outcome of treatment by re-administering to the client objective tests of partner relational conflicts; evaluate the results and provide feedback to the client.

25. Administer a survey to assess the client's degree of satisfaction with treatment.

__. _____
   _____

__. _____
   _____

__. _____
   _____

__. _____
   _____

__. _____
   _____

__. _____
   _____

DIAGNOSTIC SUGGESTIONS:

Axis I:	V61.1	Partner Relational Problem
	V62.81	Relational Problem NOS
	V61.1	Physical Abuse of an Adult

V61.1   Sexual Abuse of an Adult

_____   _____

_____   _____

Axis II: 301.7   Antisocial Personality Disorder
                  301.20   Schizoid Personality Disorder
                  301.81   Narcissistic Personality Disorder

_____   _____

_____   _____

PEER GROUP NEGATIVITY

BEHAVIORAL DEFINITIONS

1. Associates with friends and relatives who are chemically dependent, and who encourage joining them in addictive behavior.
2. Has peers who are involved in the sale of illegal substances, and who encourage joining them in criminal behavior.
3. Reports that peer group is not supportive of recovery from addiction.
4. Is involved in a gang that is supportive of criminal activity and addiction.
5. States peers do not understand addiction or the need for recovery.
6. Reports that peers laugh and joke about recovery, and continue to abuse substances.
7. Peers engage in and encourage gambling.

—. _____
   _____
   _____
—. _____
   _____
   _____
—. _____
   _____

LONG-TERM GOALS

1. Maintain a program of recovery, free of addiction and the negative influences of peers.
2. Understand that continuing to associate with the current peer group increases the risk for relapse.
3. Learn the skills necessary to develop a new peer group that is drug-free and supportive of working a program of recovery.

4. Attend recovery group meetings regularly, and help others who are addicted.
5. Educate family members about addiction and the need for recovery.
6. Encourage family members who are addicted to seek treatment.

—. _____
   _____
   _____

—. _____
   _____
   _____

—. _____
   _____

SHORT-TERM OBJECTIVES	THERAPEUTIC INTERVENTIONS
1. Verbalize the powerlessness and unmanageability that result from peer group negativity and addictive behavior. (1)	1. Using a 12-step recovery program's Step One exercise, help the client to see the powerlessness and unmanageability that result from peer group negativity and addictive behavior.
2. Complete psychological testing or objective questionnaires for assessing the client's identification with the values of a negative peer group. (2)	2. Administer to the client psychological instruments designed to objectively assess the client's identification with the values of a negative peer group (e.g., Family Environment Scale [FES]); give the client feedback regarding the results of the assessment.
3. Identify several times when peer group negativity led to addictive behavior. (3, 4)	3. Help the client to see the relationship between his/her peer group and addictive behavior, particularly how often the peer group encouraged the addictive behavior.
	4. Assign the client to list instances when peers encouraged addictive behavior.
4. List times when peer group negativity led to criminal activity. (5)	5. Assign the client to list times when the peer group led him/her into criminal activity.

5. Verbalize an acceptance of the need for breaking ties with the current peer group. (6, 7, 8, 9)

6. Reinforce the client's verbalized intent to break ties with the current peer group; empathize with the difficulty in leaving friends behind and making new friends.

7. Help the client to grieve the loss of the old peer group, and to make plans to develop new friends in recovery.

8. Help the client to see the reasons why continuing to associate with the current peer group increases his/her risk for relapse.

9. Assist the client in listing the negative consequences associated with continuing ties to the current peer group.

6. Verbalize how peer group negativity and addictive behavior meet the 12-step recovery program's concept of *insanity*. (10)

10. Using a 12-step recovery program's Step Two exercise, help the client to see how peer group negativity and addiction meet the 12-step program's concept of *insane*.

7. List ways in which a higher power can assist in recovery from peer group negativity and addiction. (11, 12, 13)

11. Teach the client about the 12-step recovery program's concept of a higher power and how this power can restore him/her to sanity (e.g., asking a higher power for help in recovery, becoming involved in religious activities, practicing 12-step prayers).

12. Assist the client in identifying the ways that a higher power can assist him/her (e.g., by sending power to resist temptation, by imparting spiritual direction, by giving a feeling of acceptance).

13. Using a 12-step recovery program's Step Three exercise, teach the client about turning problems over to a higher power each day; assign him/her to use this step

at least once a day, and keep a record of using Step Three.

8. Verbalize why obeying the law is essential for working a program of recovery. (5, 14)

5. Assign the client to list times when the peer group led him/her into criminal activity.

14. Teach the client about the 12-step recovery program's concept of rigorous honesty, and why obeying the law is essential in working a program of recovery.

9. Attend recovery group meetings regularly, and stay for coffee and conversation after each meeting. (15, 16)

15. Assign the client to make a written plan about how he/she plans to increase social contact with a new peer group that is positive toward recovery.

16. Encourage the client to stay for coffee and conversation after each 12-step recovery program meeting, to increase social skills and make new, positive friends.

10. Write an autobiography detailing the exact nature of the wrongs committed, and how these relate to the negative peer group and to addiction. (17)

17. Using a 12-step recovery program's Step Four inventory, assign the client to write an autobiography detailing the exact nature of his/her wrongs, and how these relate to the negative peer group and to addictive behavior.

11. Refuse to engage in addictive behavior in high-risk situations. (18, 19)

18. Using modeling, role-playing, and behavior rehearsal, teach the client how to refuse to engage in addictive behavior; practice refusal in high-risk situations for relapse (e.g., negative emotions, social pressure, interpersonal conflict, positive emotions, and testing personal control).

19. Review the client's implementation of refusal skills in high-risk situations; reinforce success, and redirect for failure.

12. Meet with a temporary sponsor and make plans to attend recovery group meetings. (20)

13. Make a list of peers who are positive and peers who are negative toward recovery efforts. (21, 22)

14. Family members indicate who in the client's peer group needs to be avoided in recovery. (23)

15. Family members verbalize what each can do to assist the client in recovery. (24, 25)

16. Complete a re-administration of objective tests of the client's identification with the values of a negative peer group as a means of assessing treatment outcome. (26)

17. Complete a survey to assess the degree of satisfaction with treatment. (27)

__. _____

    _____

__. _____

    _____

__. _____

    _____

20. Encourage and facilitate the client meeting his/her 12-step recovery program temporary sponsor, and discuss plans for recovery.

21. Help the client to make a list of all peers who are positive or negative toward recovery.

22. Assist the client in planning how to avoid or otherwise cope with peers who are unsupportive or critical of his/her recovery efforts.

23. In a family session, have the family members indicate which peers need to be avoided in recovery, and why.

24. Discuss with family members the connection between peer group negativity and addictive behavior; list the steps that the client must take to recover successfully.

25. In a family session, review what each member can do to assist the client in recovery.

26. Assess the outcome of treatment by re-administering to the client objective tests of the client's identification with the values of a negative peer group; evaluate the results and provide feedback to the client.

27. Administer a survey to assess the client's degree of satisfaction with treatment.

__. _____

    _____

__. _____

    _____

__. _____

    _____

DIAGNOSTIC SUGGESTIONS:

Axis I:	312.8	Conduct Disorder
	309.4	Adjustment Disorder with Mixed Disturbance of Emotions and Conduct
	309.3	Adjustment Disorder with Disturbance of Conduct
	_____	_____
	_____	_____
Axis II:	301.7	Antisocial Personality Disorder
	301.83	Borderline Personality Disorder
	301.81	Narcissistic Personality Disorder
	301.82	Avoidant Personality Disorder
	_____	_____
	_____	_____

POSTTRAUMATIC STRESS DISORDER (PTSD)

BEHAVIORAL DEFINITIONS

1. Has experienced a traumatic event that involved actual or threatened death or serious injury and caused a reaction of intense fear or helplessness.
2. Experiences recurrent intrusive memories or dreams of the traumatic event.
3. Acts or feels as if the trauma were recurring.
4. Experiences intense distress when exposed to reminders of the trauma.
5. Avoids stimuli that trigger traumatic memories.
6. Experiences psychic numbing to avoid feelings or thoughts of the trauma.
7. Has periods of disassociation, or inability to remember parts of the trauma.
8. Reports persistent symptoms of increased autonomic arousal (e.g., difficulty sleeping, irritability, anger outbursts, difficulty concentrating, hypervigilance, exaggerated startle response).
9. Expresses verbal threats or displays physically violent behavior.
10. Demonstrates a pattern of intimate relationship, coworker, and authority conflict.
11. Engages in addictive behavior as an escape from pain that is associated with the trauma.

—. _____
_____

—. _____
_____

—. _____
_____

LONG-TERM GOALS

1. Maintain a program of recovery that is free of addiction and posttraumatic stress.
2. Resolve the emotional effects of the past trauma, and terminate its negative impact on current behavior.
3. Understand posttraumatic stress symptoms and how they led to addiction in a self-defeating attempt to cope.
4. Learn the coping skills necessary to bring posttraumatic stress and addiction under control.
5. Terminate the destructive behaviors that serve to maintain escape and denial, while implementing behaviors that promote healing, acceptance of the past events, and responsible living.

—. _____

_____

—. _____

_____

—. _____

_____

SHORT-TERM OBJECTIVES	THERAPEUTIC INTERVENTIONS
1. Verbalize the powerlessness and unmanageability that result from PTSD and addictive behavior. (1)	1. Using a 12-step recovery program's Step One exercise, help the client to see that posttraumatic stress and addictive behavior lead to powerlessness and unmanageability.
2. Describe the traumatic events and the resultant feelings and thoughts, in the past and the present. (2)	2. Explore the past traumatic event(s) that the client has experienced and the associated feelings and thoughts.
3. Complete psychological testing or objective questionnaires for assessing PTSD. (3)	3. Administer to the client psychological instruments designed to objectively assess PTSD (e.g., Trauma Symptom Inventory [TSI], PTSD Symptom Scale– Self-Report [PSS-SR]); give the client feedback regarding the results of the assessment.

4. List times that PTSD symptoms led to addictive behavior. (4)

5. List the ways in which a 12-step recovery program can assist in recovery from PTSD and addictive behavior. (5)

6. List the feelings that lead to dissociation. (6)

7. Cooperate with a physician's evaluation as to whether psychopharmacological intervention is warranted. (7)

8. Take psychotropic medications as directed, and report as to their effectiveness and side effects. (7, 8, 9)

9. Turn posttraumatic stress and addiction over to a higher power each day. (10, 11)

4. Assign the client to list times when symptoms of Posttraumatic Stress Disorder led to addictive behavior.

5. Teach the client about the 12-step recovery program and discuss how it can assist in his/her recovery.

6. Help the client to uncover the feelings that revolve around the past traumatic event and led to dissociation.

7. Refer the client to a physician to examine the client, order psychotropic medications as indicated, titrate medications, and monitor for effectiveness and side effects.

7. Refer the client to a physician to examine the client, order psychotropic medications as indicated, titrate medications, and monitor for effectiveness and side effects.

8. Direct the medical staff to administer medications to the client as ordered by the physician, and to monitor for prescription compliance, effectiveness, and side effects.

9. Monitor the client for psychotropic prescription compliance, effectiveness, and side effects.

10. Teach the client about the 12-step recovery program's concept of a higher power, and how this can be used in recovery (e.g., attend regular religious activities, meet weekly with a spiritual advisor, practice regular prayer and meditation).

11. Using a 12-step recovery program's Step Three exercise, teach the client how to turn problems

10. Cooperate with systematic desensitization sessions, using imagery of the past trauma and current triggers for anxiety. (12, 13)

11. Identify and replace negative self-talk and catastrophizing that is associated with past trauma and current stimulus triggers for anxiety. (14, 15, 16)

12. Calmly approach the actual stimuli *in vivo* that trigger memories and feelings associated with past trauma. (17, 18)

over to a higher power; discuss how he/she felt using the step with perpetrators of past painful events, reinforcing success and redirecting for failure.

12. Using progressive relaxation, biofeedback, or hypnosis, teach the client how to relax; assign him/her to relax twice a day for 10 to 20 minutes.

13. Using imaginal systematic desensitization, have the client experience the past trauma and current triggers for anxiety until the anxious avoidance reaction is terminated.

14. Explore the client's negative self-talk that is associated with the past trauma and the predictions of unsuccessful coping or catastrophizing.

15. Assist the client in listing positive, realistic messages that can replace the negative self talk; assign daily implementation of this cognitive replacement technique.

16. Review the client's implementation of cognitive replacement technique, reinforcing success and redirecting for failure.

17. Encourage the client to approach stimuli that have been avoided, which trigger thoughts and feelings associated with the past trauma; urge the use of relaxation, deep breathing, and positive self-talk to overcome anxiety.

18. Review the client's approach to previously avoided stimuli; reinforce successful use of coping techniques and redirect for failure.

13. Sleep without being disturbed by dreams of the trauma. (12, 19)

12. Using progressive relaxation, biofeedback, or hypnosis, teach the client how to relax; assign him/her to relax twice a day for 10 to 20 minutes.

19. Monitor the client's sleep pattern, and encourage the use of relaxation and positive imagery as aids to induce sleep.

14. Express anger without rage, aggressiveness, or intimidation. (20, 21)

20. Review triggers to anger outbursts, and teach the client the negative consequences of loss of control.

21. Use role-playing and behavior rehearsal to teach the client assertive, respectful expression of angry feelings.

15. Practice stress management skills, to reduce overall stress levels and craving. (22)

22. Teach the client stress management skills (e.g., relaxation exercises, physical exercise, talking about problems, going to meetings, getting a sponsor) to reduce the level of anxiety and increase a sense of mastery over the environment.

16. Develop a written personal recovery plan that details the steps to follow to maintain abstinence from addictive behavior and to recover from posttraumatic stress. (23, 24)

23. Help the client to develop a personal recovery plan that includes attending recovery group meetings regularly, getting a sponsor, taking medications as directed, and follow-up visits with therapist or doctor.

24. Assist the client in listing reasons why he/she should faithfully adhere to a recovery plan.

17. Family members verbalize what each can do to assist the client in recovery. (25, 26)

25. Discuss with family members the connection between PTSD and addictive behavior.

26. In a family session, review what each member can do to assist the client in recovery.

18. Complete a re-administration of objective tests of PTSD as a means of assessing treatment outcome. (27)

19. Complete a survey to assess the degree of satisfaction with treatment. (28)

—. _____
   _____

—. _____
   _____

—. _____
   _____

27. Assess the outcome of treatment by re-administering to the client objective tests of PTSD; evaluate the results and provide feedback to the client.

28. Administer a survey to assess the client's degree of satisfaction with treatment.

—. _____
   _____

—. _____
   _____

—. _____
   _____

DIAGNOSTIC SUGGESTIONS:

Axis I:	309.81	Posttraumatic Stress Disorder
	300.14	Dissociative Identity Disorder
	300.6	Depersonalization Disorder
	300.15	Dissociative Disorder NOS
	309.xx	Adjustment Disorder
	995.52	Physical Abuse of Child (*victim*)
	995.53	Sexual Abuse of Child (*victim*)
	V61.21	Sexual Abuse of Child
	V61.10	Sexual Abuse of Adult (*by partner*)
	V62.83	Sexual Abuse of Adult (*by person other than partner*)
	_____	_____
	_____	_____
Axis II:	301.83	Borderline Personality Disorder
	301.9	Personality Disorder NOS
	_____	_____
	_____	_____

PSYCHOSIS

BEHAVIORAL DEFINITIONS

1. Exhibits bizarre content of thought (e.g., delusions of grandeur, persecution, reference, influence, control, somatic sensations, infidelity).
2. Verbalizes illogical form of thought and/or speech (e.g., loose association of ideas in speech, incoherence; illogical thinking; vague, abstract, or repetitive speech; neologisms, perseverations, clanging).
3. Reports perceptual disturbance (e.g., hallucinations, primarily auditory but occasionally visual or olfactory).
4. Demonstrates disturbed affect (e.g., blunted, none, flattened, or inappropriate).
5. Expresses lost sense of self (e.g., loss of ego boundaries, lack of identity, blatant confusion).
6. Presents with diminished volition (e.g., inadequate interest, drive, or ability to follow a course of action to its logical conclusion; pronounced ambivalence toward or cessation of goal-directed activity).
7. Experiences relationship withdrawal (e.g., withdrawal from involvement with external world and preoccupation with egocentric ideas and fantasies, feelings of alienation).
8. Demonstrates psychomotor abnormalities (e.g., marked decrease in reactivity to environment; various catatonic patterns, such as stupor, rigidity, excitement, posturing, or negativism; unusual mannerisms or grimacing).
9. Displays inability to adequately care for own physical needs, which is potentially harmful to self.
10. Presents as potentially harmful to self or others.
11. Engages in substance abuse, which exacerbates psychotic symptoms.

—. _____

_____

—. _____

_____

—. _____

_____

LONG-TERM GOALS

1. Control or eliminate active psychotic symptoms, such that supervised functioning is positive and medication is taken consistently.
2. Significantly reduce or eliminate hallucinations and/or delusions.
3. Eliminate acute, reactive, psychotic symptoms, and return to normal functioning in affect, thinking, and relating.
4. Stabilize functioning adequate to allow treatment in outpatient setting.
5. Develop adaptive methods to cope with symptoms, and seek treatment when necessary.
6. Terminate substance abuse.

—. _____

_____

—. _____

_____

—. _____

_____

SHORT-TERM OBJECTIVES

1. Accept and understand that distressing symptoms are due to a mental illness and to addictive behavior. (1, 2, 3)

THERAPEUTIC INTERVENTIONS

1. Determine if the client's psychosis is of a brief, reactive nature, or is chronic, with prodromal and reactive elements.

2. Explore the client's family history for serious mental illness and addictive behavior.

3. Evaluate the severity of the client's addiction, as well as disturbance of reality perception and frequency of intrusive irrational thoughts; refer him/her for inpatient care, if necessary.

2. Complete psychological testing or objective questionnaires for assessing psychosis. (4)

4. Administer to the client psychological instruments designed to objectively assess psychosis (e.g., Minnesota Multiphasic Personality Inventory-2 [MMPI-2], Psychiatric Research Interview for Substance and Mental Disorders [PRISM]); give the client feedback regarding the results of the assessment.

3. Cooperate with a psychiatric evaluation to assess the need for psychotropic medication. (5)

5. Refer the client to a psychiatrist to evaluate the need for antipsychotic medications; if indicated, prescribe medication and adjust dosage as necessary to increase effectiveness and reduce side effects.

4. Take antipsychotic medications consistently, as ordered by physician. (6, 7)

6. Direct the staff to administer psychotropic medication to the client and to monitor for compliance, effectiveness, and side effects.

7. Teach the client the need for consistently taking psychotropic medication; monitor for prescription compliance, effectiveness, and side effects.

5. Comply with an examination to evaluate for brain tumors, dementia, or other contributing organic factors. (8, 9)

8. Physician provides physical exam to the client, to evaluate for organic factors that may contribute to psychosis.

9. Perform neuropsychological testing to evaluate the client for organicity.

6. Describe auditory and visual hallucinations to staff, and accept a reality-based perception from others. (10)

10. Gently provide an alternative, reality-based perception to the client when hallucinations are described.

7. Verbalize delusional thoughts regarding irrational fear of harm from others and of other distortions of reality regarding powers or traits of self or others. (11, 12)

11. Ask the client to verbalize irrational beliefs and to assess their content.

12. Calmly and matter-of-factly confront delusional thoughts, offering a reality-based explanation without debating it.

8. Verbalize a trust of others that is contrary to earlier beliefs of persecution or plotting of harm to self. (7, 13)

7. Teach the client the need for consistently taking psychotropic medication; monitor for prescription compliance, effectiveness, and side effects.

13. Encourage the client to focus on the reality of the external world, versus his/her distorted perceptions and beliefs.

9. Display progress toward reality orientation, appropriate affect, organized thought, and improved relational skills. (14, 15)

14. Reinforce the client for calm, normal appearance, behavior, and speech; gently confront bizarre behaviors (e.g., talking to himself/herself, laughing or crying inappropriately, posturing, facial grimaces, incoherent speech, blank staring).

15. Reduce the level of the client's stress and stimulation in the milieu by speaking calmly, keeping noise levels low, maintaining a structure and routine that are predictable, and engaging him/her in simple tasks that distract him/her from internal focus.

10. Engage in social interaction that is reality-based, coherent, and characterized by appropriate affect, subject-focused, logical, and organized. (16, 17, 18, 19)

16. Demonstrate acceptance to the client through a calm, nurturing manner, consistent eye contact, and active listening.

17. Provide supportive therapy to alleviate the client's fears and reduce feelings of alienation.

18. Encourage others to engage the client in social interaction, and to give feedback as to the appropriateness of social skills.

19. Reinforce the client for initiating appropriate social interaction with others.

11. Implement a plan for constructive activities for each day. (20, 21)

20. Prompt the client to complete basic activities of daily living (ADLs) to promote caring for

12. Attend a therapy group and demonstrate appropriate social skills. (22, 23)

13. Replace pacing and other agitation behaviors with calm, appropriate sitting and a relaxed demeanor. (7, 24, 25)

14. Attend recreational therapy activities, and follow the rules of interaction while reporting feeling nonthreatened. (26)

15. Attend an occupational therapy group, and participate with actions that show initiative, logic, follow-through, and abstract reasoning. (27)

16. Engage in an art therapy group discussion to identify feelings, enhance reality focus, and increase social contact. (28, 29)

own basic needs; review and reinforce for progress.

21. Assign the client the task of daily preparing a list of activities that are planned; review and reinforce for progress.

22. Direct the client to attend group therapy, and then ask for a report on the content of the group and his/her contribution.

23. Lead group therapy and draw the client into interaction, reinforcing him/her for calm, logical, coherent participation in group process.

7. Teach the client the need for consistently taking psychotropic medication; monitor for prescription compliance, effectiveness, and side effects.

24. Gently confront the client's agitation behavior, and calmly reassure him/her of his/her safety.

25. Reinforce the client for a more relaxed demeanor and for sitting calmly and normally.

26. Direct the client to attend recreational therapy activities that are nonthreatening, simple to master, and encourage a low level of social interaction; reinforce for success and redirect for failure.

27. Direct occupational therapy activity that diverts the client from internal cognitive focus and provides for structured social interaction and a sense of accomplishment on the completion of a task.

28. Conduct an art therapy group, in which the client is encouraged to express feelings through various art media.

17. Sleep in a normal pattern of 6 to 9 hours per night without agitation, fears, or disruption. (30)

18. Family to verbalize an understanding that the client's bizarre behavior and irrational thoughts are due to mental illness. (31, 32, 33)

19. Verbalize an understanding and acceptance of the need for a structured, supervised living situation after discharge for intensive treatment. (34)

20. Verbalize an awareness of symptom levels that are indicative of decompensation, and methods to contact staff, clinician, and/or family/significant other if the symptoms increase in intensity. (35, 36)

21. Verbalize an understanding of the need for current medica-

29. Lead a group discussion, in which the client is encouraged to share the meaning of his/her artwork.

30. Direct the client to sleep at expected times, and reinforce him/her for compliance.

31. Arrange family therapy sessions to educate the family members regarding the client's illness, treatment, and prognosis.

32. Within a family therapy session, encourage family members to share their feelings of frustration, guilt, fear, or grief regarding the client's mental illness and behavior patterns.

33. Hold family therapy sessions to reduce the atmosphere of criticism and hostility toward the client, and to promote compassion, empathy, and support for him/her.

34. Arrange for an appropriate level of supervised, residential care for the client.

35. Educate the client regarding critical symptoms that are indicative of decompensation, and urge initiation of clinical contact if intense positive symptoms of psychosis appear and interfere with daily functioning.

36. Provide the client with written instructions and phone numbers to use if the symptoms become intense.

7. Teach the client the need for consistently taking psychotropic

tions, the importance of compliance and correct dosage, and the identification of benefits and side effects. (7, 37)

22. Family members verbalize what each can do to assist the client in recovery. (38, 39)

23. Complete a re-administration of objective tests of psychosis as a means of assessing treatment outcome. (40)

24. Complete a survey to assess the degree of satisfaction with treatment. (41)

—. _____
   _____

—. _____
   _____

—. _____
   _____

medication; monitor for prescription compliance, effectiveness, and side effects.

37. Educate the client and/or the family/significant other about the importance of ongoing medication compliance, proper dosage, refilling prescriptions, safety factors, and side effect recognition.

38. Discuss with family members the connection between psychosis and addictive behavior.

39. In a family session, review what each member can do to assist the client in recovery.

40. Assess the outcome of treatment by re-administering to the client objective tests of psychosis; evaluate the results and provide feedback to the client.

41. Administer a survey to assess the client's degree of satisfaction with treatment.

—. _____
   _____

—. _____
   _____

—. _____
   _____

DIAGNOSTIC SUGGESTIONS:

Axis I:	291.x	Alcohol-Induced Psychotic Disorder
	292.xx	Other (or Unknown) Substance-Induced Disorder
	295.xx	Schizophrenia
	296.xx	Major Depressive Disorder
	296.xx	Bipolar I Disorder
	297.1	Delusional Disorder

298.8	Brief Psychotic Disorder
295.40	Schizophreniform Disorder
310.1	Personality Change Due to (Axis III Disorder)
_____	_____
_____	_____

RELAPSE PRONENESS

BEHAVIORAL DEFINITIONS

1. Reports a history of multiple addiction treatment attempts and subsequent relapse.
2. Frequently expresses negative emotions, increasing the risk for continued addiction.
3. Friends or family members engage in addictive behavior.
4. Describes interpersonal conflicts, which increase the risk for relapse.
5. Reports experiencing social pressure, which encourages substance abuse.
6. Has never worked a program of recovery long enough to maintain abstinence.
7. Has a history of mental illness, increasing risk for relapse.

—. _____
   _____
   _____
—. _____
   _____
   _____
—. _____
   _____

LONG-TERM GOALS

1. Develop coping skills to use when experiencing high-risk situations and/or craving.
2. Resolve interpersonal conflicts, and learn healthy communication skills.
3. Develop a new peer group that is supportive of recovery.
4. Learn refusal skills for use when tempted into addictive behavior.
5. Practice a program of recovery that includes regular attendance at recovery group meetings, working with a sponsor, and helping others in recovery.

—. _____
_____
—. _____
_____
—. _____
_____

SHORT-TERM OBJECTIVES

THERAPEUTIC INTERVENTIONS

1. Write a detailed chemical use history, describing treatment attempts and the specific situations surrounding relapse. (1)

2. Complete psychological testing or objective questionnaires for assessing addiction relapse. (2)

3. Verbalize an understanding of why relapse continues to occur. (3, 4)

4. Verbalize the powerlessness and unmanageability that result from addiction and relapse. (5)

1. Assign the client to write a chemical use history, describing his/her attempts at recovery and the situations surrounding relapse.

2. Administer to the client psychological instruments designed to objectively assess addiction relapse (e.g., Substance Abuse Relapse assessment [SARA]); give the client feedback regarding the results of the assessment.

3. Teach the client the high-risk situations that lead to relapse (e.g., negative emotions, social pressure, interpersonal conflict, positive emotions, tests of personal control).

4. Help the client to understand why he/she keeps relapsing (e.g., failure to work a daily program of recovery, failure to go to meetings, poor coping skills for high-risk situation, mental illness, interpersonal problems, poor recovery environment).

5. Using a 12-step recovery program's Step One exercise, help the client to see the powerlessness and unmanageability that result from addiction and relapse.

5. Verbalize that continued alcohol/drug abuse meets the 12-step program concept of *insanity*. (6)

6. Verbalize reasons why it is essential to work a daily program of recovery to maintain abstinence. (4, 7, 8)

7. List ways in which a higher power can assist in recovery from addiction. (9, 10)

8. Make a written plan to increase reinforcement when attending recovery group meetings. (11, 12, 13)

6. Using a 12-step recovery program's Step Two exercise, help the client to see the insanity of his/her disease, then teach him/her that a higher power can restore him/her to sanity.

4. Help the client to understand why he/she keeps relapsing (e.g., failure to work a daily program of recovery, failure to go to meetings, poor coping skills for high-risk situation, mental illness, interpersonal problems, poor recovery environment).

7. Help the client to understand why is it essential to implement a daily program of recovery to maintain abstinence.

8. Using the client's relapse history, help him/her to understand the reasons why his/her recovery program failed.

9. Teach the client how to use the 12-step recovery program's Step Three, and assign him/her to practice turning problems over to a higher power each day; have the client record each situation and discuss these with the primary therapist.

10. Teach the client how a higher power can assist in recovery (e.g., attending religious activities, practicing regular prayer and meditation).

11. Probe the reasons why the client discontinues going to 12-step recovery program meetings consistently.

12. Help the client to develop a plan that will increase the rewards obtained at recovery groups (e.g.,

9. Implement a plan to deal with each situation that represents a high risk for relapse. (14, 15)

10. Practice healthy communication skills. (16)

11. Implement the application of conflict resolution skills to interpersonal conflicts. (17)

12. Practice refusal skills in the face of enticement to engage in addictive behavior. (18)

concentrate on helping others, go for coffee after the meeting, socialize, stick with the winners).

13. Assign the client to a 12-step recovery program contact person, and begin to attend recovery group meetings with him/her regularly; encourage both individuals to make the outing fun, rather than a boring obligation.

14. Help the client to make a written plan that details the coping skills (e.g., go to a meeting, call a sponsor, call the 12-step recovery program hotline, call the counselor, talk to someone) to use when in a high-risk situation (e.g., negative emotions, social pressure, interpersonal conflict, strong positive emotions, tests of personal control).

15. Review the client's implementation of coping skills for high-risk situations in his/her daily life; reinforce success and redirect for failure.

16. Teach the client healthy communication skills (e.g., active listening, using "I" messages, reflecting, sharing feelings).

17. Teach the client conflict-resolution skills. Using modeling, role-playing, and behavior rehearsal, have him/her practice handling conflict in high-risk situations.

18. Using modeling, role-playing, and behavior rehearsal, teach the client how to say no to alcohol/drugs; practice refusal in several high-risk situations.

13. Cooperate with an examination by a physician to see if pharmacological intervention is warranted. (19)

19. Refer the client to a physician to examine the client, order medications as indicated, titrate medications, and monitor for side effects.

14. Take all medication as directed, and report as to the effectiveness and side effects. (19, 20)

19. Refer the client to a physician to examine the client, order medications as indicated, titrate medications, and monitor for side effects.

20. Direct the staff to administer medications as ordered by the physician and to monitor the psychotropic medications for compliance, effectiveness, and side effects.

15. Make an emergency card that has phone numbers to call when in a high-risk situation. (21)

21. Help the client to make an emergency card to carry at all times that has the phone numbers of people to call when he/she is at high risk for relapse.

16. Agree to enter the structured continuing-care treatment setting that is necessary to maintain abstinence. (22)

22. Help the client to decide on an aftercare placement that is structured enough to help him/her maintain abstinence (e.g., halfway house, group home, outpatient treatment, day care, partial hospitalization).

17. Develop a written personal recovery plan. (23)

23. Help the client to develop a written continuing care plan that includes honesty, attending recovery group meetings regularly, getting a sponsor, and any other treatment that is needed to maintain abstinence.

18. Family members verbalize what each can do to assist the client in recovery. (24, 25)

24. Discuss with family members the connection between relapse proneness and addictive behavior.

25. In a family session, review what each member can do to assist the client in recovery.

19. Complete a re-administration of objective tests of addiction relapse as a means of assessing treatment outcome. (26)

20. Complete a survey to assess the degree of satisfaction with treatment. (27)

—. _____
   _____

—. _____
   _____

—. _____
   _____

26. Assess the outcome of treatment by re-administering to the client objective tests of addiction relapse; evaluate the results and provide feedback to the client.

27. Administer a survey to assess the client's degree of satisfaction with treatment.

—. _____
   _____

—. _____
   _____

—. _____
   _____

DIAGNOSTIC SUGGESTIONS:

Axis I:	312.8	Conduct Disorder
	296.xx	Bipolar I Disorder
	296.89	Bipolar II Disorder
	301.13	Cyclothymic Disorder
	314	Attention-Deficit/Hyperactivity Disorder
	313.81	Oppositional Defiant Disorder
	_____	_____
	_____	_____
Axis II:	301.0	Paranoid Personality Disorder
	301.20	Schizoid Personality Disorder
	301.22	Schizotypal Personality Disorder
	301.7	Antisocial Personality Disorder
	301.83	Borderline Personality Disorder
	301.81	Narcissistic Personality Disorder
	301.82	Avoidant Personality Disorder
	_____	_____
	_____	_____

SELF-CARE DEFICITS*—PRIMARY

BEHAVIORAL DEFINITIONS

1. Presents with chronic chemical dependence that has eroded motivation and discipline necessary for adequate self-care.
2. Demonstrates substandard hygiene and grooming, as evidenced by strong body odor, disheveled hair, or dirty clothing.
3. Fails to use basic hygiene techniques (e.g., bathing, brushing teeth, washing clothes).
4. Presents with medical problems due to poor hygiene.
5. Maintains poor diet due to deficiencies in cooking, meal preparation, or food selection.
6. Has poor interaction skills, as evidenced by limited eye contact, insufficient attending, and awkward social responses.
7. Has inadequate knowledge or functioning in basic skills around the home (e.g., cleaning floors, washing dishes, disposing of garbage, keeping fresh food available).
8. Reports loss of relationships, employment, or other social opportunities due to poor hygiene and/or inadequate attention to grooming.

___. _____

_____

___. _____

_____

___. _____

_____

* Most of the content of this chapter (with minor revisions) is taken from D. J. Berghuis and A. E. Jongsma, Jr., *The Severe and Persistent Mental Illness Treatment Planner* (New York: Wiley, 2000). Copyright © 2000 by D. J. Berghuis and A. E. Jongsma, Jr.

LONG-TERM GOALS

1. Discontinue substance abuse and increase functioning in self-care.
2. Understand the need for good hygiene and implement healthy personal hygiene practices.
3. Learn basic skills for maintaining a clean, sanitary living space.
4. Regularly shower or bathe, shave, brush teeth, care for hair, and use deodorant.
5. Experience increased social acceptance because of improved appearance and/or improved functioning in self-care.

—. _____

_____

_____

—. _____

_____

_____

—. _____

_____

SHORT-TERM OBJECTIVES

1. Describe current functioning in self-care, and how this relates to substance abuse. (1, 2, 3)

2. Complete or give permission for a significant other to complete a survey of the client's

THERAPEUTIC INTERVENTIONS

1. Request that the client prepare an inventory of positive and negative functioning regarding self-care, including the relationship between lack of self-care and substance abuse.

2. Ask the client to identify a trusted individual from whom he/she can obtain helpful feedback regarding daily hygiene and cleanliness; coordinate feedback from this individual to the client.

3. Assess the client's basic nutritional knowledge and skills, usual diet, and nutritional deficiencies; refer to a dietitian, if necessary.

4. Administer to the client or a significant other an objective psychological instrument (e.g., In-

level of implementation of self-care skills. (4)

3. List five negative effects of substance abuse and of not giving enough effort to self-care. (5, 6, 7, 8)

4. Verbalize insight into the secondary gain that is associated with decreased self-care functioning. (9)

5. Prioritize those self-care areas upon which to focus effort and improve functioning. (2, 10, 11)

dependent Living Scales by Loeb) to assess the client's degree of implementation of self-care skills; give the client feedback regarding the results of the assessment.

5. Ask the client to identify two painful experiences in which rejection was experienced (e.g., broken relationships, loss of employment) due to the lack of performance of basic self-care.

6. Help the client to visualize or imagine the possible positive changes that could result from decreased substance abuse and increased attention to appearance and other aspects of self-care.

7. Review with the client the medical risks (e.g., dental problems, risk of infection, lice) that are associated with substance abuse, poor hygiene, or lack of attention to other aspects of self-care.

8. Assist the client in expressing emotions related to impaired performance in self-care (e.g., embarrassment, depression, low self-esteem).

9. Reflect the possible secondary gain (i.e., less involvement in potentially difficult social situations) that is associated with decreased self-care functioning.

2. Ask the client to identify a trusted individual from whom he/she can obtain helpful feedback regarding daily hygiene and cleanliness; coordinate feedback from this individual to the client.

10. Ask the client to identify or describe those self-care behaviors

that are desired but are not present in his/her current repertoire.

11. Facilitate the client prioritizing the implementation of self-care behaviors or the learning of skills that are necessary to implement these behaviors.

6. Cooperate with a referral for an assessment of intelligence and neuropsychological deficits. (12)

12. Refer the client for an assessment of cognitive deficits (e.g., low intelligence, brain damage) that may contribute to his/her lack of attention to self-care.

7. Participate in a remediation program to teach self-care skills. (13)

13. Recommend remediation programs to the client (e.g., a self-care skill-building group, didactic group, behavior-shaping program) that is focused on removing self-care deficits.

8. Acknowledge self-care deficits as a symptom of chronic chemical dependence or mental illness. (14)

14. Reflect or interpret poor performance in self-care as an indicator of chronic chemical dependence or psychiatric decompensation; share observations with the client, with caregivers, and with other staff.

9. Stabilize, through the use of psychotropic medications, psychotic and other severe and persistent mental illness symptoms that interfere with self-care. (15, 16, 17)

15. Arrange for an evaluation of the client by a physician to determine if a prescription for psychotropic medication is warranted.

16. Educate the client about the proper use and the expected benefits of psychotropic medication.

17. Monitor the client for compliance with the prescribed psychotropic medication, and for its effectiveness and possible side effects.

10. Remediate the medical effects that have resulted from a history of a lack of self-care performance. (18, 19)

18. Arrange for a full physical examination of the client; encourage the physician to prescribe any necessary self-care remediation behaviors.

11. Implement skills that are related to basic personal hygiene on a consistent, daily basis. (20, 21, 22, 23)

19. Refer the client to a dentist to determine dental treatment needs; coordinate ongoing dental treatment.

20. Provide the client with written or video educational material for basic personal hygiene skills (e.g., *The Complete Guide to Better Dental Care* by Taintor and Taintor, *The New Wellness Encyclopedia* by the editors of the University of California-Berkeley).

21. Refer the client to a designated staff for one-to-one training in basic hygiene needs and techniques.

22. Conduct or refer the client to a psychoeducational group for teaching personal hygiene skills; use the group setting to help teach the client to give and receive feedback about hygiene skill implementation.

23. Encourage and reinforce the client for performing basic hygiene skills on a regular schedule (e.g., at the same time and in the same order each day).

12. Utilize a self-monitoring system to increase the frequency of regular use of basic hygiene skills. (24, 25)

24. Help the client to develop a self-monitoring program (e.g., a check-off chart for self-care needs).

25. Provide the client with regular feedback about progress in his/her use of self-monitoring to improve personal hygiene.

13. Utilize community resources to improve personal hygiene and grooming. (26, 27)

26. Review the use of community resources with the client (e.g., laundromat/dry cleaner, hair salon/barber) that can be used to improve personal appearance.

27. Coordinate for the client to tour community facilities for cleaning and pressing clothes, cutting and styling hair, or purchasing soap and deodorant, with an emphasis on increasing the client's understanding of this service and how it can be used.

14. Cooperate with treatment for substance abuse and/or mental illness that interferes with the ability to care for self. (28, 29, 30)

28. Assess the client for substance abuse or severe mental illness that exacerbates poor self-care performance.

29. Refer the client to Alcoholics Anonymous (AA), Narcotics Anonymous (NA), or other substance abuse treatment options. (See the Substance Abuse/Dependence chapter in this *Planner.*)

30. Provide integrated, coordinated mental health and substance abuse treatment services.

15. Implement basic skills for running and maintaining a home or apartment. (31, 32)

31. Facilitate family members, friends, and caregivers who are willing to train the client in basic housekeeping skills; monitor and reinforce the client's progress.

32. Teach the client basic housekeeping skills, utilizing references such as *Mary Ellen's Complete Home Reference Book* by Pinkham and Burg or *The Cleaning Encyclopedia* by Aslett.

16. Implement basic cooking skills and eat nutritionally balanced meals daily. (33, 34)

33. Educate the client on basic cooking techniques (e.g., *The Good Housekeeping Illustrated Cookbook,* by the editors of *Good Housekeeping, How to Cook Everything* by Bittman) or refer the client to a community-based education cooking class or seminar.

17. Engage in physical exercise several times per week. (18, 35, 36, 37, 38)

34. Monitor the client's follow-through regarding a dietitian's recommendations for changes in the client's cooking and eating practices.

18. Arrange for a full physical examination of the client; encourage the physician to prescribe any necessary self-care remediation behaviors.

35. Refer the client to an activity therapist, or make recommendations regarding physical fitness activities that are available in the community or through health clubs.

36. Assist the client in setting specific exercise goals, and monitor his/her participation in exercise and physical fitness activities.

37. Provide educational material (e.g., *Fitness and Health* by Sharkey, *ACSM Fitness Book* by American College of Sports Medicine) to increase the client's knowledge of physical fitness needs.

38. Coordinate or facilitate membership for the client at a local health club or YMCA/YWCA.

18. Complete or give permission to a significant other to complete a re-administration of a survey of the client's implementation of self-care skills, as a means of assessing treatment outcome. (39)

39. Assess the outcome of treatment by re-administering to the client or a significant other an objective survey of the client's level of implementation of self-care skills; give the client feedback regarding the results of the assessment.

19. Complete a survey to assess the degree of satisfaction with treatment. (40)

40. Administer a survey to assess the client's degree of satisfaction with treatment.

—. _____

_____

—. _____

_____

—. _____   —. _____
   _____   _____
—. _____   —. _____
   _____   _____

DIAGNOSTIC SUGGESTIONS:

Axis I:

297.1	Delusional Disorder
295.xx	Schizophrenia
295.10	Schizophrenia, Disorganized Type
295.30	Schizophrenia, Paranoid Type
295.90	Schizophrenia, Undifferentiated Type
295.60	Schizophrenia, Residual Type
295.70	Schizoaffective Disorder
296.xx	Bipolar I Disorder
296.89	Bipolar II Disorder

_____   _____

_____   _____

Axis II:

317	Mild Mental Retardation

_____   _____

_____   _____

SELF-CARE DEFICITS*—SECONDARY

BEHAVIORAL DEFINITIONS

1. Has a history of addictive behavior and chronic mental illness, which leads to a lack of effective independent activities of daily living (IADLs; e.g., transportation, banking, shopping, use of community services, other skills necessary for living more independently).
2. Verbalizes anxiety regarding increase in IADLs.
3. Lacks knowledge of community resources to aid in recovery.
4. Fails to respond appropriately in emergency situations.
5. Chronic addiction, paranoia, psychosis, or other severe and persistent mental illness symptoms negatively affect ability to use community resources independently.
6. Lacks familiarity with daily living resources (e.g., banking, stores, other services).
7. Does not pay attention to and organize personal responsibilities, resulting in unpaid bills and/or missed appointments.
8. Fails access to community resources (e.g., 12-step groups, worship centers, libraries, recreational areas, businesses).
9. External restrictions have been placed on access to community resources due to chronic addiction and/or bizarre behaviors.
10. Has a history of allowing or expecting others to take responsibility for performing own IADLs.

—. _____

_____

—. _____

_____

* Most of the content of this chapter (with minor revisions) is taken from D. J. Berghuis and A. E. Jongsma, Jr., *The Severe and Persistent Mental Illness Treatment Planner* (New York: Wiley, 2000). Copyright © 2000 by D. J. Berghuis and A. E. Jongsma, Jr.

—. _____
   _____

LONG-TERM GOALS

1. Develop a program of recovery and increase knowledge of community resources.
2. Timely, appropriate, and safe responses to emergency situations.
3. Participate in recovery and increase functioning independently.
4. Consistent use of available addiction recovery and/or mental health community resources.
5. Increased organization of and attention to daily routines, resulting in personal responsibilities being fulfilled.
6. Take responsibility for own IADLs to level of own potential, and develop resources for help from others.

—. _____
   _____
—. _____
   _____
—. _____
   _____

SHORT-TERM OBJECTIVES

1. Describe powerlessness and unmanageability over addiction and/or mental illness and over current functioning in performing IADLs and the negative affects of substance abuse. (1, 2, 3)

THERAPEUTIC INTERVENTIONS

1. Request that the client prepare an inventory of his/her positive and negative experiences with attempting to perform IADLs while addicted.

2. Ask the client to identify two areas in which he/she has experienced success in recovery and in becoming more independent in the community.

3. Solicit from the client two areas in which addiction has led to failure in becoming more independent.

2. Complete or give permission for a significant other to complete a survey of the client's IADLs. (4)

3. Identify barriers to recovery and to increasing IADLs. (3, 5, 6)

4. Prioritize IADL areas upon which to focus effort and improve functioning. (1, 7, 8)

5. Apply for Supplemental Security Income (SSI) if necessary, and agree to work with a family or mental health community advocate. (9)

6. Participate in remediation program to teach IADL skills and recovery from addiction. (10)

4. Administer to the client or a significant other an objective survey (e.g., Independent Living Scales, by Loeb) to assess the client's IADLs; give the client feedback regarding the results of the assessment.

3. Solicit from the client two areas in which addiction has led to failure in becoming more independent.

5. Examine problematic IADL areas with the client, to identify any patterns of addictive behavior or cognitions that cause failure at independent functioning.

6. After obtaining the client's permission to release information, obtain feedback from family members, friends, and caregivers about the client's addiction and performance of IADLs.

1. Request that the client prepare an inventory of his/her positive and negative experiences with attempting to perform IADLs while addicted.

7. Ask the client to identify or describe those IADLs which are desired but not present in current repertoire.

8. Assist the client in prioritizing IADLs and the skills that must be learned to implement these IADLs.

9. Help the client choose a family or mental health community advocate, and apply for SSI, if necessary.

10. Recommend programs to the client (e.g., skill-building groups, 12-step meetings, token

economies or behavior-shaping programs) that are focused on removing deficits of IADL performance.

7. Increase frequency and appropriateness of recovery activities and social interaction. (11, 12, 13)

11. Explore the client's anxiety regarding social contacts, participation at recovery group meetings, and increasing independence.

12. Assist the client in learning the skills necessary for using appropriate social behavior in recovery (see Social Anxiety/Skills Deficit chapter in this *Planner*).

13. Provide positive feedback and encouragement to the client's attempts to increase social interaction and participate in a program of recovery.

8. Develop and implement a regular schedule for performance of routine IADLs and recovery from addiction. (14, 15)

14. Aid the client in developing a specific schedule for completing IADLs (e.g., go to 12-step group on Thursday, arrange finances on Monday morning, go to grocery store on Tuesday).

15. Teach the client about situations in which he/she should break from his/her established routine (e.g., do banking on a different day due to holiday, do weekly cleaning one day earlier in order to attend desired social function).

9. Acknowledge IADL deficits as a symptom of chronic addiction and/or mental illness being inadequately controlled or treated. (16, 17)

16. Educate the client about the expected or common symptoms of his/her mental illness and addiction (e.g., persistent intoxication or drug abuse, man excitement behaviors, negative symptoms of schizophrenia), which may negatively impact basic IADL functioning.

17. Reflect or interpret poor performance in IADLs as an indicator

10. Comply with an evaluation by a physician for psychotropic medication, and take medication as prescribed. (18, 19, 20, 21, 22)

of psychiatric decompensation or addiction relapse; share observations with the client, caregivers, and medical staff.

18. Arrange for an evaluation of the client by a physician for a prescription for psychotropic medications.

19. Educate the client about the proper use and expected benefits of psychotropic medications, including naltrexone and accamprosate; model procedures for the procurement of medications, and identify a person to monitor medication compliance.

20. Monitor the client's psychotropic medication compliance and its effectiveness and possible side effects; report any significant problems to the medical staff.

21. Develop an agreement with the client regarding the level of responsibility and independence he/she must display to trigger a decrease in clinician's monitoring of medications.

22. Coordinate an agreement between the client, pharmacist, and clinician regarding circumstances that would trigger the transfer of medication monitoring back to the clinician (e.g., the client's failure to pick up monthly prescription, client trying to refill a prescription too soon).

11. Obtain necessary transportation to work, 12-step meetings, medical appointments, leisure opportunities, or other desired destinations. (23)

23. Brainstorm possible transportation resources with the client (e.g., public transportation, personal vehicle, agency resources, friends and family, walking, bicycling); encourage and reinforce the

client's independent use of these resources.

12. Use public transportation in a safe, socially appropriate, and efficient manner. (24, 25, 26)

24. Familiarize the client with available public transportation options through discussion, written schedules, and accompanied use of community services.

25. Review typical expectations for using public transportation, including payment, time schedule, and social norms for behavior.

26. Ride with the client to various destinations on public transportation until he/she is adequately comfortable in doing so alone.

13. Identify, attain, and manage adequate sources of financial income. (27, 28)

27. Assist the client in identifying and attaining adequate sources of income or eligibility for welfare assistance.

28. Develop a budget with the client, based on resources and needs.

14. Use banking resources to facilitate financial independence. (29, 30, 31)

29. Review procedures for and advantages of the use of banking systems to assist the client with IADLs, including increased security, financial organization, and convenience paying bills; caution the client about hazards related to banking (e.g., credit debt, overdrawn checking account charges).

30. Coordinate a helping relationship between specific bank staff and the client; with proper permission to release information, provide information to bank staff about the client's needs and disabilities.

31. Encourage the client to use specific staff at a specific bank branch in order to develop a more personal and understanding relationship.

15. Utilize the services of a choice of stores in the community. (32, 33)

32. Familiarize the client with retail resources available in his/her area, through a review of newspaper advertisements and a tour of the business districts in the community.

33. Role-play situations which commonly occur while shopping at a store (e.g., getting a sponsor, asking for assistance, declining a pushy salesperson, returning a defective item); provide the client with feedback about his/her functioning in these situations.

16. Attend 12-step meetings and other support groups. (34, 35)

34. Review places, times, and locations of support groups for the client (e.g., 12-step meetings, religious groups, community agencies).

35. Go with the client to 12-step meetings and other groups at which he/she is uncomfortable or uncertain, gradually decreasing support.

17. Identify and contact alternative resources before contacting emergency response staff. (36, 37, 38)

36. Teach the client the appropriate use of specific emergency service professionals, including their responsibilities and limitations.

37. Provide the client with an easy-to-read list of emergency telephone numbers.

38. Brainstorm alternative resources that are available to the client for use, instead of "nuisance" calls to emergency response staff (e.g., contact a support group member when lonely instead of going to the emergency room, contact family first if feeling ill).

18. Request assistance from others when attempting to implement IADLs. (39, 40)

39. Ask the client to identify a list of personal resources that he/she can use for assistance in carrying out

IADLs (e.g., family and friends, support group members, neighbors).

40. Role-play how to approach strangers for basic assistance (e.g., asking for directions); provide feedback to the client about his/her approach, personal hygiene or dress, and how appearance and manner affect the stranger's comfort level (see the Social Anxiety/Skills Deficit chapter in this *Planner*).

19. Complete or give permission to a significant other to complete a re-administration of a survey of the client's IADLs, as a means of assessing treatment outcome. (41)

41. Assess the outcome of treatment by re-administering to the client or a significant other an objective survey of the client's IADLs; give the client feedback regarding the results of the assessment.

20. Complete or give permission to a significant other to complete a survey to assess the degree of satisfaction with treatment. (42)

42. Administer a survey to the client or significant other to assess the client's degree of satisfaction with treatment.

—. _____

—. _____

—. _____

—. _____

—. _____

—. _____

—. _____

—. _____

DIAGNOSTIC SUGGESTIONS:

Axis I:	291.2	Alcohol-Induced Persisting Dementia
	303.90	Alcohol Dependence
	304.80	Polysubstance Dependence
	297.1	Delusional Disorder
	295.xx	Schizophrenia
	295.70	Schizoaffective Disorder

296.xx   Bipolar I Disorder
296.89   Bipolar II Disorder

_____   _____

_____   _____

Axis II: 317   Mild Mental Retardation

_____   _____

_____   _____

SEXUAL PROMISCUITY

BEHAVIORAL DEFINITIONS

1. Engages in repeated acts of sexual intimacy with partner with whom there is no meaningful emotional or lasting social connections.
2. Reports a preoccupation with sexual thoughts.
3. Has a history of sexually acting out that is potentially self-damaging (e.g., unprotected sex, hiring prostitutes, cruising the streets for sex, many different sexual partners).
4. Demonstrates a pattern of sexual behavior that seeks immediate gratification.
5. Engages in prostitution.
6. Lacks control over self-destructive sexual behavior.
7. Uses sexual behavior to cope or escape from stress or to reduce tension.
8. Overreacts to mildly sexually oriented stimulation.
9. Reports a sense of tension or affective arousal before engaging in sexual behavior, and a reduction of tension after completing the sexual act.
10. Engage in illegal sexual acts with a minor.
11. Concomitant substance abuse accompanies the impulsive, emotionally detached sexual encounters.
12. Chemical dependence leads to an exchange of sex for mood-altering drugs.

—. _____

_____

—. _____

_____

—. _____

_____

LONG-TERM GOALS

1. Maintain a program of recovery that is free from sexual promiscuity and addictive behavior.
2. Reduce the frequency of sexual promiscuity, and increase the frequency of meaningful sexual behavior.
3. Reduce thoughts that trigger sexual promiscuity, and increase self-talk that controls behavior.
4. Learn to stop, think, and plan before acting.
5. Learn stress reduction techniques to manage stress without the use of sexually promiscuous behavior.
6. Terminate substance abuse that accompanies sexual promiscuity.

—. _____
   _____
   _____
—. _____
   _____
   _____
—. _____
   _____

SHORT-TERM OBJECTIVES

1. Verbalize an understanding of the powerlessness and unmanageability that result from sexual promiscuity and addiction. (1)

2. Describe the history and nature of the sexual promiscuity. (2)

3. Complete psychological testing or objective questionnaires for assessing sexual promiscuity. (3)

THERAPEUTIC INTERVENTIONS

1. Using a 12-step recovery program's Step One exercise, help the client to understand how sexual promiscuity and addiction lead to powerlessness and unmanageability.

2. Explore the client's history and nature of sexual promiscuity.

3. Administer to the client psychological instruments designed to objectively assess sexual promiscuity (e.g., Derogatis Interview for Sexual Functioning [DISF], Multiphasic Sex Inventory II [MSI-II], Sexual Adjustment Inventory [SAI]); give the client feedback regarding the results of the assessment.

4. Identify the negative consequences of sexual promiscuity and addiction. (4, 5)

4. Assist the client in making connections between his/her sexual promiscuity and the negative consequences that he/she has experienced.

5. Assign the client to write a list of the negative consequences that occurred because of his/her sexual promiscuity and addiction.

5. Identify various times when sexual promiscuity led to addictive behavior. (6)

6. Explore times when the client acted too quickly on impulses, resulting in sexually promiscuous and addictive behavior.

6. Verbalize how sexual promiscuity and addictive behavior meet the 12-step recovery program's criteria for *insanity*. (7)

7. Using a 12-step recovery program's Step Two exercise, help the client to see that doing the same things over and over again and expecting different results meets the program's definition of *insanity*.

7. Increase the frequency of reviewing behavioral decisions with a trusted friend or family member for feedback regarding the consequences before the decision is enacted. (8)

8. Conduct a session with the spouse, significant other, sponsor, or family member and the client to develop a contract for the client receiving feedback prior to engaging in sexually promiscuous acts.

8. Identify the biopsychosocial elements that have contributed to sexual promiscuity. (9)

9. Probe the client's biopsychosocial history and help him/her to see the possible causes for his/her sexual promiscuity (e.g., family patterns of promiscuity, low self-esteem, sexual abuse, mental illness).

9. Comply with a physician's evaluation regarding the necessity for psychopharmacological intervention, and take all medications as prescribed. (10, 11)

10. Refer the client to a physician for an examination, to order medication as indicated, titrate medications, and monitor for side effects.

11. Monitor for effectiveness and side effects when the client takes prescribed medications.

10. Identify and replace thoughts that trigger impulsive sexual behavior. (12, 13)

12. Help the client to uncover dysfunctional thoughts that lead to sexual promiscuity; teach him/her to replace each one with an accurate, positive, self-enhancing, and adaptive thought.

13. Help the client to develop a list of positive, accurate, and self-enhancing thoughts to read to himself/herself each day, particularly when feeling tense or disparaged.

11. Implement adaptive stress-reduction techniques. (14, 15)

14. Use modeling, role-playing, and behavior rehearsal to teach the client adaptive stress-reduction techniques (e.g., talking to someone about the problem, taking a time out, calling the sponsor, going to a meeting, engaging in exercise, practicing relaxation).

15. Teach the client relaxation techniques (e.g., progressive relaxation, self-hypnosis, biofeedback); assign him/her to relax whenever feeling tense or anxious.

12. Implement the assertive formula, "I feel.... When you ... I would prefer it if ..." (16, 17)

16. Using modeling, role-playing, and behavior rehearsal, teach the client how to use the assertive formula, "I feel.... When you ... I would prefer it if ..." in conflict situations.

17. Review implementation of assertiveness, feelings about it, as well as the consequences of it; redirect as necessary.

13. Implement stopping, thinking, and planning before acting. (18, 19)

18. Using modeling, role-playing, and behavior rehearsal, teach the client how to use "stop, think, and plan before acting" in various current situations.

14. Verbalize an understanding of a 12-step program's Step Three, regarding the role of a higher power and how this step can be used in recovery from sexual promiscuity and addiction. (20)

15. Write an autobiography detailing the exact nature of wrongs that were committed, and relate each of these wrongs to sexual promiscuity. (21)

16. Disclose any history of sexual abuse in childhood, and relate that experience to current patterns of sexual behavior. (22, 23)

17. Verbalize why a meaningful relationship is necessary for true sexual intimacy. (24)

18. Identify those factors that contribute to difficulty with establishing intimate, trusting relationships. (25)

19. Review the client's use of "stop, think, and plan before acting" in day-to-day living, and identify the positive consequences; redirect as necessary.

20. Using a 12-step recovery program's Step Three exercise, teach the client how to turn his/her will and life over to the care of a higher power; discuss how this step can be beneficial in recovery from sexual promiscuity and addictive behavior (e.g., understanding God's forgiveness and grace, practicing regular prayer, turning cravings over to God).

21. Using a 12-step recovery program's Step Four exercise, assign the client to write an autobiography of the exact nature of his/her wrongs, and to relate these wrongs to sexual promiscuity and addiction.

22. Explore the client's history of sexual abuse.

23. Relate the client's childhood sexual abuse to his/her current pattern of sexual promiscuity; refer the client for ongoing counseling that is focused on overcoming the effects of the sexual abuse.

24. Teach the client the importance of a meaningful relationship, to allow for true intimacy in a sexual encounter.

25. Explore the client's history of rejection or neglect, which may have led to an inability to form and/or maintain trusting, close, intimate relationships.

19. Identify triggers to sexual promiscuity and coping behaviors for each trigger. (26, 27)

20. List personal advantages of monogamous sexual intimacy. (28)

21. Develop and write out a continuing care program that includes the recovery group's meetings and any further therapy that is necessary for recovery. (29)

22. Complete a re-administration of objective tests of sexual promiscuity as a means of assessing treatment outcome. (30)

23. Complete a survey to assess the degree of satisfaction with treatment. (31)

___. _____
   _____
___. _____
   _____
___. _____
   _____

26. Assist the client in identifying thoughts and situations that trigger urges to act out sexually.

27. Develop with the client adaptive behaviors to cope with trigger situations.

28. Assist the client in identifying a list of personal advantages for him/her becoming monogamous in sexually intimate behavior (e.g., increased self-esteem, greater emotional intimacy, development of trust and respect from others, living within a spiritual value system, reduced health risk).

29. Help the client to develop an aftercare plan that includes attending recovery groups regularly, getting a sponsor, and any further therapy that is necessary to recover from sexual promiscuity and any other addictive behavior.

30. Assess the outcome of treatment by re-administering to the client objective tests of sexual promiscuity; evaluate the results and provide feedback to the client.

31. Administer a survey to assess the client's degree of satisfaction with treatment.

___. _____
   _____
___. _____
   _____
___. _____
   _____

DIAGNOSTIC SUGGESTIONS:

Axis I:	296.xx	Bipolar I Disorder
	296.89	Bipolar II Disorder
	302.2	Pedophilia
	312.8	Conduct Disorder
	309.3	Adjustment Disorder with Disturbance of Conduct
	312.30	Impulse-Control Disorder NOS
	_____	_____
	_____	_____
Axis II:	301.7	Antisocial Personality Disorder
	301.83	Borderline Personality Disorder
	301.81	Narcissistic Personality Disorder
	_____	_____
	_____	_____

SOCIAL ANXIETY/SKILLS DEFICIT*

BEHAVIORAL DEFINITIONS

1. Acknowledges never having learned social skills that would decrease anxiety and increase confidence.
2. Expresses excessive fear and worry about social circumstances that has no factual or logical basis.
3. Admits to constant worry about social interactions, which prevents feeling comfortable in group meetings.
4. Tends to feel blamed by others for the slightest imperfection or mistake.
5. Reports symptoms of autonomic hyperactivity in social situations (e.g., cardiac palpitations, shortness of breath, sweaty palms, dry mouth, trouble swallowing, nausea, diarrhea).
6. Demonstrates symptoms of motor tension (e.g., restlessness, tiredness, shakiness, muscle tension).
7. Reports symptoms of hypervigilance in social settings (e.g., feeling constantly on edge, difficulty concentrating, sleep problems, irritability).
8. Uses addictive behavior in an attempt to control anxiety symptoms.
9. Lacks the necessary social skills to initiate and maintain relationships.
10. Alienates self from others due to socially inappropriate behavior.

—. _____
_____
—. _____
_____
—. _____
_____

*Most of the content of this chapter (with minor revisions) is taken from R. R. Perkinson and A. E. Jongsma, Jr., *The Addiction Treatment Planner, 2nd Edition* (New York: Wiley, 2001). Copyright © 2001 by R. R. Perkinson and A. E. Jongsma, Jr., and from A. E. Jongsma, Jr., and L. M. Peterson, *The Complete Adult Psychotherapy Treatment Planner, 3rd Edition* (New York: Wiley, 2003). Copyright © 2003 by A. E. Jongsma, Jr. and L. M. Peterson. Reprinted with permission.

LONG-TERM GOALS

1. Interact socially without excessive anxiety.
2. Develop the social skills that are necessary to reduce excessive anxiety in social situations, and terminate reliance on addiction as a coping mechanism.
3. Maintain a program of recovery that is free from excessive social anxiety and addiction.
4. Decrease thoughts that trigger anxiety, and increase positive, self-enhancing self-talk.
5. Learn the relationship between anxiety and addiction.
6. Form relationships that will enhance a recovery support system.

—. _____
   _____
   _____
—. _____
   _____
   _____
—. _____
   _____

SHORT-TERM OBJECTIVES

1. Keep a daily journal of social anxiety rating, including the situations that cause anxious feelings and the negative thoughts that fueled social anxiety. (1)

2. Complete psychological testing or objective questionnaires for assessing social anxiety and social skills. (2)

THERAPEUTIC INTERVENTIONS

1. Assign the client to keep a daily record of social anxiety, including a description of each situation that caused anxious feelings, the rating of anxiety, using Subjective Units of Distress (SUDs), and thoughts that triggered the anxiety; process the journal material, help the client uncover the dysfunctional, distorted thoughts that fueled the social anxiety.

2. Administer to the client tests designed to assess social anxiety and social skills (e.g., Social Phobia and Anxiety Inventory [SPAI], Social Reticence Scale [SRS], Social Skills Inventory [SSI]); score and give feedback to the client.

3. Acknowledge the powerlessness and unmanageability that are caused by excessive social anxiety and addiction. (3, 4, 5)

3. Help the client to see how social anxiety and powerlessness over addiction have made his/her life unmanageable.

4. Teach the client about the relationship between social anxiety and addiction (i.e., how the substance was used to treat the anxious symptoms, and why more substance use became necessary).

5. Teach the client about the 12-step program concept of *insanity*, and help him/her to see how engaging in the same ineffective, self-defeating, and dysfunctional patterns of behavior in an attempt to overcome social anxiety and addiction is insane.

4. List specific worries, and use logic and reasoning to label these worries as irrational. (6, 7)

6. Assist the client in understanding the irrational nature of his/her thoughts, which underlies his/her social fears.

7. Help the client to identify and list his/her specific worries, and then facilitate his/her use of logic and reasoning to challenge the irrational thoughts that are associated with the fears.

5. Implement positive self-talk to replace distorted thoughts and beliefs and to reduce or eliminate social anxiety. (8, 9, 10)

8. Help the client to develop reality-based cognitive messages that can replace distorted thoughts and will increase self-confidence in coping with social fears and anxieties.

9. Reinforce the client's use of more realistic, positive messages to himself/herself in interpreting life events.

10. Assign the client to read *What to Say When You Talk to Yourself* by Helmstetter; process key ideas with the therapist.

6. List 10 positive, self-enhancing statements to be read several times per day, particularly when feeling anxious. (10, 11)

10. Assign the client to read *What to Say When You Talk to Yourself* by Helmstetter; process key ideas with the therapist.

11. Assist the client in developing a list of 10 self-affirming statements to read to himself/herself several times per day, particularly when feeling anxious.

7. Comply with a physician's evaluation to determine if psychopharmacological intervention is warranted, and take any medications as directed. (12, 13)

12. Physician to determine if psychopharmacological intervention is warranted, to order medication, titrate medication, and monitor for side effects.

13. Monitor the client for psychotropic medication prescription compliance, effectiveness, and side effects.

8. Report on instances when worries and anxieties were turned over to a higher power. (14, 15, 16)

14. Teach the client the benefits of turning his/her will and life over to the care of a higher power of his/her own understanding.

15. Using a Step Three exercise from a 12-step recovery program, teach the client how to turn problems, worries, and anxieties over to a higher power, and trust that the higher power is going to help him/her resolve the situation.

16. Review and reinforce the client's implementation of turning social anxiety over to a higher power.

9. Relate the fears that were learned in the family of origin, or other painful experiences, to current social anxiety level. (17, 18, 19, 20)

17. Probe the client's family-of-origin history for experiences in which social anxiety was learned; help him/her relate these past events to current thoughts, feelings, and behaviors.

18. Encourage and support the client in verbally expressing and clarifying his/her feelings that are associated with past rejection

experiences, harsh criticism, abandonment, or trauma.

19. Assign the client to read the books *Healing the Shame That Binds You* by Bradshaw and *Facing Shame* by Fossum and Mason; process key concepts with the therapist.

20. Ask the client to write an autobiography, detailing the exact nature of his/her painful experiences, as well as wrongs toward others; then, teach him/her how to begin to forgive others and himself/herself.

10. Develop a leisure program that will increase pleasurable activities and affirm self. (21)

21. Help the client to develop a plan of engaging in pleasurable leisure activities (e.g., clubs, hobbies, church, sporting activities, social activities, games) that will increase his/her enjoyment of life, affirm himself/herself, and reduce stress.

11. Practice relaxation techniques twice a day for 10 to 20 minutes. (22)

22. Use relaxation techniques (e.g., progressive relaxation, guided imagery, biofeedback) to teach the client how to relax completely; assign him/her to relax twice a day for 10 to 20 minutes.

12. Exercise at least three times a week at a training heart rate for at least 20 minutes. (23)

23. Using current physical fitness levels, increase the client's exercise by 10 percent a week, until he/she is exercising three times a week at a training heart rate for at least 20 minutes.

13. Write a specific plan to follow when anxious and tempted to engage in addictive behaviors to reduce stress. (8, 15, 22, 23, 24)

8. Help the client to develop reality-based cognitive messages that can replace distorted thoughts and will increase self-confidence in coping with social fears and anxieties.

15. Using a Step Three exercise from a 12-step recovery program, teach

the client how to turn problems, worries, and anxieties over to a higher power, and trust that the higher power is going to help him/her resolve the situation.

22. Use relaxation techniques (e.g., progressive relaxation, guided imagery, biofeedback) to teach the client how to relax completely; assign him/her to relax twice a day for 10 to 20 minutes.

23. Using current physical fitness levels, increase the client's exercise by 10 percent a week, until he/she is exercising three times a week at a training heart rate for at least 20 minutes.

24. Help the client to develop an alternative constructive plan of action (e.g., implement relaxation exercises, engage in physical exercise, call a sponsor, go to a meeting, call the counselor, talk to someone) when feeling anxious and/or craving substance use.

14. Increase the frequency of speaking up with confidence in social situations. (25, 26, 27)

25. Use role-playing and behavior rehearsal to teach assertiveness skills, to help the client to communicate thoughts, feelings, and needs more openly and directly.

26. Recommend that the client read books on overcoming social anxiety (e.g., *Intimate Connections* by Burns or *Shyness* by Zimbardo).

27. Teach the client the basics of good communication (e.g., eye contact, attentive active listening, asking questions to draw out the speaker, using "I" messages); refer him/her to a social skills training class, if indicated.

15. Identify and re-implement successful social skills from the past. (28, 29, 30)

28. Ask the client to list and process positive experiences from previous social experiences.

29. Utilize a brief, solution-oriented approach to identify a time when the client socialized with enjoyment and little anxiety, then create a situation that involves the same elements, and have the client use this social coping skill consistently in the following weeks.

30. Monitor the client's solution-oriented approach to his/her social anxiety; reinforce success and redirect for failure.

16. Initiate one social contact per day with a familiar person for increasing lengths of time. (31)

31. Assign the client to initiate one conversation daily with a familiar person, increasing time from 1 minute to 5 minutes per interaction; review and process the outcome.

17. Verbally report positive outcomes of participation in social and support groups. (32, 33, 34, 35)

32. Ask the client to attend and participate in available social and recreational activities within the treatment program and/or the community.

33. Refer the client to a self-help group (i.e., AA, NA, Emotions Anonymous, Recovery) and to self-disclose twice in each session; process the experience.

34. Instruct the client to attend a communication improvement seminar or a Dale Carnegie course.

35. Monitor, encourage, redirect, and give positive feedback to the client as he/she increases his/her interaction with others.

18. Initiate a social contact with a stranger. (36, 37)

36. Encourage and support the client in his/her effort to initiate and build social relationships.

19. Identify ways he/she is like other people, and therefore is acceptable to others. (38, 39)

37. Facilitate a role-play with the client around initiating a conversation with another person for the first time; process the experience.

38. Assign the client to read books on self-understanding (e.g., *Born To Win* by James and Jongeward, *Pulling Your Own Strings* by Dyer, or *I'm OK You're OK* by Harris and Harris) to help him/her see himself/herself more clearly and in a more hopeful light.

39. Assist the client in recognizing how he/she is like or similar to others.

20. Complete a re-administration of objective tests of progress in overcoming social skills deficits and/or social anxiety as a means of assessing treatment outcome. (40)

40. Assess the outcome of treatment by re-administering to the client objective tests of social skills and/or social anxiety (e.g., Liebowitz Social Anxiety Scale, Brief Social Phobia Scale); evaluate the results and provide feedback to the client.

21. Complete a survey to assess the degree of satisfaction with treatment. (41)

41. Administer a survey to assess the client's degree of satisfaction with treatment.

__. _____
   _____
__. _____
   _____
__. _____
   _____

__. _____
   _____
__. _____
   _____
__. _____
   _____

DIAGNOSTIC SUGGESTIONS:

Axis I:	300.23	Social Phobia
	300.4	Dysthymic Disorder
	309.21	Separation Anxiety Disorder
	292.89	Substance-Induced Anxiety Disorder

296.90	Mood Disorder NOS
300.01	Panic Disorder without Agoraphobia
300.21	Panic Disorder with Agoraphobia
300.02	Generalized Anxiety Disorder
309.24	Adjustment Disorder with Anxiety
309.28	Adjustment Disorder with Mixed Anxiety and Depressed Mood

_____   _____

_____   _____

Axis II:

301.0	Paranoid Personality Disorder
301.83	Borderline Personality Disorder
301.82	Avoidant Personality Disorder
301.6	Dependent Personality Disorder

_____   _____

_____   _____

SPIRITUAL CONFUSION

BEHAVIORAL DEFINITIONS

1. Verbalizes confusion about spiritual matters, leading to a negative attitude about recovery.
2. Upholds religious convictions that are negative toward addiction and toward a twelve-step program of recovery.
3. Fears that God is angry, preventing a connection with a higher power.
4. Refuses to seek conscious contact with God because of anger toward God.
5. Is actively involved in a religious system that is not supportive of a twelve-step recovery program.
6. Lacks understanding of the need for a higher power.
7. Maintains spiritual beliefs that are negative toward the existence of a higher power.
8. Anger at God leads to a rejection of any religious system or personal spiritual development.

—. _____

_____

—. _____

_____

—. _____

_____

LONG-TERM GOALS

1. Maintain a program of recovery, free of addiction and spiritual confusion.
2. Resolve spiritual conflicts, allowing for a meaningful relationship with a higher power.

3. Understand the relationship between spiritual confusion and addiction.
4. Accept that a higher power can assist in relieving addiction.
5. Develop a concept of a higher power that is loving and supportive to re-covery.
6. Learn the difference between religion and spirituality.

—. _____
   _____
   _____

—. _____
   _____
   _____

—. _____
   _____

SHORT-TERM OBJECTIVES

1. Describe the thoughts and feelings associated with the role of spirituality in personal life. (1)

2. Complete psychological testing or objective questionnaires for assessing spiritual confusion. (2)

3. Verbalize the powerlessness and unmanageability that result from spiritual confusion and addictive behavior. (3)

4. Verbalize an understanding of how spiritual confusion contributed to addictive behavior and how addiction led to spiritual confusion. (4, 5, 6)

THERAPEUTIC INTERVENTIONS

1. Explore the client's spiritual journey, religious training, thoughts, and feelings toward a higher power, and current spiritual practices.

2. Administer to the client psychological instruments designed to objectively assess spiritual confusion (e.g., Spiritual Well-Being Scale [SWBS]); give the client feedback regarding the results of the assessment.

3. Using a 12-step recovery program's Step One exercise, help the client to accept that he/she is powerless over spiritual confusion and addictive behavior, and that his/her life is unmanageable.

4. Probe the client's history of spiritual confusion, and show him/her how this confusion contributed to addiction and a negative attitude toward recovery.

5. Help the client to identify how addiction led to spiritual confusion.

5. Verbalize how spiritual confusion leads to a negative attitude toward working a 12-step program of recovery. (7)

6. Verbalize an understanding of the 12-step recovery program's concept of "God as we understand Him." (8)

7. Verbalize how many different religions and cultures can work in a 12-step program of recovery. (9)

8. Verbalize an understanding of a higher power's grace and willingness to forgive. (10, 11, 12)

9. List ways in which a higher power can assist in recovery from spiritual confusion and addiction. (13)

10. Verbalize an understanding of the concept of God's plan. (14)

6. Using a 12-step recovery program's Step Two exercise, help the client to see the *insanity* of his/her spiritual confusion and addictive behavior.

7. Show the client how negative attitudes toward spiritual matters make recovery difficult.

8. Teach the client about the 12-step recovery program's concept of "God as we understand Him," and how this relates to his/her spiritual confusion.

9. Teach the client how many different religions and cultures can implement a similar 12-step program of recovery.

10. Teach the client that the higher power will forgive him/her for the wrongs that he/she has committed.

11. Assign the client to read books on the process of forgiveness (e.g., *Forgive and Forget* by Smedes).

12. Assign the client to read *Addiction and Grace* by May; process key ideas.

13. Teach the client about the importance of a higher power in a 12-step program, and list many ways that a higher power can assist him/her (e.g., attend regular religious activities, speak weekly with a spiritual advisor, practice regular prayer and meditation).

14. Assign the client to read page 449 in the Alcoholics Anonymous *Big Book;* then, teach him/her how everything that happens in the world is a part of God's good plan.

11. Verbalize the need to begin a spiritual journey, as outlined in the 12 steps. (15, 16, 17)

15. Arrange for the client to meet a clergyperson who is familiar with 12-step recovery programs, and encourage the client to share his/her thoughts and feelings about a higher power.

16. Arrange for the client to meet with a contact person, or temporary sponsor, and discuss the 12-step recovery program, spiritual confusion, and addiction.

17. Assign the client to read "How It Works" in the Alcoholics Anonymous *Big Book* and to discuss the three pertinent ideas that are outlined at the end of the chapter: (1) "We were alcoholic and could not manage our own lives;" (2) "Probably no human power could have relieved our alcoholism;" and (3) "God could and would have if He were sought."

12. Make a written plan to continue a spiritual journey as outlined in the 12 steps. (18)

18. Using the 12 steps as a guide, help the client to make a written plan to continue his/her spiritual journey.

13. Write a letter to a higher power, sharing feelings and asking for specific needs in recovery. (19)

19. Assign the client to write a letter to a higher power, sharing how he/she thinks and feels and asking for what he/she wants to aid him/her in recovery; process the content of the letter.

14. Express a decision to turn own will and life over to a higher power, as it is understood. (20)

20. Using a 12-step recovery program's Step Three exercise, teach the client how to turn problems over to a higher power.

15. Practice prayer and meditation at least once a day. (21, 22, 23)

21. Assign the client to read Chapter 11 in AA's *Twelve Steps and Twelve Traditions*. Teach the client how to pray (talk to God) and meditate (listen for God); then, assign him/her to pray and meditate at least once each day.

22. Assign the client to keep a prayer journal, writing down his/her prayers and new insights gained about the higher power's will for his/her life.

23. Assign the client to ask God to come into his/her life each day and then ask, "God, what is the next step in my relationship with you?" Have the client write down each insight that he/she has gained from God, and share these with the primary therapist.

16. Develop a written personal recovery plan. (24)

24. Help the client to develop a personal recovery plan that includes regular attendance at recovery groups, getting a sponsor, helping others in recovery, and any other treatment that is necessary to recover from spiritual confusion and addiction.

17. Family members verbalize what each can do to assist the client in recovery. (25, 26)

25. Discuss with family members the connection between spiritual confusion and addictive behavior; outline the steps the client must take to successfully recover.

26. In a family session, review what each member can do to assist the client in recovery.

18. Complete a re-administration of objective tests of spiritual confusion as a means of assessing treatment outcome. (27)

27. Assess the outcome of treatment by re-administering to the client objective tests of spiritual confusion; evaluate the results and provide feedback to the client.

19. Complete a survey to assess the degree of satisfaction with treatment. (28)

28. Administer a survey to assess the client's degree of satisfaction with treatment.

__. _____

_____

__. _____

_____

—. _____   —. _____

_____   _____

—. _____   —. _____

_____   _____

DIAGNOSTIC SUGGESTIONS:

Axis I: V62.89   Religious or Spiritual Problem

V62.4   Acculturation Problem

_____   _____

_____   _____

SUBSTANCE ABUSE/DEPENDENCE

BEHAVIORAL DEFINITIONS

1. Demonstrates a maladaptive pattern of substance use, manifested by increased tolerance and withdrawal.
2. Fails to stop or cut down use of mood-altering drug once started, despite the verbalized desire to do so and the negative consequences continued use brings.
3. Presents with blood work (e.g., elevated liver enzymes, electrolyte imbalance) and physical indicators (e.g., stomach pain, high blood pressure, malnutrition) that reflect the results of a pattern of heavy substance use.
4. Denies that chemical dependence is a problem, despite feedback from significant others that the use of the substance is negatively affecting them and others.
5. Experiences frequent blackouts when using.
6. Continues substance use despite knowledge of experiencing persistent physical, legal, financial, vocational, social, and/or relationship problems that are directly caused by the use of the substance.
7. Demonstrates increased tolerance for the drug, as there is the need to use more to become intoxicated or to recall the desired effect.
8. Exhibits physical withdrawal symptoms (e.g., shaking, seizures, nausea, headaches, sweating, anxiety, insomnia, depression) when going without the substance for any length of time.
9. Has a history of arrests for addiction-related offenses (e.g., driving under the influence [DUI], minor in possession [MIP], assault, possession/ delivery of a controlled substance, shoplifting, breaking and entering [B&E]).
10. Reports suspension of important social, recreational, or occupational activities because they interfere with using.

—. _____
_____

—. _____
_____

—. _____

_____

LONG-TERM GOALS

1. Accept the powerlessness and unmanageability over mood-altering substances, and participate in a recovery-based program.
2. Establish a sustained recovery, free from the use of all mood-altering substances.
3. Establish and maintain total abstinence, while increasing knowledge of the disease and the process of recovery.
4. Acquire the necessary 12-step skills to maintain long-term sobriety from all mood-altering substances, and live a life free of substance abuse.
5. Improve quality of life by maintaining an ongoing abstinence from all mood-altering chemicals.

—. _____

_____

—. _____

_____

—. _____

_____

SHORT-TERM OBJECTIVES

1. Provide honest and complete information for a chemical dependence biopsychosocial history. (1)

2. Complete psychological testing or objective questionnaires for assessing substance abuse/dependence. (2)

THERAPEUTIC INTERVENTIONS

1. Complete a thorough family and personal biopsychosocial history that focuses on addiction.

2. Administer to the client psychological instruments designed to objectively assess substance abuse/dependence (e.g., Substance Abuse Subtle Screening Inventory-3 [SASSI-3], Addiction Severity Index [ASI], Substance Use Disorders Diagnostic Schedule-IV [SUDDS-IV]); give the client feedback regarding the results of the assessment.

3. Cooperate with a medical assessment and an evaluation of the necessity for pharmacological intervention. (3, 4)

3. Refer the client to a physician to perform a physical exam and write treatment orders including, if necessary, prescription of medications.

4. Ask the physician to monitor the effectiveness and side effects of medication, titrating as necessary.

4. Take prescribed medications as directed by the physician, and report as to compliance, effectiveness, and side effects. (5, 6)

5. Direct the staff to administer the client's prescription medications.

6. Monitor the client's prescribed psychotropic medications for compliance, effectiveness, and side effects.

5. Report acute withdrawal symptoms. (7)

7. Assess and monitor the client's condition during withdrawal, using a standardized procedure (e.g., Clinical Institute of Withdrawal Scale) as needed.

6. Attend didactic sessions and read assigned material in order to increase knowledge of addiction and of the process of recovery. (8, 9, 10)

8. Assign the client to attend a chemical dependence didactic series to increase his/her knowledge of the patterns and effects of chemical dependence; ask him/her to identify and process several key points attained from each didactic.

9. Ask the client to read substance abuse literature (e.g., *Cannabis and Cognitive Functioning* by Solowij, *Cocaine Addiction* by Washton, or *Alcohol Abuse* by Sales); process with the therapist five key points that were gained from the reading.

10. Require the client to read pages 1 to 52 in the Alcoholics Anonymous *Big Book* and to gather five key points from it to process with the therapist.

7. Attend group therapy sessions focused on addiction. (11, 12)

11. Assign the client to attend group therapy that is focused on addiction issues.

12. Direct group therapy that facilitates the sharing of causes for, consequences of, feelings about, and alternatives to addiction.

8. Verbally admit to powerlessness over mood-altering substances. (13)

13. Assign the client to complete a 12-step recovery program's Step One paper, admitting to powerlessness over mood-altering chemicals, and present it in group or individual therapy for feedback.

9. Verbalize an understanding of the problems that are caused by the use of mood-altering substances and, therefore, the need to stay in treatment. (14, 15)

14. Ask the client to make a list of the ways in which chemical abuse has negatively impacted his/her life; process the list with the therapist or group.

15. Assist the client in listing reasons why he/she should stay in chemical dependence treatment and be abstinent from addiction.

10. Verbalize a recognition that mood-altering chemicals were used as the primary coping mechanism to escape from stress or pain, and that that resulted in negative consequences. (16)

16. Explore with the client how addiction was used to escape from stress, physical and emotional pain, and boredom; confront the negative consequences of this pattern.

11. List the negative emotions that were caused by or exacerbated by substance dependence. (17)

17. Probe the client's sense of shame, guilt, and low self-worth that have resulted from addictive behavior and its consequences.

12. Develop a list of the social, emotional, and family factors that contributed to substance dependence. (1, 18)

1. Complete a thorough family and personal biopsychosocial history that focuses on addiction.

18. Using the biopsychosocial history, assist the client in understanding the familial, emotional, and social factors that contributed to the development of chemical dependence.

13. List lies that were used to hide substance dependence. (19)

19. Help the client to see the dishonesty that goes along with addiction; ask him/her to list lies

14. Verbalize the ways in which a higher power can assist in recovery. (20)

15. Practice healthy communication skills to reduce stress and to increase positive social interaction. (21)

16. Practice problem-solving skills. (22)

17. List the reasons for substance abuse, and list the ways in which the same things can be attained in an adaptive manner. (23)

18. Develop a written leisure skills program to decrease stress and improve health. (24)

19. Practice stress management skills to attain a feeling of relaxation and comfort. (25)

20. Complete a 12-step recovery program's Step Four inventory, and share with a clergyperson or someone else in the program. (26)

21. Make a written plan to cope with each high-risk or relapse

told to hide substance abuse; teach the client why honesty is essential to recovery.

20. Teach the client about the 12-step recovery program's concept of a higher power, and how this can assist in recovery (e.g., attending religious activities, practicing regular prayer and meditation).

21. Teach the client healthy communication skills (e.g., using "I" messages, reflecting, active listening, empathy, being reinforcing, sharing).

22. Using modeling, role-playing, and behavior rehearsal, teach the client how to solve problems in an organized fashion (i.e., write the problem, think accurately, list the options of action, evaluate alternatives, act, monitor results).

23. Assist the client in clarifying why he/she was using substances; teach him/her how to get good things out of life without mood-altering substances.

24. Assign the client to list the pleasurable activities that he/she plans to pursue in recovery.

25. Using progressive relaxation or biofeedback, teach the client how to relax; assign him/her to relax twice a day for 10 to 20 minutes.

26. Assign the client to complete a 12-step recovery program's Step Four inventory; make arrangements for him/her to share this with a clergyperson or someone else in recovery.

16. Explore with the client how addiction was used to escape from

trigger situation.
(16, 23, 27, 28)

stress, physical and emotional pain, and boredom; confront the negative consequences of this pattern.

23. Assist the client in clarifying why he/she was using substances; teach him/her how to get good things out of life without mood-altering substances.

27. Using a 12-step recovery program's relapse prevention exercise, help the client uncover his/her triggers for relapse.

28. Teach the client about high-risk situations (e.g., negative emotions, social pressure, interpersonal conflict, positive emotions, test of personal control); assist him/her in making a written plan to cope with each high-risk situation.

22. Practice saying no to alcohol and drugs. (29)

29. Using modeling, role-playing, and behavior rehearsal, teach the client how to say no to alcohol and drugs; practice saying no in the client's high-risk situations.

23. Write a personal recovery plan that includes attending recovery group meetings regularly, getting a sponsor, participating in aftercare, and helping others in recovery. (30)

30. Help the client to develop a personal recovery plan that includes attending recovery group meetings regularly, getting a sponsor, aftercare, and helping others in recovery.

24. Take a personal inventory at the end of each day, listing the problems in recovery, the plans to address these problems, and things for which to be grateful for that day. (31)

31. Encourage the client to take a personal inventory each night, listing the problems that he/she had that day, making a plan to deal with any problems, and then listing five things for which he/she was grateful that day.

25. Family members verbalize an understanding of their role in the disease and the process of recovery. (32, 33, 34, 35)

32. Teach the family members the family aspects of the addiction process and the recovery process.

26. Family members decrease the frequency of enabling behaviors. (36, 37)

27. Complete a re-administration of objective tests of substance abuse/dependence as a means of assessing treatment outcome. (38)

28. Complete a survey to assess the degree of satisfaction with treatment. (39)

__. _____

   _____

__. _____

   _____

__. _____

   _____

33. Direct the client's family to attend Alanon, Naranon, or Tough Love meetings.

34. Ask the client's family to attend the family education component of the treatment program.

35. Assign appropriate reading that will increase the family members' knowledge of the disease and recovery process (e.g., *Bradshaw on the Family* by Bradshaw, *Adult Children of Alcoholics* by Woititz, or *It Will Never Happen to Me* by Black).

36. Educate the client's family in the dynamics of enabling and of tough love; monitor the family for enabling behaviors, and redirect them in the family sessions if appropriate.

37. Help the client to list three things that each family member can do to assist him/her in recovery.

38. Assess the outcome of treatment by re-administering to the client objective tests of substance abuse/dependence; evaluate the results and provide feedback to the client.

39. Administer a survey to assess the client's degree of satisfaction with treatment.

__. _____

   _____

__. _____

   _____

__. _____

   _____

DIAGNOSTIC SUGGESTIONS:

Axis I:		
	305.60	Cocaine Abuse
	305.30	Hallucinogen Abuse
	305.90	Inhalant Abuse
	305.50	Opioid Abuse
	305.90	Phencyclidine Abuse
	305.40	Sedative, Hypnotic, or Anxiolytic Abuse
	303.90	Alcohol Dependence
	305.20	Cannabis Abuse
	305.70	Amphetamine Abuse
	305.00	Alcohol Abuse
	304.40	Amphetamine Dependence
	304.30	Cannabis Dependence
	304.20	Cocaine Dependence
	304.50	Hallucinogen Dependence
	304.60	Inhalant Dependence
	304.00	Opioid Dependence
	304.90	Phencyclidine Dependence
	304.10	Sedative, Hypnotic, or Anxiolytic Dependence
	304.80	Polysubstance Dependence

_____   _____

_____   _____

SUBSTANCE-INDUCED DISORDERS

BEHAVIORAL DEFINITIONS

1. Experiences memory impairment (amnestic disorder) that persists beyond expected period of substance intoxication or withdrawal effects.
2. Experiences memory impairment and cognitive disturbance (dementia) that persist beyond expected period of substance intoxication or withdrawal effects.
3. Lacks clear awareness of the environment, deficient in ability to focus attention, has memory dysfunction, language and/or perceptual disturbance (delirium) that developed during or shortly after substance intoxication or withdrawal.
4. Experiences hallucinations or delusions that persist beyond expected period of substance intoxication or withdrawal effects.
5. Exhibits depressed mood that developed during or shortly after substance intoxication or withdrawal.
6. Exhibits markedly expansive mood that developed during or shortly after substance intoxication or withdrawal.
7. Reports prominent anxiety, panic attacks, or obsessions that developed during or shortly after substance intoxication or withdrawal.
8. Reports sleep disturbance that developed during or shortly after substance intoxication or withdrawal.
9. Presents with sexual dysfunction that developed during or shortly after substance intoxication or withdrawal.

—. _____
_____

—. _____
_____

—. _____
_____

LONG-TERM GOALS

1. Learn the importance of working a twelve-step program, and maintain a program of recovery from addiction and substance-induced disorders.
2. Restore normal sleep pattern, improve long- and short-term memory, and maintain abstinence from addiction.
3. Recover clear memory and an awareness of environment, realistic perceptions, coherent communication, focused attention, and abstain from addiction.
4. Reduce anxiety symptoms significantly, and abstain from addictive behavior.
5. Expansive mood returns to normal level, depressed mood elevated to normal functioning, and abstinence from addiction is maintained.
6. Participate in medical management of substance-induced disorder and addiction.

—. _____
   _____
—. _____
   _____
—. _____
   _____

SHORT-TERM OBJECTIVES

1. Verbalize an understanding that the signs and symptoms of the substance- induced disorder are caused by chemical dependence. (1, 2, 3)

THERAPEUTIC INTERVENTIONS

1. Welcome the client to treatment and explain that he/she is in a safe place; encourage him/her to stay in treatment long enough to begin recovery.

2. Gather information regarding the client's recent substance abuse behavior and history of chemical dependence.

3. Teach the client about his/her substance-induced disorder, and directly relate signs and symptoms to chemical abuse; indicate that the symptoms will ameliorate if the client remains abstinent.

2. Complete psychological testing or objective questionnaires for assessing substance-induced disorders. (4)

4. Administer to the client psychological instruments designed to objectively assess substance-induced disorders (e.g., Beck Depression Inventory [BDI], Beck Anxiety Inventory [BAI], Clinical Institute Withdrawal Scale [CIWS], Narcotics Withdrawal Scale [NWS], Mental Status Examination, Cognitive Screening Capacity Examination, etc.); give the client feedback regarding the results of the assessment.

3. Report to the staff any thoughts of causing harm to self or others. (5)

5. Assess the client's potential for harm to self or others, and take precautionary steps if needed; encourage reporting to the staff any future thoughts of causing harm to self or others.

4. Verbalize feelings that surround substance-induced disorder and addiction. (6)

6. Encourage the client to share the feelings that surround substance-induced disorder and addiction.

5. Submit to a physician's physical examination to assess bodily functions and the need for psychotropic medications. (7)

7. Refer the client to a physician to examine the client, write treatment orders as indicated, titrate medications, and monitor for effectiveness and side effects.

6. Take prescribed medications as directed by the physician, and report symptoms and side effects to the medical staff. (8)

8. Direct the staff to carry out orders as directed by the physician and to monitor the client's symptoms and the effectiveness and side effects of the prescribed medication.

7. Intake fluids and nourishment as indicated by the medical staff. (9)

9. Encourage the client to take fluids and nourishment as ordered by the physician.

8. Stay with a staff member during severe symptoms of substance-induced disorder, intoxication, or withdrawal. (10)

10. Assign a staff member to stay with the client during severe substance-induced disorder, intoxication, or withdrawal.

9. Reduce environmental stimulation to decrease excessive

11. Adjust the client's environment until there is minimal stimulation

anxiety, perceptual disturbances, and irritability. (11)

10. Talk with a treatment peer that
is further along in the program,
and discuss plans for recovery.
(12)

11. Verbalize the need for further treatment and develop
a written plan to address
substance-induced disorder
and addiction. (13, 14)

12. Family members verbalize an
understanding of the connection between substance-induced
disorder and addiction. (15, 16)

13. Complete a re-administration
of objective tests of substance-
induced disorders as a means
of assessing treatment outcome. (17)

14. Complete a survey to assess
the degree of satisfaction with
treatment. (18)

___. _____
_____

___. _____
_____

___. _____
_____

that might exacerbate excessive
anxiety, perceptual disturbances,
and irritability.

12. Ask treatment peers to encourage
the client during the early stages
of recovery.

13. Teach the client about twelve-step
recovery, and encourage him/her
to stay in treatment.

14. Help the client develop a written
plan to treat his/her substance-
induced disorder and addiction.

15. In a family session, explain the
connection between substance-
induced disorder and addictive
behavior.

16. Help the client to list three things
that each family member can do
to assist him/her in recovery.

17. Assess the outcome of treatment
by re-administering to the client
objective tests of substance-
induced disorder; evaluate the
results and provide feedback to
the client.

18. Administer a survey to assess the
client's degree of satisfaction with
treatment.

___. _____
_____

___. _____
_____

___. _____
_____

DIAGNOSTIC SUGGESTIONS:

Axis I:		
	291.0	Alcohol Intoxication Delirium
	291.0	Alcohol Withdrawal Delirium
	291.2	Alcohol-Induced Persisting Dementia
	291.1	Alcohol-Induced Persisting Amnestic Disorder
	291.5	Alcohol-Induced Psychotic Disorder, with Delusions
	291.3	Alcohol-Induced Psychotic Disorder, with Hallucinations
	291.89	Alcohol-Induced Mood Disorder
	291.89	Alcohol-Induced Anxiety Disorder
	291.8	Alcohol-Induced Sexual Dysfunction
	291.8	Alcohol-Induced Sleep Disorder

_____   _____

_____   _____

SUBSTANCE INTOXICATION/ WITHDRAWAL

BEHAVIORAL DEFINITIONS

1. Demonstrates cognitive, behavioral, or emotional changes (e.g., alcohol on breath, belligerence, mood lability, cognitive impairment, impaired judgment, slurred speech, ataxia) shortly after ingestion or exposure to a substance.
2. Presents with abnormal autonomic reactivity (e.g., elevated or decreased vital signs, tachycardia, dilated or constricted pupils, diaphoresis, flushed face) subsequent to the introduction of a mood-altering substance into the body.
3. Admits to recently abusing a mood-altering chemical.
4. Presents with urine, blood screen, or breathalyzer results that indicate recent substance use.
5. Exhibits psychological symptoms caused by substance withdrawal (e.g., irritability, anxiety, anger, emotional lability, depression, hallucinations, delusions).
6. Reports that intoxication or withdrawal symptoms cause significant impairment in work, school, or play.
7. Experiences a preoccupation with strong cravings, leaving treatment and using mood-altering chemicals.

—. _____

_____

—. _____

_____

—. _____

_____

LONG-TERM GOALS

1. Stabilize condition medically, behaviorally, emotionally, and cognitively, and return to functioning within normal parameters.
2. Recover from substance intoxication/withdrawal, and participate in a chemical dependency assessment.
3. Understand the severity of and reasons for the substance use, and enter a program of recovery.
4. Comply with assessments of substance intoxication and withdrawal.
5. Enter a program of recovery necessary to bring addiction under control.
6. Understand the extent of the danger to self and others when intoxicated.

—. _____

_____

—. _____

_____

—. _____

_____

SHORT-TERM OBJECTIVES

1. Verbalize an acceptance of the need to be in a safe place to recover from substance intoxication/withdrawal. (1, 2)

2. Complete psychological testing or objective questionnaires for assessing intoxication/withdrawal. (3)

3. Verbalize an agreement to cooperate with the medical

THERAPEUTIC INTERVENTIONS

1. Welcome the client to the treatment setting; explain substance intoxication and the procedures that will be used to arrest symptoms.

2. Teach the client the importance of staying in treatment to recover from substance intoxication and possible withdrawal.

3. Administer to the client psychological instruments designed to objectively assess substance intoxication/withdrawal (e.g., Clinical Institute of Withdrawal Scale, Narcotic Withdrawal Scale); give the client feedback regarding the results of the assessment.

4. Inform the client of what he/she can expect during intoxication

management of substance
intoxication/withdrawal. (4)

4. Sign a release of information
to allow significant others to be
informed about admission and
condition. (5)

5. Cooperate with a physician
evaluation and take all medications as prescribed. (6)

6. Report as to medication compliance, effectiveness, and side
effects. (7, 8)

7. Provide information for a
biopsychosocial assessment of
the extent of addiction/depen-
dence. (9)

8. Agree to stay with a staff member or treatment buddy during
severe intoxication/withdrawal.
(10)

9. Report any change in symptoms of intoxication/
withdrawal to the medical staff.
(3, 11)

and withdrawal, and encourage
him/her to cooperate with medical
management; ask him/her to sign
a consent-to-treat form.

5. Encourage the client to sign a
release of information; contact
significant others to gain support
for the client's admission to treatment.

6. Refer the client to a physician
to examine him/her, educate
about substance intoxication and
withdrawal, order medications as
appropriate, titrate medications,
and monitor for effectiveness and
side effects.

7. Direct the medical staff to carry
out the orders of the physician
and to administer medications as
directed.

8. Monitor the client's medications
for compliance, effectiveness, and
side effects.

9. Complete a biopsychosocial assessment to determine the extent
of the client's addiction and the
need for treatment.

10. Assign a staff member to remain
with the client until he/she is
through intoxication and withdrawal.

3. Administer to the client psychological instruments designed to
objectively assess substance intox-
ication/withdrawal (e.g., Clinical
Institute of Withdrawal Scale,
Narcotic Withdrawal Scale); give
the client feedback regarding the
results of the assessment.

11. Teach the client what signs and
symptoms he/she may experience

during substance intoxication and/or withdrawal; encourage him/her to report any significant change in symptoms to the medical staff.

10. Blood work shows no presence of mood-altering substances. (12)

11. Vital signs stabilized within normal parameters. (13)

12. Demonstrate that cognitive, behavioral, and emotional functioning have returned to preintoxication status. (3, 14)

12. Monitor the client's status via blood tests, and report findings in the clinical chart.

13. Monitor the client's vital signs and document the findings in his/her chart.

3. Administer to the client psychological instruments designed to objectively assess substance intoxication/withdrawal (e.g., Clinical Institute of Withdrawal Scale, Narcotic Withdrawal Scale); give the client feedback regarding the results of the assessment.

14. Evaluate the client's cognitive, behavioral, and emotional status as detoxification progresses, reporting the results on his/her chart.

13. Share the feelings that surround admission for substance intoxication/withdrawal. (9, 15, 16, 17)

9. Complete a biopsychosocial assessment to determine the extent of the client's addiction and the need for treatment.

15. Probe the client's feelings that surround his/her substance intoxication and admission for addiction treatment.

16. Teach the client that substance withdrawal means substance dependence; help him/her to make plans for treatment and recovery.

17. Share the results of a chemical dependence assessment, and discuss options for the treatment of addiction/dependence.

14. Verbalize thoughts of causing harm to self or others. (18, 19)

18. Assess danger to the client or others; encourage him/her to report

15. Learn and cooperate with the rules of the treatment program. (20)

16. In a family session, discuss the connection between withdrawal symptoms and addiction. (21)

17. Read letters of support from family members. (22)

18. Complete a re-administration of objective tests of substance intoxication/withdrawal as a means of assessing treatment outcome. (23)

19. Complete a survey to assess the degree of client's satisfaction with treatment. (24)

18. any thoughts of causing harm to himself/herself or others.

19. Help the client to reduce environmental stimulation to a level that will not exacerbate symptoms and not increase agitation.

20. Teach the client the rules of the treatment program; encourage him/her to follow the rules while in treatment.

21. In a family session, discuss withdrawal symptoms and their connection with addiction.

22. Encourage the family members to write letters of support to the client; have him/her read the letters.

23. Assess the outcome of treatment by re-administering to the client objective tests of substance intoxication/withdrawal; evaluate the results and provide feedback to the client.

24. Administer a survey to assess the client's degree of satisfaction with treatment.

__. _____
   _____

__. _____
   _____

__. _____
   _____

__. _____
   _____

__. _____
   _____

__. _____
   _____

DIAGNOSTIC SUGGESTIONS:

Axis I:	303.00	Alcohol Intoxication
	292.89	Amphetamine Intoxication
	305.90	Caffeine Intoxication
	292.89	Cannabis Intoxication

292.89	Cocaine Intoxication
292.89	Hallucinogen Intoxication
292.89	Opioid Intoxication
292.89	Phencyclidine Intoxication
292.89	Sedative, Hypnotic, or Anxiolytic Intoxication
291.81	Alcohol Withdrawal
292.0	Amphetamine Withdrawal
292.0	Cocaine Withdrawal
292.0	Opioid Withdrawal
292.0	Sedative, Hypnotic, or Anxiolytic Withdrawal
292.81	Other (or unknown) Substance Intoxication
292.0	Other (or unknown) Substance Withdrawal

_____   _____

_____   _____

SUICIDAL IDEATION

BEHAVIORAL DEFINITIONS

1. Reports recurrent thoughts of and preoccupation with death.
2. Reports recurrent or ongoing suicidal ideation without any plans.
3. Expresses ongoing suicidal ideation with a specific plan.
4. Presents with chemical dependency or addiction that exacerbates depression, hopelessness, and suicidal ideation.
5. Reports losses due to addiction (e.g., financial, familial, vocational), which leave the client feeling suicidal and hopeless about his/her life.
6. Verbalizes belief that everyone would be better of if he/she was dead.
7. Has a history of suicide attempts.
8. Verbalizes profound feelings of helplessness, hopelessness, and worthlessness.
9. Reports the loss of a significant other to suicide or death, and has recurrent fantasies about joining the other person.
10. Expresses a bleak, hopeless attitude regarding life, coupled with recent losses that support this belief (e.g., divorce, death of spouse, illness, loss of job).

—. _____
   _____
   _____
—. _____
   _____
   _____
—. _____
   _____

LONG-TERM GOALS

1. Resolve preoccupation with death, find new hope, and enter a program of recovery, free of addiction and suicidal ideation.

2. Terminate all suicidal urges, express hope for the future, and remain abstinent from all mood-altering substances.
3. Placement at the level of care necessary to protect the client from his/her suicidal impulses.
4. Understand the relationship between suicidal ideation and addiction.
5. Develop a sense of worth to other addicts and family members.

—. _____

_____

—. _____

_____

—. _____

_____

SHORT-TERM OBJECTIVES

1. Verbalize specific suicidal thoughts, feelings, plans, and actions. (1, 2)

2. Complete psychological testing or objective questionnaires for assessing suicidal ideation. (3)

3. Sign a no-self-harm contract and agree to contact a staff member if feeling suicidal. (4)

THERAPEUTIC INTERVENTIONS

1. Assess the dangerousness of the suicidal ideation by asking the client to share suicidal feelings, thoughts, plans, and behaviors.

2. Explore the client's reasons for suicidal ideation: feelings of helplessness, hopelessness, and worthlessness.

3. Administer to the client psychological instruments designed to objectively assess suicidal ideation (e.g., Beck Depression Inventory II [BDI-II], Beck Scale for Suicide Ideation [BSS]); give the client feedback regarding the results of the assessment.

4. Have the client sign a no-self-harm contract that states that he/she will do nothing to harm himself/herself while in treatment, and that he/she will contact a staff member if feeling suicidal.

4. Agree to the level of care that is necessary to protect self from suicidal impulses. (5, 6)

5. Discuss the levels of care that are available (e.g., locked room, staying close by a staff member, transfer to a more intensive level of care); admit the client to the level of care that will be necessary to protect him/her from suicidal impulses.

6. Assign a staff member to stay with the client until his/her suicidal threat is resolved.

5. Verbalize an understanding of how suicide risk is magnified by addiction. (7)

7. Assist the client in understanding how feelings of shame, loss, and hopelessness are exacerbated by addictive behavior.

6. Identify the losses sustained because of addiction. (8)

8. Review the losses (e.g., marital, familial, social, legal, financial, health, occupational) that have resulted from addictive behavior and have led to suicidal hopelessness.

7. Verbalize feeling a sense of importance to family members and other addicts in recovery. (9, 10)

9. Help the client to see the meaning behind the 12-step recovery program's saying, "What we cannot do alone, we can do together;" help the client to see that other addicts need his/her support in recovery.

10. Review the client's role of importance to family and friends; confront minimization or discounting.

8. Meet the physician for an assessment for the need for psychotropic medication. (11)

11. Refer the client to a physician to examine him/her, discuss suicidal ideation and addiction, order medications as indicated, titrate medications, and monitor for side effects.

9. Take all medications as directed. (12, 13)

12. Direct the staff to administer the client's prescribed medications.

13. Monitor the client's medication for compliance, effectiveness, and side effects.

10. Keep a record of self-defeating thoughts, and replace each dysfunctional thought with positive, self-enhancing self-talk. (14, 15)

14. Assist the client in developing an awareness of his/her cognitive messages that reinforce hopelessness and helplessness; assign him/her to keep a daily record of self-defeating thoughts (e.g., thoughts of hopelessness, helplessness, worthlessness, catastrophizing, negatively predicting the future).

15. Challenge each of the client's self-defeating thoughts for accuracy; replace each dysfunctional thought with a thought that is positive and self-enhancing.

11. List the reasons for new hope for the future. (16, 17, 18)

16. Provide the client with reasons for new hope in recovery (e.g., being in treatment offers hope, working with trained professionals who can act as an advocate, other addicts can encourage him/her, staff members are supportive).

17. Encourage the client regarding the excellent chances for recovery from addiction and depression if he/she works the 12-step program.

18. Assign the client to read "the promises" on pages 83 and 84 of the Alcoholics Anonymous (AA) *Big Book;* encourage him/her to verbalize hope for the future.

12. List reasons for wanting to live. (10, 19, 20)

10. Review the client's role of importance to family and friends; confront minimization or discounting.

19. Help the client to list reasons to live (e.g., positive people, places, things that are a part of his/her life).

20. Assign the client to write a list of the positive people, places, and things in his/her life.

13. Verbalize new hope for resolving interpersonal conflicts because of being in addiction treatment. (21, 22)

21. Help the client to see the new hope that addiction treatment brings to the resolution of interpersonal conflicts.

22. Meet with the client and a significant other with whom there is conflict, to begin a process of conflict resolution.

14. Verbalize an understanding of the 12-step *attitude of gratitude*; list five things to be grateful for each day. (23)

23. Teach the client about the 12-step recovery program's concept of the *attitude of gratitude*; assign him/her to list five things for which he/she is grateful for each day.

15. Verbalize coping strategies that will elevate depressed mood. (24)

24. Assist the client in developing coping strategies for suicidal ideation (e.g., more physical exercise, less internal focus, increased social involvement, more expression of feelings).

16. Encourage someone else in recovery at least once a day. (18, 25)

18. Assign the client to read "the promises" on pages 83 and 84 of the Alcoholics Anonymous *Big Book;* encourage him/her to verbalize hope for the future.

25. Assign the client to encourage someone in treatment each day; record each event and discuss with the therapist.

17. Verbalize an understanding of the 12-step program's concept of a higher power, and how this can be used to recover from suicidal ideation and addictive behavior. (26, 27)

26. Teach the client about the 12-step recovery program's concept of a higher power; encourage the client to ask a higher power for direction each day.

27. Assign the client to read Chapter 11 in the *Twelve Steps and Twelve Traditions* (AA); encourage him/her to pray and meditate at least once each day.

18. List three things that each family member can do to assist the client in recovery. (28, 29)

28. In a family session, have the client discuss the connection between suicidal ideation and addiction.

19. Complete a re-administration of objective tests of suicidal ideation as a means of assessing treatment outcome. (30)

20. Complete a survey to assess the degree of satisfaction with treatment. (31)

—. _____
   _____

—. _____
   _____

—. _____
   _____

29. Help the client to list three things that each family member can do to assist him/her in recovery; assign the client to share these with the family members and report back to the therapist.

30. Assess the outcome of treatment by re-administering to the client objective tests of suicidal ideation; evaluate the results and provide feedback to the client.

31. Administer a survey to assess the client's degree of satisfaction with treatment.

—. _____
   _____

—. _____
   _____

—. _____
   _____

DIAGNOSTIC SUGGESTIONS:

Axis I:	296.xx	Major Depressive Disorder
	300.4	Dysthymic Disorder
	296.xx	Bipolar I Disorder
	296.89	Bipolar II Disorder
	309.xx	Adjustment Disorder
	291.89	Alcohol-Induced Mood Disorder
	292.84	Amphetamine-Induced Mood Disorder
	292.84	Cocaine-Induced Mood Disorder
	292.84	Inhalant-Induced Mood Disorder
	292.84	Opioid-Induced Mood Disorder
	_____	_____
	_____	_____
Axis II:	301.83	Borderline Personality Disorder
	_____	_____
	_____	_____

TREATMENT RESISTANCE

BEHAVIORAL DEFINITIONS

1. Verbalizes severe denial of addiction in spite of strong evidence of loss of control, withdrawal symptoms, and many negative consequences of addiction.
2. Substitutes a secondary problem as the focus of concern rather than admit that addiction is the primary problem.
3. Demonstrates anger toward family members, court, or employer for giving an ultimatum for treatment.
4. Refuses to cooperate with the staff and remains a constant risk of leaving treatment Against Medical Advice.
5. Is verbally abusive toward others, irritable, restless, and angry.
6. Demonstrates dishonesty to self and others rather than to the facts regarding own addiction.
7. Constantly uses the telephone to make demands of a friend or family member to come and take him/her out of treatment.
8. Refuses to talk to or bond with treatment peers.

—. _____
   _____
   _____
—. _____
   _____
   _____
—. _____
   _____

LONG-TERM GOALS

1. Accept the truth about the problems that addiction has caused, and enter a program of recovery.
2. Accept the powerlessness and unmanageability that addiction has brought to life, and actively engage in the treatment process.

3. Learn the facts about addiction, and make a logical decision about the treatment necessary to arrest it.
4. Cooperate with addiction assessments and accept the diagnosis and treatment plan.
5. Resolve anger at others and accept responsibility for the problems caused by addiction and for the need for treatment.
6. Cooperate with medical management for withdrawal, and agree to enter a 12-step program of recovery.

—. _____
_____
—. _____
_____
—. _____
_____

SHORT-TERM OBJECTIVES

1. Share the feelings that surround admission to treatment. (1, 2)

2. Cooperate with a biopsychosocial assessment and accept the treatment recommendations. (3)

3. Complete psychological testing or objective questionnaires for assessing treatment resistance. (4)

THERAPEUTIC INTERVENTIONS

1. Probe the reasons why the client is resisting treatment; check for the accuracy of his/her beliefs about addiction.

2. Encourage the client to share the fear, sadness, shame, and anger that he/she feels about coming for treatment.

3. Conduct a biopsychosocial assessment, and collect laboratory results and collateral information from friends and relatives; share these results with the client.

4. Administer to the client psychological instruments designed to objectively assess treatment resistance (e.g., Correctional Treatment Resistance Scale, Therapeutic Reactance Scale [TRS]); give the client feedback regarding the results of the assessment.

4. Cooperate with a physician's examination. (5)

5. Refer the client to a physician to examine the client and share the results of the client's history and physical, pointing out signs and symptoms of prolonged and excessive addiction.

5. Listen to the results of the assessments, and make a rational, informed choice about the treatment that is needed to arrest addiction. (6, 7, 8)

6. Using the biopsychosocial and medical assessments, help the client to make an informed choice about addiction treatment.

7. Discuss the levels of care that are available (e.g., recovery group meetings, counseling, outpatient treatment, intensive outpatient, day treatment, residential treatment) and help the client to make an informed decision about entering treatment.

8. Teach the client about the treatment process, and encourage him/her to stay in treatment as long as necessary to bring the addiction under control.

6. Provide data for a State of Change assessment. (9)

9. Assess the client's position in the State of Change by Prochaska and DiClemente; provide feedback of results.

7. List times when addictive behavior led to negative consequences. (10)

10. Help the client to see the extent of his/her addiction by assisting him/her in listing a number of negative consequences that have resulted from addictive behavior.

8. Concerned family members, friends, employer, and/or coworkers express their concerns about the client's addiction. (11, 12)

11. Ask the client to sign releases of information and to meet with his/her employer, family, friends, and/or coworkers to enlist their support for him/her to remain in treatment.

12. Ask concerned family, friends, employer, and coworkers to write letters, stating specific instances when the client's addiction hurt

them, and to share what they are going to do if the client refuses treatment; if possible, have each person read the letters to the client in a group setting.

9. Sign a release of information to the probation, parole, or court services worker so information can be shared concerning treatment. (13)

13. Ask the client to sign a release of information, and contact his/her probation, parole, or court services worker to elicit support for treatment.

10. Discuss the reasons for treatment resistance with treatment peers, and listen to their feedback. (14, 15)

14. In a group setting, encourage the client to share why he/she does not want to remain in treatment; facilitate other clients' confrontation of denial and support for the need for treatment.

15. Encourage the client to discuss with peers and staff his/her plans to leave treatment.

11. Stay with a staff member or treatment buddy until the threat of leaving treatment resolves. (16)

16. Assign a staff member or treatment peer to stay with the client until the risk of leaving treatment is resolved.

12. List lies that were told to hide addiction. (17)

17. Help the client to admit to the lies that he/she told to hide his/her addiction.

13. Develop a written personal recovery plan that includes the treatment that is necessary to maintain abstinence. (18)

18. Help the client to develop a written personal recovery plan detailing the treatment that is necessary to maintain abstinence.

14. Make a list of things that each family member can do to assist the client in recovery. (19, 20)

19. In a family session, teach the family the role of denial in treatment resistance and addiction.

20. Help the client to list three things that each family member can do to assist in recovery; facilitate a sharing of these with family members.

15. Complete a re-administration of objective tests of treatment resistance as a means of assessing treatment outcome. (21)

21. Assess the outcome of treatment by re-administering to the client objective tests of treatment resistance; evaluate the results and provide feedback to the client.

16. Complete a survey to assess the degree of satisfaction with treatment. (22)

22. Administer a survey to assess the client's degree of satisfaction with treatment.

—. _____
  _____

—. _____
  _____

—. _____
  _____

—. _____
  _____

—. _____
  _____

—. _____
  _____

DIAGNOSTIC SUGGESTIONS:

Axis I:	305.00	Alcohol Abuse
	305.70	Amphetamine Abuse
	305.20	Cannabis Abuse
	305.60	Cocaine Abuse
	305.30	Hallucinogen Abuse
	305.90	Inhalant Abuse
	305.50	Opioid Abuse
	305.40	Sedative, Hypnotic, or Anxiolytic Abuse
	303.90	Alcohol Dependence
	304.40	Amphetamine Dependence
	304.30	Cannabis Dependence
	304.20	Cocaine Dependence
	304.50	Hallucinogen Dependence
	304.60	Inhalant Dependence
	304.00	Opioid Dependence
	304.10	Sedative, Hypnotic, or Anxiolytic Dependence
	304.80	Polysubstance Dependence
	305.90	Phencyclidine Abuse
	304.90	Phencyclidine Dependence

_____ _____

_____ _____

Axis II: 301.7   Antisocial Personality Disorder

_____ _____

_____ _____

Appendix A

BIBLIOTHERAPY SUGGESTIONS

Adult Child of an Alcoholic Traits

Al-Anon Family Group. (1994). *From Survival to Recovery: Growing Up in an Alcoholic Family.* Virginia Beach, VA: Al-Anon Family Group.

Bowden, J. D., Gravitz, H. L., Wegscheider, C., & Bowden, J. D. (1987). *Recovery: A Guide for Adult Children of Alcoholics.* New York: Fireside.

Kritsberg, W. (1998). *The Adult Children of Alcoholics Syndrome: From Discovery to Recovery.* New York: Bantam Books.

Woititz, J. G. (1990). *Adult Children of Alcoholics.* Palm Coast, FL: Health Communications.

Anger

Alberti, R., & Emmons, M. (2001). *Your Perfect Right: Assertiveness and Equality in Your Life and Relationships* (8th ed.). Atascadero, CA: Impact Publishers.

Bilodeau, L. (1992). *The Anger Workbook.* Minneapolis, MN: Compare Publications.

Gottlieb, M. (1999). *The Angry Self: A Comprehensive Approach to Anger Management.* Redding, CT: Zeig, Tucker & Theisen.

Harbin, T. J. (2000). *Beyond Anger: A Guide for Men: How to Free Yourself from the Grip of Anger and Get More Out of Life.* New York: Marlowe & Co.

Lee, J., & Stott, B. (1995). *Facing the Fire: Experiencing and Expressing Anger Appropriately.* New York: Bantam Doubleday Dell.

Lerner, H. (1997). *The Dance of Anger: A Woman's Guide to Changing the Patterns of Intimate Relationships.* New York: HarperCollins.

McKay, M., Rogers, P. D., & McKay, J. (1989). *When Anger Hurts: Quieting the Storm Within.* Oakland, CA: New Harbinger Publications.

Rosellini, G., & Worden, M. (1986). *Of Course You're Angry.* San Francisco: Harper Hazelden.

Rubin, T. I. (1969). *The Angry Book.* New York: Macmillan.

Smedes, L. (1991). *Forgive and Forget: Healing the Hurts We Don't Deserve.* San Francisco: Harper.

Weisinger, H. (1985). *Dr. Weisinger's Anger Work Out Book.* New York: Quill.

Williams, R., & Williams, V. (1998). *Anger Kills: Seventeen Strategies for Controlling the Hostility That Can Harm Your Health.* New York: Harper Mass Market Paperbacks.

Antisocial Behavior

Bilodeau, L. (1992). *The Anger Workbook.* Minneapolis, MN: Compare Publications.

Gottlieb, M. (1999). *The Angry Self: A Comprehensive Approach to Anger Management.* Redding, CT: Zeig, Tucker & Theisen.

Sharp, B. (2000). *Changing Criminal Thinking: A Treatment Program.* Lanham, MD: American Correctional Association.

Wolman, B. (1999). *Antisocial Behavior: Personality Disorders from Hostility to Homicide.* Amherst, NY: Prometheus Books.

Anxiety

Antony, M., & Swinson, R. (2000). *The Shyness & Social Anxiety Workbook: Proven Techniques for Overcoming Your Fears.* Oakland, CA: New Harbinger Publishers.

Bradshaw, J. (1988). *Healing the Shame That Binds You.* Deerfield Beach, FL: Health Communications.

Burns, D. (1985). *Intimate Connections: The New Clinically Tested Program for Overcoming Loneliness.* New York: William Morrow.

Dayhoff, S. (2000). *Diagonally Parked in a Parallel Universe: Working Through Social Anxiety.* Placitas, NM: Effectiveness-Plus Publications.

Goldman, C., & Babior, S. (1996). *Overcoming Panic, Anxiety, & Phobias: New Strategies to Free Yourself from Worry and Fear.* Duluth, MN: Whole Person Associates.

Helmstetter, S. (1986). *What to Say When You Talk to Yourself.* New York: Fine Communications.

Hofmann, S., & Dibartolo, P. (Eds.). (2000). *From Social Anxiety to Social Phobia: Multiple Perspectives.* Needham Heights, MA: Allyn & Bacon.

Peurifoy, R. (1995). *Anxiety, Phobias, and Panic: A Step-by-Step Program for Regaining Control of Your Life.* New York: Warner Books.

Rapee, R. (1999). *Overcoming Shyness and Social Phobia: A Step-by-Step Guide.* Northvale, NJ: Jason Aronson.

Zimbardo, P. (1987). *Shyness: What It Is and What to Do About It.* Reading, MA: Addison-Wesley.

Attention-Deficit/Hyperactivity Disorder (ADHD)

Barkley, R. A. (2000). *Taking Charge of ADHD: The Complete, Authoritative Guide for Parents.* New York: Guilford.

Hollowell, E. M., & Ratey, J. J. (1995). *Driven to Distraction: Recognizing and Coping With Attention Deficit Disorder from Childhood Through Adulthood.* New York: Simon & Schuster.

Ingersoll, B. (1995). *Distant Drums, Different Drummers: A Guide for Young People with ADHD.* Buffalo, NY: Cape Publishing.

Kelly, K., & Ramundo, P. (1996). *You Mean I'm Not Lazy, Stupid or Crazy?!: A Self-Help Book for Adults with Attention Deficit Disorder.* New York: Fireside.

Murphy, K. R., & Levert, S. (1995). *Out of the Fog: Treatment Options and Coping Strategies for Adult Attention Deficit Disorder.* New York: Hyperion.

Quinn, P. O., & Stern, J. M. (1992). *Putting on the Brakes: Young People's Guide to Understanding Attention Deficit Hyperactive Disorder.* Washington, DC: Magination.

Attention-Deficit/Inattentive Disorder (ADD)

Barkley, R. A. (2000). *Taking Charge of ADHD: The Complete, Authoritative Guide for Parents.* New York: Guilford.

Hollowell, E. M., & Ratey, J. J. (1995). *Driven to Distraction: Recognizing and Coping With Attention Deficit Disorder from Childhood Through Adulthood.* New York: Simon & Schuster.

Ingersoll, B. (1995). *Distant Drums, Different Drummers: A Guide for Young People with ADHD.* Buffalo, NY: Cape Publishing.

Kelly, K., & Ramundo, P. (1996). *You Mean I'm Not Lazy, Stupid or Crazy?!: A Self-Help Book for Adults with Attention Deficit Disorder.* New York: Fireside.

Murphy, K. R., & Levert, S. (1995). *Out of the Fog: Treatment Options and Coping Strategies for Adult Attention Deficit Disorder.* New York: Hyperion.

Quinn, P. O., & Stern, J. M. (1992). *Putting on the Brakes: Young People's Guide to Understanding Attention Deficit Hyperactive Disorder.* Washington, DC: Magination.

Borderline Traits

Kreisman, J. J., & Straus, H. (1991). *I Hate You—Don't Leave Me: Understanding Borderline Personality Disorder.* New York: Avon.

Mason, P. T., Kreger, R., & Siever, L. J. (1998). *Stop Walking on Eggshells; Coping When Someone You Care About Has Borderline Personality Disorder.* Oakland, CA: New Harbinger Publications.

Moskovitz, R. A. (1996). *Lost in the Mirror: An Inside Look at Borderline Personality Disorder.* Dallas, TX: Taylor Publishers.

Santoro, J., & Cohen, R. (1997). *The Angry Heart: Overcoming Borderline and Addictive Disorders: An Interactive Self-Help Guide.* Oakland, CA: New Harbinger Publications.

Thornton, M. F., Peterson, E. W., & Barley, W. D. (1997). *Eclipses: Behind the Borderline Personality Disorder.* Madison, AL: Monte Sano Publishers.

Childhood Trauma

Barnhill, J. W., Rosen, R. K., & Granet, R. (1999). *Why Am I Still So Afraid: Understanding Post Traumatic Stress Disorder.* New York: Dell Publication Co.

Bradshaw, J. (1988). *Healing the Shame That Binds You.* Deerfield Beach, FL: Health Communications.

Draper, P. L. (1996). *Haunted Memories: Healing the Pain of Childhood Abuse.* Old Tappan, NJ: Fleming H. Revell Co.

Flannery, R. B., Jr. (1995). *Post-Traumatic Stress Disorder: The Victims Guide to Healing and Recovery.* New York: Crossroad/Herder & Herder.

Gambrill, E., & Richey, C. (1985). *Taking Charge of Your Social Life.* New York: Wadsworth Publishing.

Gil, E. (1984). *Outgrowing the Pain: A Book for and About Adults Abused as Children.* New York: Dell Publishing.

Kushner, H. (1981). *When Bad Things Happen to Good People.* New York: Schocken Books.

Matsakis, A. (1996). *I Can't Get Over It: A Handbook for Trauma Survivors.* Oakland, CA: New Harbinger Publications.

Matsakis, A. (1998). *Trust After Trauma: A Guide to Relationships for Survivors and Those Who Love Them.* Oakland, CA: New Harbinger Publications.

Schiraldi, G. R. (1999). *The Post-Traumatic Stress Disorder Sourcebook: A Guide to Healing, Recovery and Growth.* Lincolnwood, IL: Lowell House.

Smedes, L. (1991). *Forgive and Forget: Healing the Hurts We Don't Deserve.* San Francisco: Harper.

Chronic Pain

Benson, H. (1979). *The Mind/Body Effect.* New York: Simon & Schuster.

Burns, D. (1989). *The Feeling Good Handbook.* New York: Plume.

Burns, D. (1993). *Ten Days to Self Esteem!* New York: William Morrow.

Caudill, M. (1995). *Managing Pain before It Manages You.* New York: Guilford.

Duckro, P., Richardson, W., & Marshall, J. (1995). *Taking Control of Your Headaches.* New York: Guilford.

Hunter, M. (1996). *Making Peace with Chronic Pain.* New York: Brunner/Mazel.

Siegel, B. (1989). *Peace, Love and Healing.* New York: Harper & Row.

Dangerousness/Lethality

Jamison, K. P, & Jamison, K. R. (2000). *When Night Falls.* New York: Vintage Books.

McKay, M., Rogers, P. D., & McKay, J. (1989). *When Anger Hurts: Quieting the Storm Within.* Oakland, CA: New Harbinger Publications.

Sells, S. (2002). *Parenting Your Out of Control Teenager: 7 Steps to Reestablish Authority and Reclaim Love.* New York: St. Martin's Press.

Dependent Traits

Alberti, R., & Emmons, M. (1990). *Your Perfect Right.* San Luis Obispo, CA: Impact.

Alcoholics Anonymous. (1974). *Big Book*. New York: Alcoholics Anonymous General Services Office.

Beattie, M. (1987). *Codependent No More: How to Stop Controlling Others and Start Caring for Yourself*. San Francisco: Harper.

Drews, T.R. (1980). *Getting Them Sober: A Guide for Those Living with Alcoholism*. South Plainfield, NJ: Bridge Publishing.

Evans, P. (1992). *The Verbally Abusive Relationship*. Holbrook, MA: Bob Adams Inc.

Helmfelt, R., Minirth, F., & Meier, P. (1985). *Love Is a Choice*. Nashville, TN: Nelson.

Norwood, R. (1985). *Women Who Love Too Much*. Los Angeles: Tarcher.

Pittman, F. (1998). *Grow Up!* New York: Golden Books.

Walker, L. (1979). *The Battered Woman*. New York: Harper & Row.

Whitfield, C. (1990). *A Gift to Myself: A Personal Guide to Healing My Child Within*. Deerfield Beach, FL: Health Communications.

Whitfield, C. (1993). *Boundaries and Relationships: Knowing, Protecting, and Enjoying the Self*. Deerfield Beach, FL: Health Communications.

Depression

Beck, A.T., Rush, J.A., Shaw, B.F., & Emery, G. (1979). *Cognitive Therapy of Depression*. New York: Guilford.

Burns, D. (1990). *The Feeling Good Handbook*. New York: Plume.

Cronkite, K. (1995). *On the Edge of Darkness: Conversations About Conquering Depression*. New York: Delta.

Golant, M., & Golant, S.K. (1997). *What to Do When Someone You Love Is Depressed: A Self-help and Help Others Guide*. New York: Villard.

O'Connor, R. (1999). *Undoing Depression: What Therapy Doesn't Teach You and Medication Can't Give You*. New York: Berkley Publishing Group.

Rosen, L.E., & Amador, X.F. (1996). *When Someone You Love Is Depressed: How to Help Your Loved One Without Losing Yourself*. New York: Fireside.

Thorn, J., & Rothstein, L. (1993). *You are Not Alone: Words of Experience and Hope for the Journey Through Depression*. New York: Harperperennial.

Yapko, M. (1998). *Breaking the Patterns of Depression*. New York: Main Street Books.

Eating Disorders

Claude-Pierre, P. (1999). *The Secret Language of Eating Disorders: The Revolutionary New Approach*. New York: Vintage Books.

Costin, C. (1999). *The Eating Disorder Source Book: A Comprehensive Guide to the Causes, Treatments, and Prevention of Eating Disorders*. Los Angeles: Lowell House.

Jantz, G.L. (1995). *Hope, Help, and Healing for Eating Disorders: A New Approach to Treating Anorexia, Bulimia, and Overeating*. Wheaton, IL: Harold Shaw Publishers.

Sacker, I.M., & Zimmer, M.A. (1995). *Dying to Be Thin: Understanding & Defeating Anorexia & Bulimia*. New York: Warner Books.

Siegel, M. (1997). *Surviving an Eating Disorder: Strategies for Family and Friends.* New York: HarperCollins.

Family Conflicts

Beattie, M. (1987). *Codependent No More.* Center City, MN: Hazelden.
Covey, S. R., & Covey, S. M. (1998). *The 7 Habits of Highly Effective Families: Building a Beautiful Family Culture in a Turbulent World.* New York: Golden Books.
Page, S., & Page, S. (1998). *How One of You Can Bring the Two of You Together: Breakthrough Strategies to Resolve Conflicts and Reignite Your Love.* New York: Bantam Doubleday Dell.
Robinson, J. (1997). *Communication Miracles for Couples: Easy and Effective Tools to Create More Love and Less Conflict.* New York: Conari Publishing.
Sherven, J., & Sniechowski, J. (1997). *The New Intimacy: Discovering the Magic at the Heart of Your Differences.* Palm Coast, FL: Health Communications.
Weinhold, B., & Weinhold, J. (1989). *Breaking Free of the Co-Dependency Trap.* Walpole, NH: Stillpoint Publishing.

Gambling

Berman, L., & Siegel, M. (1998). *Behind the 8-Ball: A Guide for Families of Gamblers.* San Jose, CA: Excel Press.
Chamberlain, L. & McCowan, W. G. (2000). *Best Possible Odds: Contemporary Treatment Strategies for Gambling Disorders.* New York: Wiley.
Eadington, W. R., & Cornelius, J. A. (2000). *The Downside: Problem and Pathological Gambling.* Las Vegas, NV: University of Nevada Press.
Federman, E. J., Drebing, C. E., & Krebs, C. (2000). *Don't Leave It to Chance: A Guide for Families of Problem Gamblers.* Oakland, CA: New Harbinger Publications.
Herscovitch, A. (1999). *Alcoholism and Pathological Gambling: Similarities and Differences.* Holmes Beach, FL: Learning Publications.
May, G. G. (1991). *Addiction and Grace.* San Francisco: Harper.

Grief/Loss Unresolved

Alcoholics Anonymous World Service. (2001). *The Big Book* (4th ed.). New York: Alcoholics Anonymous World Service.
Caplan, S., & Lang, G. (1995). *Grief's Courageous Journey: A Workbook.* Oakland, CA: New Harbinger Publications.
Childs-Gowell, E. (1992). *Good Grief Rituals: Tools for Healing: A Healing Companion.* Barrytown, NY: Station Hill Press.
Colgrove, M., Bloomfield, H., & McWilliams, P. (1991). *How to Survive the Loss of a Love.* Los Angeles: Prelude Press.

Harris-Lord, J., & Wheeler, E. (1991). *No Time for Goodbyes: Coping With Sorrow, Anger, and Injustice After a Tragic Death.* New York: Pathfinder Publications.

James, J., & Friedman, R. (1998). *The Grief Recovery Handbook: The Action Program for Moving Beyond Death, Divorce, and Other Losses.* New York: HarperCollins.

Kushner, H. (1981). *When Bad Things Happen to Good People.* New York: Schocken Books.

Obershaw, R. (1998). *Cry Until You Laugh: Comforting Guidance for Coping With Grief.* Minneapolis, MN: Fairview Publications.

Schiff, N. (1977). *The Bereaved Parent.* New York: Crown.

Smedes, L. (1991). *Forgive and Forget: Healing the Hurts We Don't Deserve.* San Francisco: Harper.

Westberg, G. (1986). *Good Grief: A Constructive Approach to the Problem of Loss.* Minneapolis, MN: Fortress Press.

Zonnebelt-Smeenge, S., & DeVries, R. (1998). *Getting to the Other Side of Grief: Overcoming the Loss of a Spouse.* Grand Rapids, MI: Baker.

Impulsivity

Garber, S., Freedman Spizman, R., & Garber, M. (1995). *Is Your Child Hyperactive? Inattentive? Impulsive? Distractable?: Helping the ADD/Hyperactive Child.* New York: Villard Books.

Melody, P., & Miller, A. (1992). *Facing Love Addiction: Giving Yourself the Power to Change the Way You Love & The Love Connection to Codependence.* San Francisco: Harper.

Shapiro, L., & Shore, L. (1993). *Sometimes I Drive My Mom Crazy, but I Know She's Crazy About Me: A Self-Esteem Book for Overactive and Impulsive Children.* Memphis, TN: Center for Applied Psychology.

Legal Problems

Kheel, T. (1999). *The Keys to Conflict Resolution: Proven Methods of Settling Disputes Voluntarily.* New York: Four Walls Eight Windows.

Mnookin, R., Peppet, S., & Tulumello, A. (2000). *Beyond Winning: Negotiating to Create Value in Deals and Disputes.* Cambridge, MA: Harvard University Press.

Seidenberg, R., & Dawes, W. (1997). *The Father's Emergency Guide to Divorce-Custody Battle.* Takoma Park, MD: JES Books.

Smith, G., & Abrahms, S. (1998). *What Every Woman Should Know About Divorce and Custody: Judges, Lawyers, and Therapists Share Winning Strategies on How to Keep the Kids, the Cash and the Family.* New York: Perigee.

Stewart, J. (2000). *The Child Custody Book: How to Protect Your Children and Win Your Case.* Atascadero, CA: Impact Publishers.

Strohm, R. (Ed.). (1997). *Solving Your Financial Problems: Getting Out of Debt,*

Repairing Your Credit and Dealing With Bankruptcy (Layman's Law Guide). Broomall, PA: Chelsea House Publishing.

Living Environment Deficiency

Alberti, R., & Emmons, M. (1990). *Your Perfect Right.* San Luis Obispo, CA: Impact.

Forward, S., & Frazier, D. (1998). *Emotional Blackmail.* New York: HarperCollins.

Gordon, S. (1981). *The Teenage Survival Book.* New York: Times Books.

Kaplan, L. (1997). *Coping with Peer Pressure.* Center City, MN: Hazelden.

Kritsberg, W. (1998). *The Adult Children of Alcoholics Syndrome: From Discovery to Recovery.* New York: Bantam Books.

Sachs, S. (1997). *Street Gang Awareness: A Resource Guide for Parents and Professionals.* Minneapolis, MN: Fairview Press.

Mania/Hypomania

Bradley, L. (2000). *Manic Depression: How to Live While Loving a Manic Depressive.* Houston, TX: Emerald Ink Publications.

Granet, R., & Ferber, E. (1999). *Why Am I Up, Why Am I Down?: Understanding Bipolar Disorder.* New York: Dell.

Mondimore, F. (1999). *Bipolar Disorder: A Guide for Patients and Families.* Baltimore: Johns Hopkins University Press.

Olson, B., & Olson, M. (1999). *Win the Battle: The 3-Step Lifesaving Formula to Conquer Depression and Bipolar Disorder.* Worchester, MA: Chandler House Press.

Papolos, D., & Papolos, J. (1999). *The Bipolar Child: The Definitive and Reassuring Guide to Childhood's Most Misunderstood Disorder.* New York: Broadway Books.

Waltz, M. (2000). *Bipolar Disorders: A Guide to Helping Children and Adolescents.* Sebastopol, CA: O'Reilly & Associates.

Medical Issues

Cousins, N. (1991). *Anatomy of an Illness as Perceived by the Patient.* New York: Bantam Doubleday.

Dollemore, D., & Feinstein, A. (Eds.). (1996). *Symptoms: Their Causes & Cures: How to Understand and Treat 265 Health Concerns.* New York: Bantam Books.

Griffith, W., & Pederson, M. (1992). *Complete Guide to Symptoms, Illnesses & Surgery for People Over 50.* New York: Perigee.

Winter, H., & Griffith, M. (2000). *The Complete Guide to Symptoms, Illnesses, and Surgery.* New York: Perigee.

Narcissistic Traits

Brown, N. (1998). *The Destructive Narcissistic Pattern.* Westport, CT: Praeger Publications.

Donaldson-Pressman, S., & Pressman, R. (1997). *The Narcissistic Family: Diagnosis and Treatment.* San Francisco: Jossey-Bass.

Forrest, G. (1995). *Alcoholism, Narcissism and Psychopathology.* Leonia, NJ: Jason Aronson.

Golomb, E. (1995). *Trapped in the Mirror: Adult Children of Narcissists in Their Struggle for Self.* New York: HarperCollins.

Lowen, A. (1997). *Narcissism: Denial of the True Self.* Greenwich, CT: Touchstone.

Schwartz-Salant, N. (1982). *Narcissism and Character Transformation: The Psychology of Narcissistic Character Disorders.* Toronto, ON: Inner City Books.

Solomon, M. (1992). *Narcissism and Intimacy: Love and Marriage in an Age of Confusion.* New York: W. W. Norton.

Nicotine Abuse/Dependence

American Psychiatric Association Practice Guideline for the Treatment of Patients With Nicotine Dependence. (1996). Washington, DC: American Psychiatric Press.

Ashelman, M. W. (2000). *Stop Smoking Naturally.* New York: NTC/Contemporary Publishing.

Baer, A. (1998). *Quit Smoking for Good: A Supportive Program for Permanent Smoking Cessation.* Freedom, CA: Crossing Press.

Burton, D. (1986). *American Cancer Society's Freshstart: 21 Days to Stop Smoking.* New York: Pocket Books.

Fisher, E. B., & Koop, C. E. (1998). *American Lung Association 7 Steps to a Smoke Free Life.* New York: Wiley.

Lynch, B. S., & Bonnie, R. (Eds.). (1994). *Growing Up Tobacco Free: Preventing Nicotine Addiction in Children and Youths.* Washington, DC: National Academy Press.

Rogers, J., & Rubinstein, J. (1995). *You Can Stop Smoking.* New York: Pocket Books.

Occupational Problems

Gill, L. (1999). *How to Work With Just About Anyone: A 3-Step Solution for Getting Difficult People to Change.* New York: Fireside.

Hirsh, S., & Kise, J. (1996). *Work it Out: Clues for Solving People Problems at Work.* Palo Alto, CA: Davies-Black Publishing.

Johnson, S. (1998). *Who Moved My Cheese?: An Amazing Way to Deal With Change in Your Work and in Your Life.* New York: Putnam Publishing Group.

Lloyd, K. (1999). *Jerks at Work: How to Deal With People Problems and Problem People.* Franklin Lakes, NJ: Career Press.

Scanlon, W. (1991). *Alcoholism and Drug Abuse in the Workplace.* Westport, CT: Praeger Publications.

Opioid Dependence

Bressler, D. (1979). *Free Yourself From Pain.* New York: Simon & Schuster.

Catalono, E. M., & Hardin, K. N. (1996). *The Chronic Pain Control Workbook: A Step-By-Step Guide for Coping With and Overcoming Pain.* Oakland, CA: New Harbinger Press.

Inaba, D. S., & Cohen, W. E. (2004). *Uppers Downers, All Arounders.* Ashland, OR: CNS Publications.

Inciardi, J. A. (2001). *The War on Drugs III: The Continuing Saga of the Mysteries and Miseries of Intoxication, Addiction, Crime, and Public Policy.* New York: Allyn & Bacon.

Jamison, R. N. (1996). *Learning to Master Your Chronic Pain.* Sarasota, FL: Professional Resource Press.

Leith, L. (1998). *Exercising Your Way to Better Mental Health.* Morgantown, WV: Fitness Information Technology.

Narcotics Anonymous World Service. (1988). *Narcotics Anonymous.* Los Angeles: Narcotics Anonymous World Service.

Oppositional Defiant Disorder

Alberti, R., & Emmons, M. (2001). *Your Perfect Right: Assertiveness and Equality in Your Life and Relationships* (8th ed.). Atascadero, CA: Impact Publishers.

Bodenhamer, G. (1884). *Back in Control: How to Get Your Children to Behave.* New York: Simon & Schuster Trade.

Greene, R. W. (1998). *The Explosive Child: A New Approach for Understanding and Parenting Easily Frustrated, "Chronically Inflexible" Children.* New York: HarperCollins.

Hepp, E., Fleishman, M., & Espeland, P. (1996). *Fighting Invisible Tigers: A Stress Management Guide for Teens.* Minneapolis, MN: Free Spirit Publishing.

Kindlon, D., Thompson, M., Kindlon, D., & Barker, T. (2000). *Raising Cain: Protecting the Emotional Life of Boys.* New York: Ballantine Publishing Group.

McCoy, K., & Wibbelsman, C. (1995). *A Teenagers Guide to Friends, Failure, Sexuality, Love, Rejection, Addiction, Peer Pressure, Families, Loss, Depression, Change, and Other Challenges of Living.* New York: Berkley Publishing Group.

Riley, D. (1997). *The Defiant Child: A Parents Guide to Oppositional Defiant Disorder.* Dallas, TX: Taylor Publishing Company.

Parent-Child Relational Problem

Bodenhamer, G. (1884). *Back in Control: How to Get Your Children to Behave.* New York: Simon & Schuster Trade.

Dreikurs, R., & Soltz, V. (1964). *Children the Challenge.* New York: Hawthorne Books.

Hepp, E., Fleishman, M., & Espeland, P. (1996). *Fighting Invisible Tigers: A Stress Management Guide for Teens.* Minneapolis, MN: Free Spirit Publishing.

McCoy, K., & Wibbelsman, C. (1995). *A Teenagers Guide to Friends, Failure, Sexuality, Love, Rejection, Addiction, Peer Pressure, Families, Loss, Depression, Change, and Other Challenges of Living.* New York, NY: Berkley Publishing Group.

Sells, S. P. (1998). *Treating the Tough Adolescent: A Family Based, Step-by-Step Guide.* New York: Guilford.

Seixas, J. S., & Youcha, G. (1985). *Children of Alcoholics: A Survivor's Manual.* New York: Crown Publishers.

Steinberg, L., & Levine, A. (1997). *You and Your Adolescent: A Parent's Guide for Ages 10 to 20.* New York: HarperCollins.

Partner Relational Conflicts

Asker, S. (1999). *Plan B: How to Get Unstuck from Work, Family, and Relationship Problems.* New York: Perigee.

Beck, A. (1989). *Love is Never Enough: How Couples Can Overcome Misunderstanding, Resolve Conflicts, and Solve Relationship Problems Through Cognitive Therapy.* New York: HarperCollins.

Crenshaw, R. (1981). *Expressing Your Feelings: The Key to an Intimate Relationship.* New York: Irvington Publications.

Page, S. (1998). *How One of You Can Bring the Two of You Together: Breakthrough Strategies to Resolve your Conflicts and Reignite Your Love.* New York: Bantam Doubleday.

Robinson, J. (1997). *Communication Miracles for Couples: Easy and Effective Tools to Create More Love and Less Conflict.* Berkeley, CA: Conari Press.

Stern, S. (1999). *He Just Doesn't Get It: Simple Solutions to the Most Common Relationship Problems.* New York: Pocket Books.

Peer Group Negativity

Kaplan, L. (1997). *Coping with Peer Pressure.* Center City, MN: Hazelden.

Kritsberg, W. (1998). *The Adult Children of Alcoholics Syndrome: From Discovery to Recovery.* New York: Bantam Books.

Gordon, S. (1981). *The Teenage Survival Book.* New York: Times Books.

Sachs, S. (1997). *Street Gang Awareness: A Resource Guide for Parents and Professionals.* Minneapolis, MN: Fairview Press.

Scott, S. (1997). *How to Say No and Keep Your Friends: Peer Pressure Reversal for Teens and Preteens.* Amherst, MA: Human Resourse Development Press.

Posttraumatic Stress Disorder (PTSD)

Coffey, R. (1998). *Unspeakable Truths and Happy Endings: Human Cruelty and the New Trauma Therapy.* Towson, MD: Sidran Press.

Flannery, R. B., Jr. (1995). *Post-Traumatic Stress Disorder: The Victim's Guide to Healing and Recovery.* New York: Crossroad/Herder & Herder.

Freyd, J. (1998). *Betrayal Trauma: The Logic of Forgetting Childhood Abuse.* Cambridge, MA: Harvard University Press.

Matsakis, A. (1996). *I Can't Get Over It: A Handbook for Trauma Survivors.* Oakland, CA: New Harbinger Publications.

Matsakis, A. (1998). *Trust After Trauma: A Guide to Relationships for Survivors and Those Who Love Them.* Oakland, CA: New Harbinger Publications.

Rosenbloom, D., Williams, M., & Watkins, B. E. (1999). *Life After Trauma: A Workbook for Healing.* New York: Guilford.

Schiraldi, G. (1999). *The Post-Traumatic Stress Disorder Sourcebook: A Guide to Healing, Recovery, and Growth.* Lincolnwood, IL: Lowell House.

Psychosis

Adamec, C., & Jaffe, D. (1996). *How to Live With a Mentally Ill Person: A Handbook of Day-to-Day Strategies.* New York: Wiley.

Granet, R., & Ferber, E. (1999). *Why Am I Up, Why Am I Down?: Understanding Bipolar Disorder.* New York: Dell.

Mondimore, F. (1999). *Bipolar Disorder: A Guide for Patients and Families.* Baltimore: Johns Hopkins University Press.

Mueser, K. (1994). *Coping with Schizophrenia: A Guide for Families.* Oakland, CA: New Harbinger Publications.

Olson, B., & Olson, M. (1999). *Win the Battle: The 3-Step Lifesaving Formula to Conquer Depression and Bipolar Disorder.* Worchester, MA: Chandler House Press.

Papolos, D., & Papolos, J. (1999). *The Bipolar Child: The Definitive and Reassuring Guide to Childhood's Most Misunderstood Disorder.* New York: Broadway Books.

Torrey, F. (1995). *Surviving Schizophrenia: A Manual for Families, Consumers and Providers.* New York: Harperperennial Library.

Waltz, M. (2000). *Bipolar Disorders: A Guide to Helping Children and Adolescents.* Sebastopol, CA: O'Reilly & Associates.

Weinstein, A. (1996). *Madness, Psychosis, and Addiction (Lecture 7).* Chantilly, VA: The Teaching Company.

Relapse Proneness

Dorsman, J. (1998). *How to Quit Drugs for Good: A Complete Self-Help Guide.* Roseville, CA: Prima Publishing.

Duwors, G. (2000). *White Knuckles & Wishful Thinking: Learning From the Moment of Relapse in Alcoholism and Other Addictions.* Kirkland, WA: Hogrefe and Huber Publishers.

Gorski, T., & Miller, M. (1986). *Staying Sober: A Guide for Relapse Prevention.* Scottdale, PA: Herald Publishing House.

Gorski, T. (1987). *Passages Through Recovery: An Action Plan for Preventing Relapse.* Center City, MN: Hazelden.

Washton, A. (1991). *Cocaine Addiction: Treatment, Recovery, and Relapse Prevention.* New York: W. W. Norton.

Washton, A., & Boundy, D. (1990). *Willpower's Not Enough: Understanding and Recovering from Addictions of Every Kind.* New York: HarperCollins.

Self-Care Deficits—Primary

American College of Sports Medicine. (1998). *ACSM Fitness Book.* Champaign, IL: Human Kinetics.

Bittman, M. (1998). *How to Cook Everything.* New York: Macmillan.

The Editors of Good Housekeeping. (1989). *The Good Housekeeping Illustrated Cookbook.* New York: Hearst Books.

The Editors of the University of California-Berkeley (1995). *The New Wellness Encyclopedia.* New York: Houghton-Mifflin Co.

Pinkham, M., & Burg, D. (1993). *Mary Ellen's Complete Home Reference Book.* New York: Three Rivers Press.

Sharkey, B. (1991). *Fitness and Health.* Champaign, IL: Human Kinetics.

Taintor, J., & Taintor, M. (1999). *The Complete Guide to Better Dental Care.* New York: Checkmark Books.

Self-Care Deficits—Secondary

American College of Sports Medicine. (1998). *ACSM Fitness Book.* Champaign, IL: Human Kinetics.

Aslett, D. (1984). *The Cleaning Encyclopedia: Your A to Z Illustrated Guide to Cleaning Like the Pros.* New York: Dell.

Bittman, M. (1998). *How to Cook Everything.* New York: Macmillan.

The Editors of Good Housekeeping. (1989). *The Good Housekeeping Illustrated Cookbook.* New York: Hearst Books.

The Editors of the University of California-Berkeley. (1995). *The New Wellness Encyclopedia.* New York: Houghton-Mifflin Co.

Pinkham, M., & Burg, D. (1993). *Mary Ellen's Complete Home Reference Book.* New York: Three Rivers Press.

Sharkey, B. (1991). *Fitness and Health.* Champaign, IL: Human Kinetics.

Taintor, J., & Taintor, M. (1999). *The Complete Guide to Better Dental Care.* New York: Checkmark Books.

Sexual Promiscuity

Carnes, P. (1991). *Don't Call it Love: Recovery from Sexual Addiction.* New York: Bantam Books.

Carnes, P. J. (1992). *Out of the Shadows: Understanding Sexual Addiction.* Center City, MN: Hazelden.

Means, M. (1999). *Living With Your Husband's Secret Wars.* Grand Rapids, MI: Fleming H. Revell Co.

Melody, P., & Miller, A. W. (1992). *Facing Love Addiction: Giving Yourself the Power to Change the Way You Love—The Love Connection to Codependence.* San Francisco: Harper.

Money, J. (1989). *Lovemaps: Clinical Concepts of Sexual/Erotic Health and Pathology, Paraphilia, and Gender Transposition in Childhood, Adolescents and Maturity.* Amherst, NY: Prometheus Books.

Social Anxiety/Skills Deficit

Antony, M., & Swinson, R. (2000). *The Shyness & Social Anxiety Workbook: Proven Techniques for Overcoming Your Fears.* Oakland, CA: New Harbinger Publishers.

Bradshaw, J. (1988). *Healing the Shame That Binds You.* Deerfield Beach, FL: Health Communications.

Burns, D. (1985). *Intimate Connections: The New Clinically Tested Program for Overcoming Loneliness.* New York: William Morrow.

Burns, D. (1993). *Ten Days to Self-Esteem!* New York: William Morrow.

Dayhoff, S. (2000). *Diagonally Parked in a Parallel Universe: Working Through Social Anxiety.* Placitas, NM: Effectiveness-Plus Publications.

Dyer, W. (1978). *Pulling Your Own Strings.* New York: Thomas Crowell.

Fossum, M. A., & Mason, M. J. (1986). *Facing Shame: Families in Recovery.* New York: W. W. Norton.

Harris, A., & Harris, T. (1969). *I'm OK You're OK.* New York: Harper & Row.

Helmstetter, S. (1986). *What to Say When You Talk to Yourself.* New York: Fine Communications.

James, M., & Jongeward, D. (1971). *Born to Win.* Reading, MA: Addison-Wesley.

Rapee, R. (1999). *Overcoming Shyness and Social Phobia: A Step-by-Step Guide.* Northvale, NJ: Jason Aronson.

Zimbardo, P. (1987). *Shyness: What It Is and What to Do About It.* Reading, PA: Addison-Wesley.

Spiritual Confusion

Carter, L. (1997). *The Choosing to Forgive Workbook.* Nashville, TN: Thomas Nelson.

Foster, R. (1988). *Celebration of Discipline: The Path to Spiritual Growth.* San Francisco: Harper & Row.

Graham, B. (1984). *Peace With God.* Dallas, TX: Word.

May, G. (1991). *Addiction and Grace.* San Francisco: Harper.

Parachin, J. (1999). *Engaged Spirituality: Ten Lives of Contemplation and Action.* St. Louis, MO: Chalice Press.

Perkinson, R. (2000). *God Talks To You.* Bloomington, IN: 1stBooks.

Smedes, L. (1991). *Forgive and Forget: Healing the Hurts We Don't Deserve.* San Francisco: Harper.

Willard, D. (1988). *The Spirit of the Disciplines.* New York: Harper & Row.

Substance Abuse/Dependence

Alcoholics Anonymous. (2001). New York: Alcoholics Anonymous General Service Office.

Inaba, D. S., & Cohen, W. E. (2001). *Uppers, Downers, All Arounders.* Ashland, OR: CNS Productions.

Perkinson, R. R. (2001). *Chemical Dependency Counseling: A Practical Guide* (2nd ed.). Thousand Oaks, CA: Sage Publications.

Perkinson, R. R. (2004). *Treating Alcoholism: How to Help Your Clients Get on the Road to Recovery.* Hoboken, NJ: Wiley.

Sales, P. (1999). *Alcohol Abuse: Straight Talk Straight Answers.* Honolulu, HI: Ixia Publications.

Solowji, N. (1998). *Cannabis and Cognitive Functioning.* New York: Cambridge University Press.

Washton, A. (1991). *Cocaine Addiction: Treatment, Recovery, and Relapse Prevention.* New York: W. W. Norton.

Substance-Induced Disorders

Antony, M., & Swinson, R. P. (2000). *The Shyness & Social Anxiety Workbook: Proven Techniques for Overcoming Your Fears.* Oakland, CA: New Harbinger Publishers.

Burns, D. (1990). *The Feeling Good Handbook.* New York: Plume.

Cronkite, K. (1995). *On the Edge of Darkness: Conversations About Conquering Depression.* New York: Delta.

Dayhoff, S. A. (2000). *Diagonally Parked in a Parallel Universe: Working Through Social Anxiety.* Placitas, NM: Effectiveness-Plus Publications.

Goldman, C., & Babior, S. (1996). *Overcoming Panic, Anxiety, & Phobias: New Strategies to Free Yourself from Worry and Fear.* Duluth, MN: Whole Person Associates.

O'Connor, R. (1999). *Undoing Depression: What Therapy Doesn't Teach You and Medication Can't Give You.* New York: Berkley Publishing Group.

Peurifoy, R. Z. (1995). *Anxiety, Phobias, and Panic: A Step-by-Step Program for Regaining Control of Your Life.* New York: Warner Books.

Rapee, R. M. (1999). *Overcoming Shyness and Social Phobia: A Step-by-Step Guide.* Northvale, NJ: Jason Aronson.

Thorn, J., & Rothstein, L. (1993). *You are Not Alone: Words of Experience and Hope for the Journey Through Depression.* New York: Harperperennial.

Yapko, M. (1998). *Breaking the Patterns of Depression.* New York: Main Street Books.

Substance Intoxication/Withdrawal

Alcoholics Anonymous World Services. (1976). *Alcoholics Anonymous.* New York: Alcoholics Anonymous World Services.

Alcoholics Anonymous World Services. (1981). *Twelve Steps and Twelve Traditions.* New York: Alcoholics Anonymous World Services.

Denning, P., & Marlatt, A. (2000). *Practicing Harm Reduction Psychotherapy: An Alternative Approach to Addictions.* New York: Guilford.

Fanning, P. (1996). *The Addiction Workbook: A Step-by-Step Guide to Quitting Alcohol and Drugs.* Oakland, CA: New Harbinger Publications.

May, G. (1991). *Addiction and Grace.* San Francisco: Harper.

Perkinson, R. (1997). *Chemical Dependency Counseling: A Practical Guide.* Thousand Oaks, CA: Sage Publications.

West, J., & Ford, B. (1997). *The Betty Ford Center Book of Answers: Help for Those Struggling With Substance Abuse and for the People Who Love Them.* New York: Pocket Books.

World Service Office. (1988). *Narcotics Anonymous.* Van Nuys, CA: World Service Office.

Suicidal Ideation

Arena, J. (1996). *Step Back from The Exit: 45 Reasons to Say No to Suicide.* Milwaukee, WI: Zebulon Press.

Burns, D. (1990). *The Feeling Good Handbook.* New York: Plume.

Cronkite, K. (1995). *On the Edge of Darkness: Conversations About Conquering Depression.* New York: Delta.

Ellis, T. E., & Newman, C. F. (1996). *Choosing to Live: How to Defeat Suicide Though Cognitive Therapy.* Oakland, CA: New Harbinger Publications.

Jamison, K. R. (2000). *Night Falls Fast: Understanding Suicide.* New York: Vintage Books.

O'Connor, R. (1999). *Undoing Depression: What Therapy Doesn't Teach You and Medication Can't Give You.* New York: Berkley Publishing Group.

Thorn, J., & Rothstein, L. (1993). *You are Not Alone: Words of Experience and Hope for the Journey Through Depression.* New York: Harperperennial.

Yapko, M. (1998). *Breaking the Patterns of Depression.* New York: Main Street Books.

Treatment Resistance

Alcoholics Anonymous World Services. (1976). *Alcoholics Anonymous.* New York: Alcoholics Anonymous World Services.

Alcoholics Anonymous World Services. (1981). *Twelve Steps and Twelve Traditions.* New York: Alcoholics Anonymous World Services.

Fanning, P. (1996). *The Addiction Workbook: A Step-by-Step Guide to Quitting Alcohol and Drugs.* Oakland, CA: New Harbinger Publications.

May, G. G. (1991). *Addiction and Grace.* San Francisco: Harper.

West, J. W., & Ford, B. (1997). *The Betty Ford Center Book of Answers: Help for Those Struggling With Substance Abuse and for the People Who Love Them.* New York: Pocket Books.

World Service Office. (1988). *Narcotics Anonymous.* Van Nuys, CA: World Service Office.

Appendix B

INDEX OF *DSM-IV-TR* CODES ASSOCIATED WITH PRESENTING PROBLEMS

Acculturation Problem   V62.4
  Living Environment Deficiency
  Spiritual Confusion

Acute Stress Disorder   308.3
  Anxiety
  Grief/Loss Unresolved

Adjustment Disorder   309.xx
  Posttraumatic Stress Disorder
    (PTSD)
  Suicidal Ideation

Adjustment Disorder with Anxiety   309.24
  Medical Issues
  Occupational Problem
  Social Anxiety/Skills Deficit

Adjustment Disorder with Depressed Mood   309.0
  Depression
  Grief/Loss Unresolved
  Medical Issues
  Occupational Problem

Adjustment Disorder with Disturbance of Conduct   309.3
  Antisocial Behavior
  Grief/Loss Unresolved
  Legal Problems
  Medical Issues
  Peer Group Negativity
  Sexual Promiscuity

Adjustment Disorder with Mixed Anxiety and Depressed Mood   309.28
  Depression
  Grief/Loss Unresolved
  Social Anxiety/Skills Deficit

Adjustment Disorder with Mixed Disturbance of Emotions and Content   309.4
  Anger
  Dangerousness/Lethality
  Grief/Loss Unresolved
  Oppositional Defiant Disorder
  Peer Group Negativity

Adult Antisocial Behavior   V71.01
  Anger
  Antisocial Behavior
  Dangerousness/Lethality
  Family Conflicts
  Legal Problems

Alcohol Abuse   305.00
  Substance Abuse/Dependence
  Treatment Resistance

Alcohol Dependence   303.90
  Self-Care Deficits—Secondary
  Substance Abuse/Dependence
  Treatment Resistance

Alcohol-Induced Anxiety Disorder   **291.89**
Anxiety
Substance-Induced Disorders

Alcohol-Induced Mood Disorder   **291.89**
Substance-Induced Disorders
Suicidal Ideation

Alcohol-Induced Persisting Amnestic Disorder   **291.1**
Substance-Induced Disorders

Alcohol-Induced Persisting Dementia   **291.2**
Self-Care Deficits—Secondary
Substance-Induced Disorders

Alcohol-Induced Psychotic Disorder   **291.x**
Psychosis

Alcohol-Induced Psychotic Disorder, with Delusions   **291.5**
Substance-Induced Disorders

Alcohol-Induced Psychotic Disorder, with Hallucinations   **291.3**
Substance-Induced Disorders

Alcohol-Induced Sexual Dysfunction   **291.8**
Substance-Induced Disorders

Alcohol-Induced Sleep Disorder   **291.8**
Substance-Induced Disorders

Alcohol Intoxication   **303.00**
Substance Intoxication/
Withdrawal

Alcohol Intoxication Delirium   **291.0**
Substance-Induced Disorders

Alcohol Withdrawal   **291.8**
Substance Intoxication/
Withdrawal

Alcohol Withdrawal Delirium   **291.0**
Substance-Induced Disorders

Amphetamine Abuse   **305.70**
Substance Abuse/Dependence
Treatment Resistance

Amphetamine Dependence   **304.40**
Substance Abuse/Dependence
Treatment Resistance

Amphetamine-Induced Mood Disorder   **292.84**
Suicidal Ideation

Amphetamine Intoxication   **292.89**
Substance Intoxication/
Withdrawal

Amphetamine Withdrawal   **292.0**
Substance Intoxication/
Withdrawal

Anorexia Nervosa   **307.1**
Eating Disorders

Antisocial Personality Disorder   **301.7**
Anger
Antisocial Behavior
Attention-Deficit/Hyperactivity
Disorder (ADHD)
Attention-Deficit/Inattentive
Disorder (ADD)
Borderline Traits
Childhood Trauma
Family Conflicts
Impulsivity
Legal Problems
Occupational Problem
Oppositional Defiant Disorder
Parent-Child Relational
Problem
Partner Relational Conflicts
Peer Group Negativity
Relapse Proneness
Sexual Promiscuity
Treatment Resistance

Anxiety Disorder Not Otherwise Specified   **300.00**
Adult-Child-of-an-Alcoholic
(ACOA) Traits
Dependent Traits

**Intermittent Explosive
Disorder**   312.34
  Anger
  Antisocial Behavior
  Dangerousness/Lethality
  Impulsivity
  Legal Problems
  Oppositional Defiant Disorder

**Learning Disorder, Not
Otherwise Specified**   315.9
  Attention-Deficit/Inattentive
    Disorder (ADD)

Major Depressive Disorder   296.xx
  Borderline Traits
  Childhood Trauma
  Dangerousness/Lethality
  Eating Disorders
  Psychosis
  Suicidal Ideation

**Major Depressive Disorder,
Recurrent**   296.3x
  Chronic Pain
  Depression
  Gambling
  Grief/Loss Unresolved

**Major Depressive Disorder,
Single Episode**   296.2x
  Depression
  Grief/Loss Unresolved

**Maladaptive Health Behaviors
Affecting (Axis III Disorder)**   316
  Medical Issues

Mild Mental Retardation   317
  Self-Care Deficits—Primary
  Self-Care Deficits—Secondary

**Mood Disorder Due to ...
[Indicate the General Medical
Condition]**   293.83

**Mood Disorder, Not
Otherwise Specified**   296.90
  Anxiety
  Social Anxiety/Skills Deficit

**Narcissistic Personality
Disorder**   301.81
  Anger
  Antisocial Behavior
  Borderline Traits
  Dangerousness/Lethality
  Eating Disorders
  Impulsivity
  Legal Problems
  Narcissistic Traits
  Parent-Child Relational
    Problem
  Partner Relational Conflicts
  Peer Group Negativity
  Relapse Proneness
  Sexual Promiscuity

Neglect of Child   V61.4
  Childhood Trauma
  Living Environment Deficiency
  Parent-Child Relational
    Problem

**Neglect of Child (if focus of
clinical attention is on the
victim)**   995.5
  Childhood Trauma
  Living Environment Deficiency

Nicotine Dependence   305.10
  Nicotine Abuse/Dependence

Nicotine Withdrawal   292.0
  Nicotine Abuse/Dependence

**Obsessive-Compulsive
Disorder**   300.3
  Anxiety
  Chronic Pain
  Eating Disorders

Occupational Problem   V62.2
  Living Environment Deficiency
  Occupational Problem

Opioid Abuse   305.50
  Opioid Dependence
  Substance Abuse/Dependence
  Treatment Resistance

Appendix C

CLIENT SATISFACTION SURVEYS: RESOURCE MATERIAL

Each chapter in the book has a list of Objectives and Interventions; at the end of the list they refer to completing or administering a satisfaction survey. Following are listed references to examples of surveys which may be purchased and used for assessing client satisfaction. Dr. C. Attkisson has published considerable research on this issue, and others have used his scales in their research and agency outcome studies. Attkisson has developed scales with 3, 4, 8, 18, and 31 items.

Other surveys are also used in gathering information about clients' satisfaction with mental health services. The following are references to survey material. Some of this material is copyrighted and must be purchased, while other survey items are available for general use. Please contact the authors to ask about using their survey material.

Attkisson, C., & Pascoe, G. (1983). Patient satisfaction in health and human services. *Evaluation and Program Planning, 6*(3), 373–383.

Eisen, S. V., Shaul, J. A., Leff, H. S., Stringfellow, V., Clarridge, B. R., & Cleary, P. D. (2001). Toward a national consumer survey: evaluation of the CABHS and MHSIP instruments. *Journal of Behavioral Health Services & Research, 28*(3), 347–369.

Essex, D. W., Fox, J. A., & Groom, J. M. (1981). The development, factor analysis, and revision of a client satisfaction form. *Community Mental Health Journal, 17*(3), 226–235.

Greenfield, T., & Attkisson, C. (1989). Steps toward a multifactorial satisfaction scale for primary care and mental health service. *Evaluation and Program Planning, 12,* 271–278.

Larson, D. L., Attkisson, C. C., Hargreaves, W. A., & Nguyen, T. D. (1979). Assessment of client/patient satisfaction in human service programs: Development of a general scale. *Evaluation and Program Planning, 2,* 197–207.

Lebow, J., (1983). Research assessing consumer satisfaction with mental health treatment: A review of findings. *Evaluation and Program Planning, 6,* 237–245.

Mental Health Corporations of America. (1995). *Customer Survey–Form C.* Tallahassee, FL: Mental Health Corporations of America.

Appendix D

ASAM SIX ASSESSMENT DIMENSIONS: A CHECKLIST EXAMPLE

Dimension 1: Detoxification/Withdrawal (Acute Intoxication/Withdrawal Potential)

Signs and symptoms indicate the continued presence of the intoxication or withdrawal problem that required admission to the present level of care.

❑ Patient was monitored for acute withdrawal symptoms and received medication(s).
❑ Patient was monitored for acute withdrawal symptoms and did not receive medication for withdrawal.
❑ Patient completed acute detoxification and no complications were noted.
❑ Patient completed acute detoxification and withdrawal was prolonged.
❑ Patient received education on protracted withdrawal symptoms.
❑ Patient did not require detoxification at the time of admission.

COMMENTS: _____

_____

Dimension 2: Biomedical Conditions and Complications

The patient's status in Dimension 2 is characterized by *one* of the
following:

YES   NO

_____ _____   a. The interaction of the patient's biomedical condition and continued
alcohol or other drug use places the patient in imminent danger
of serious damage to physical health or concomitant biomedical
conditions *or*

_____ _____   b. A current biomedical condition requires 24-hour nursing and medical
monitoring or active treatment.

Patient was treated for the following medical problems

❑ Hypertension   ❑ Chronic Pain   ❑ Sleep Pattern   ❑ Hepatomegaly
❑ COPD/Asthma/   Syndrome   Disturbance   ❑ Headaches
   Emphysema   ❑ Diabetes   ❑ Cardiovascular   ❑ Arthritis/Gout
❑ Back Problems   ❑ Anemia   Problems   ❑ Ulcers
❑ Upper Respiratory ❑ Thyroid Problems ❑ Pancreatitis   ❑ Sinus Infection
   Infection   ❑ Urinary Tract   ❑ Bowel Problems   ❑ Hepatitis
❑ Gastritis   Infection   ❑ GERD
❑ Other _____

❑ Admission Laboratory Work Completed ❑ Repeat Laboratory Work Completed   ❑ N/A
❑ Urine Chemical Screening Completed: ❑ Positive   ❑ Negative   ❑ Not Available at the
                                                                    Present Time
❑ History and Physical Completed   ❑ TB Mantoux Given: ❑ Positive   ❑ Negative
❑ Patient was given psychotropic medications—see Dimension 3 for further information.

COMMENTS: _____

_____

Dimension 3:   Emotional/Behavioral Conditions and Complications

Affect or Mood (Check all that are appropriate):

❏ Appropriate	❏ Labile	❏ Restless	❏ Poor Impulse Control
❏ Euphoric	❏ Cooperative	❏ Pressured Speech	
❏ Sad	❏ Homicidal Plan	❏ Manic	❏ Anxious
❏ Homicidal Ideation	❏ Panic Attacks	❏ Flat	❏ Angry
❏ Poor Concentration	❏ Apathetic	❏ Suicidal Ideation	❏ Suicidal Plan
❏ Requires Ongoing Boundary Setting	❏ Aggressive	❏ Paranoid Thoughts	❏ Depressed
❏ Inappropriate	❏ Argumentative	❏ Obsessive-Compulsive Thoughts	
	❏ Irritable		

Patient had a psychiatric evaluation by a psychiatrist:

    ❏ Yes   ❏ No   ❏ Scheduled but Pending

Patient received a prescription for psychotropic medications:

    ❏ Yes   ❏ No

Medications were prescribed for the following psychiatric conditions: _____

_____

COMMENTS: _____

_____

Dimension 4:   Readiness to Change

The patient's status in this dimension is characterized by *one* of the following:

YES   NO

_____ _____   a. Despite experiencing serious consequences or effects of the addictive disorder or mental health problem, the patient does not accept or relate the addictive disorder to the severity of these problems; *or*

_____ _____   b. The patient is in need of intensive strategies, activities, and processes available only in a 24-hour structured, medically monitored setting; *or*

_____ _____   c. The patient needs ongoing, 24-hour psychiatric monitoring to assure follow-through with the treatment regimen and to deal with issues such as ambivalence about compliance with psychiatric medications.

Attendance:	❏ Poor	❏ Fair	❏ Good	❏ Excellent
Attitude:	❏ Poor	❏ Fair	❏ Good	❏ Excellent
Group Participation:	❏ Poor	❏ Fair	❏ Good	❏ Excellent
Honesty:	❏ Poor	❏ Fair	❏ Good	❏ Excellent
Acceptance:	❏ Poor	❏ Fair	❏ Good	❏ Excellent
Commitment/Motivation:	❏ Poor	❏ Fair	❏ Good	❏ Excellent

During the past week the patient worked on the following assignments (Check all that apply):

❏ Chemical Use History   ❏ Problem Assessment   ❏ Millon   ❏ Quickview
❏ BECK Depression Inventory ❏ Honesty Exercise   ❏ Step One   ❏ Step Two
❏ Step Three   ❏ Step Four   ❏ Step Five
❏ Gambling Assessments   ❏ Other _____

Patient Visited with Staff Clergy: ❏ Yes   ❏ No
Patient Attended Church: ❏ Yes   ❏ No

COMMENTS: _____

_____

Dimension 5:   Relapse, Continued Use, or Continued Problem Potential

The patient's status in this dimension is characterized by *one* of the following:

YES   NO

_____ _____   a. The patient is experiencing an acute psychiatric or substance-use crisis, marked by intensification of symptoms of his/her addictive or mental disorder, *or*

_____ _____   b. The patient is experiencing an escalation of relapse behaviors and/or reemergence of acute symptoms, *or*

_____ _____   c. The modality of treatment or protocols to address relapse require that the patient stay in treatment.

Relapse Potential is: ❑ High   ❑ Moderate   ❑ Low
Worked on a Peer Pressure Exercise: ❑ Yes   ❑ No   ❑ Pending
Worked on Identifying Relapse Triggers: ❑ Yes   ❑ No   ❑ Pending
Developed a Relapse Prevention Exercise: ❑ Yes   ❑ No   ❑ Pending
Patient Has Pending Legal Issues: ❑ Yes   ❑ No   ❑ Pending
Had Contact with Patient's
   Probation Officer: ❑ Yes   ❑ No   ❑ Pending   ❑ N/A

COMMENTS: _____

_____

Dimension 6:   Recovery Environment

The patient's status in this dimension is characterized by *one* of the following:

YES   NO

____ ____ a. The patient's current living situation is characterized by a high risk of initiation or repetition of physical, sexual, or emotional abuse, or substance use so endemic that the patient is assessed as being unable to achieve or maintain recovery at a less intensive level of care; *or*

____ ____ b. Family members or significant others living with the patient are not supportive of his/her recovery goals and are actively sabotaging treatment, *or*

____ ____ c. The patient is unable to cope, for even limited periods of time.

It is appropriate to retain the patient at the present level of care if:

____ 1. The patient is making progress, but has not yet achieved the goals articulated in the individualized treatment plan. Continued treatment at the present level of care is assessed as necessary to permit the patient to continue to work toward his/her treatment goals; *or*

____ 2. The patient is not yet making progress, but has the capacity to resolve his/her problems. He/she is actively working toward the goals articulated in his/her individualized treatment plan. Continued treatment at the present level of care is assessed as necessary to permit the patient to continue to work toward his/her treatment goals; *and/or*

____ 3. New problems have been identified that are appropriately treated at the present level of care. This level is the least intensive at which the patient's new problems can be addressed effectively.

Patient Developed a Relapse Prevention Plan:
□ Yes   □ No   □ Pending
Patient Agreed to Participate in AA/NA/GA Meetings Post Discharge:
□ Yes   □ No
Patient Given a Name for a Temporary AA/NA/GA Contact:
□ Yes   □ No   □ Pending
Patient Agreed to Attend Aftercare Meetings Post Discharge:
□ Yes   □ No   □ Pending
If Yes, At What Facility: _____
Patient Has Agreed to Attend Individual Counseling Post Discharge:
□ Yes   □ No   □ Pending   □ N/A   □ Patient Refuses
If Yes, At What Facility: _____
Patient Has Agreed to Attend Marital Counseling Post Discharge:
□ Yes   □ No   □ Pending   □ N/A   □ Patient Refuses
If Yes, At What Facility: _____

Employer Has Been Contacted:
   ❑ Yes   ❑ No   ❑ Pending   ❑ N/A   ❑ Patient Refuses
Family/Significant Other was Contacted:
   ❑ Yes   ❑ No   ❑ Pending   ❑ N/A   ❑ Patient Refuses
Family Program Scheduled:
   ❑ Yes (Dates_____)   ❑ No   ❑ Pending   ❑ Patient Refuses
Halfway House Placement Is Being Recommended for the Patient:
   ❑ Yes   ❑ No   ❑ Pending   ❑ N/A   ❑ Patient Refuses
Patient Returning Home:
   ❑ Yes   ❑ No   ❑ Pending   ❑ N/A   ❑ Patient Refuses

COMMENTS: _____
_____
_____

_____
Primary Therapist Signature   Date